JOINT VENTURES

SUBSCRIPTION NOTICE

This Wiley product is updated on a periodic basis with supplements to reflect important changes in the subject matter. If you purchased this product directly from John Wiley & Sons, Inc., we have already recorded your subscription for this update service.

If, however, you purchased this product from a bookstore and wish to receive (1) the current update at no additional charge, and (2) future updates and revised or related volumes billed separately with a 30-day examination review, please send your name, company name (if applicable), address, and the title of the product to:

Supplement Department
John Wiley & Sons, Inc.
One Wiley Drive
Somerset, NJ 08875
1–800–225–5945

For customers outside the United States, please contact the Wiley office nearest you:

Professional & Reference Division
John Wiley & Sons Canada, Ltd.
22 Worcester Road
Rexdale, Ontario M9W 1L1
CANADA
(416) 675–3580
1–800–567–4797
FAX (416) 675–6599

John Wiley & Sons, Ltd.
Baffins Lane
Chichester
West Sussex, PO19 1UD
UNITED KINGDOM
(44) (243) 779777

Jacaranda Wiley Ltd.
PRT Division
P. O. Box 174
North Ryde, NSW 2113
AUSTRALIA
(02) 805–1100
FAX (02) 805–1597

John Wiley & Sons (SEA) Pte. Ltd.
37 Jalan Pemimpin
Block B # 05–04
Union Industrial Building
SINGAPORE 2057
(65) 258–1157

JOINT VENTURES
Business Strategies for Accountants
Second Edition

Joseph M. Morris

Contributing Authors

Richard P. Graff
Coopers & Lybrand L.L.P.

Barbara A. Jenkins
Jenkins & Jenkins, PC

Ray H. Johnson
Price Waterhouse LLP

Robert Porter Lynch
The Warren Company

Daniel T. May
Coopers & Lybrand L.L.P.

Francis J. O'Brien
ICU Medical, Inc.

Robert J. Puls
Price Waterhouse LLP

John Wiley & Sons, Inc.
New York • Chichester • Weinheim • Brisbane • Singapore • Toronto

Library of Congress Cataloging in Publication Data:

Morris, Joseph M., 1949–
    Joint ventures : business strategies for accountants / Joseph M.
Morris ; contributing authors, Richard P. Graff . . . [et al.]. — 2nd
ed.
        p.   cm.
    Includes bibliographical references and index.
    ISBN 0-471-57018-4 (alk. paper)
    1. Joint ventures — Management. 2. Joint ventures — Accounting.
3. Joint ventures — Finance. 4. Joint ventures — Taxation — United
States. I. Graff, Richard P.

    HD62.47.M67 1998
658'.044 — dc21   97–31046
                                                           CIP

Printed in the United States of America
10 9 8 7 6 5 4 3 2 1

Permissions

This book contains various references to and brief quotations from materials contained in pronouncements on accounting and auditing and other published materials, which are acknowledged as follows:

Copyright by Financial Accounting Standards Board
Statements of Financial Accounting Standards
FASB Interpretations
FASB Technical Bulletins
FASB Discussion Memorandums
FASB Issues Papers
EITF Abstracts

The references to and quotations from the above pronouncements are contained herein with the permission of the Financial Accounting Standards Board. Complete copies of the above are available from the Financial Accounting Standards Board, 401 Merritt 7, Norwalk, CT 06856.

Copyright by American Institute of Certified Public Accountants
Opinions of the Accounting Principles Board
Accounting Interpretations of APB Opinions
Statements of Position
Statements on Auditing Standards and Codification of Statements on Auditing Standards
AICPA Audit and Accounting Guides
AcSEC Issues Papers

For Fitz and Fran
And Thelma and Carl

ABOUT THE AUTHOR

Joseph M. Morris is Senior Vice President, Chief Financial Officer, and a member of the board of directors of ITEX Corporation, a publicly traded NASDAQ company, which operates the largest organized commercial barter exchange. From 1988 to 1990, Mr. Morris was a project manager for the Financial Accounting Standards Board (FASB), where he was the FASB staff specialist in accounting for the software industry, in which capacity he served as the FASB staff liaison and advisor to the AICPA Task Force that developed SOP 91-1, *Software Revenue Recognition*. Mr. Morris was also responsible for the FASB's major project on Consolidations and Related Matters, which included accounting for acquisitions, joint ventures, consolidated financial statements, and parent–subsidiary and other relationships. Prior to and after his service at the FASB, Mr. Morris was Vice President–Corporate Controller of Scientific Software-Intercomp, Inc., a publicly traded NASDAQ company. Mr. Morris participates actively in various business ventures as a consultant, in some situations serving as an officer and member of the board of directors. Earlier in his career, Mr. Morris served in several financial management positions with Lone Star Industries, Inc. He started his career with Coopers & Lybrand L.L.P., where he was an audit manager. In addition to *Software Industry Accounting*, which was named the Best New Book in Accounting Practice for 1993 by the American Publishers Association, Mr. Morris has authored three other Wiley books, including *Mergers and Acquisitions — Business Strategies for Accountants*, which was named the Best New Book in Accounting Practice for 1995.

ABOUT THE CONTRIBUTORS

Richard P. Graff is a partner in the Denver office of Coopers & Lybrand, L.L.P. who has significant experience in the natural resources industry. He is chairman of the Firm's Mining and Metals Processing Industry Program within the United States and serves as a National Consulting partner on filings with the Securities and Exchange Commission. He is a business assurance partner whose client base consists primarily of public companies; many of which have international operations.

Barbara A. Jenkins is an owner and President of Jenkins & Jenkins, P.C., a Denver certified public accounting firm. The firm specializes in small business start-ups, agriculture, taxes, and litigation support. Ms. Jenkins is also a professor of accounting at Regis University. Previously, she was Financial Vice President for an international conglomerate.

Ray H. Johnson, CPA, MBA, is a retired partner of Price Waterhouse LLP. Mr. Johnson, who had a 37-year career with his firm, is an expert in joint ventures, mergers and acquisitions, and strategic alliances.

Robert Porter Lynch is President of the Warren Company, a management consulting firm in Providence, Rhode Island. One of the nation's top experts in the art of developing strategic collaborations, he is the author of the highly successful *The Practical Guide to Joint Ventures and Corporate Alliances* (John Wiley & Sons), which has been translated into several languages. He holds a master's degree in organization development from Harvard University. As an entrepreneur, he and his corporate team have been involved in developing the strategy or operationally managing over 40 strategic alliances worldwide. Mr. Lynch has served as consultant to large corporations such as AT&T, General Electric, and Scott Paper, along with numerous other companies ranging from hi-tech to insurance. Executives from over 1,000 companies have attended his seminar programs internationally. He has written articles for numerous magazines and speaks to business groups regularly.

Daniel T. May is a partner in Coopers & Lybrand L.L.P.'s Corporate Finance Group. His activities include advising clients on acquisitions, divestitures, valuation, financings, and joint ventures. He also is active in due diligence and structuring for both strategic and financial buyers. Mr. May is a frequent contributor and speaker on corporate finance topics nationally.

Francis J. O'Brien, CPA, is Chief Financial Officer, Secretary, and Treasurer of ICU Medical, Inc., a company publicly traded on the NASDAQ National Market tier of The NASDAQ Stock Market. ICU Medical designs and manufactures safe, disposable medical devices. Prior to joining ICU Medical, Mr. O'Brien was a business, financial, and litigation consultant working principally with publicly held companies in the software industry and the health care industries. Mr. O'Brien was a member of the Accounting Standards Executive Committee from 1988 to 1991 and has served on numerous AICPA and California Society of CPA committees and task forces. Mr. O'Brien started his career with Arthur Young & Company, later Ernst & Young LLP, where he was a senior partner until 1994.

Robert J. Puls is a partner in the Corporate Finance Group of Price Waterhouse LLP, where his activities including advising clients on achieving maximum benefits from the structuring of acquisitions, divestitures (including spin-offs and carve outs), and joint ventures. He also is active in managing preacquisition due diligence. Previously, he was a partner in Price Waterhouse's National Accounting Services Group where his activities included formulation of Price Waterhouse positions on accounting issues being addressed by the FASB, Emerging Issues Task Force (EITF), and other standard-setting organizations. Mr. Puls has authored numerous articles that have been published in technical accounting periodicals.

Preface

Many business activities are conducted through joint ventures of two or more parties. These arrangements require special cooperation of the parties because no one party has control. Accountants must have an array of specialized knowledge and skills to function well in joint venture situations.

Joint ventures may be structured by the formation of a separate corporate or partnership entity. Alternatively, they are sometimes conducted as joint activities of two or more parties without the formation of a separate entity. Such arrangements are usually governed by contracts between the parties.

Some aspects of this book, such as equity method and partnership accounting, are also applicable to unconsolidated entities that are not joint ventures. At present, accounting principles are generally the same for all investments in entities that do not qualify for consolidation but are above the threshold for accounting as a passive investment. Thus, although the focus of this book is on joint venture situations, portions of the book have broader applicability in the entire area of unconsolidated entities and activities.

In addition to a knowledge of specialized joint venture accounting principles, practices, and procedures, accountants need to understand the general business considerations of joint venture activities. In addition to normal accounting work in joint venture situations, accountants often do such things as due diligence work, reviewing of transaction structure and contracts, monitoring compliance with contract terms, planning for and complying with tax laws and regulations, SEC and regulatory compliance, auditing, and post joint venture formation transition and integration. In a future annual supplement, we plan to add chapters on tax and legal aspects of joint ventures.

While this book focuses heavily on accounting for investments in joint ventures and accounting and financial reporting by joint ventures, the authors have endeavored to provide a perspective that will be useful to accountants in performing all the roles they must take in a joint venture situation. The book is intended to be useful to many categories of accountants, such as chief financial officers, controllers, accounting managers, business consultants, independent accountants, tax professionals, and internal auditors. Nonaccountants may also find much of the material in this book informative and useful.

I greatly appreciate and admire the work of each contributing author and also greatly appreciate the patience, support, and confidence of the fine publishing professionals at John Wiley & Sons, especially Mr. Sheck Cho.

Joseph M. Morris

Denver, Colorado
September 1997

Contents

JOINT VENTURES

CHAPTER ONE

A General Business Perspective

Robert Porter Lynch
The Warren Company

1.1 Introduction
    (a)   The Alliance Revolution
    (b)   What Is a Joint Venture?
1.2 Why Alliances Today?
    (a)   General
    (b)   Changing Nature of Competition
    (c)   Driving Forces
    (d)   Trends
         (i) Global Economic and Competitive Forces
        (ii) Converging Technologies and Markets
       (iii) Systems Integration
       (iv) Value Migration
        (v) Globalization
       (vi) Innovative Technologies
1.3 Transformational Advantages of Joint Ventures
1.4 Freestanding, Spin-out, and Preacquisition Joint Ventures
    (a)   Freestanding Joint Ventures
    (b)   Spin-out and Preacquisition Joint Ventures

1.1   INTRODUCTION

(a) The Alliance Revolution

The 1990s have been an era of massive organizational revolutions with a re-constructive overhaul that has reordered our business structures. To survive, rigid, hierarchical giants of the past have had to become far smaller, much faster, more flexible, less hierarchical, and look and act more like small- and medium-sized companies, or face the alternative of becoming dinosaurs ready for extinction. Many multinationals, such as Chrysler, Shell, Dupont, Xerox, Hewlett Packard, IBM, and AT&T have reoriented their corporate structures to encompass multiple joint ventures in multiple markets around the globe.

Today's corporation requires tighter and closer relationships, including joining forces with allies, foreign or domestic, to assure continued growth. Some companies have recognized this need faster than others. Dupont now has over 125 international joint ventures; Corning recognizes more than 50% of its profits from joint ventures; Xerox and Chrysler extracted themselves from possible extinction using joint ventures; and Exxon Chemical expects to see 25% of its revenues from joint ventures.

During the 1800s, joint ventures were a mainstay of American business, playing a vital role in this country's formative years in the shipping, railroad, mining, and oil industries. Today the joint venture, as the most formalized member of the strategic alliance family, has taken on a significant role in stretching the realm of possibilities for innovation and financial rewards. According to a recent Booz-Allen study of over 2,500 alliances, their average return on investment (ROI) was more than 50% higher than the average return for other U.S. businesses.

Because joint ventures tend to be dynamic structures, they are often more flexible to operate. With a significantly lower cash requirement than an acquisition and the stretching of managerial and technical resources, the returns on investment from a joint venture tend to be substantially higher, therefore the venture becomes inherently less risky.

As we move into the next millennium, the joint venture will continue to emerge as a major strategic weapon to create increased competitive advantage. But, despite its proliferation, joint ventures and strategic alliances continue to be a somewhat unfamiliar tool in our strategic arsenals. This chapter will discuss an array of general business aspects of joint ventures and how to be successful in forming and managing a venture.

(b) What Is a Joint Venture?

In a general sense, a joint venture is *a separate business activity, formed and owned by two or more parties (the venturers).* A joint venture may have both a separate legal and tax identity, and often a separate management structure as well. However, the best and most dynamic of the joint ventures are truly *strategic alliances*—characterized by a far richer set of defining characteristics that make them sounder and more innovative than strictly a financial agreement. (See Exhibit 1.1.)

EXHIBIT 1.1   Characteristics of Joint Ventures

The best of joint ventures are, above all, powerful strategic alliances that have these strategic, structural, and operational characteristics:

Synergistic	By bringing two organizations together, the result should be significantly greater than if they operated independently. The venturers should see the relationship from a 1+1=3 perspective.
Strategic	The relationship is not just of tactical convenience or strictly financially motivated—it affects the venturers' long-term destiny.
Separate Management and Organization	The relationship is more than an "unpopulated tax shell," bringing together the unique talents of both organizations.
Tight Operating Linkages	Typically, operational personnel of the venturers will be exchanged in and out of the venture to ensure learning is transferred from and to the venturers. Interaction between the joint venture and the venturers tends to occur at multiple levels, including the top echelons, as well as among operating personnel.
Beyond Win-Win	Successful ventures make the commitment to ensuring that the other venturer truly emerges as a winner, recognizing that by both winning, they all gain more.
Reciprocal Relationships	By sharing strengths and information, the venturers migrate value and increase the possibilities for innovation and growth.

1.2 WHY ALLIANCES TODAY?

(a) General

Alliances have been growing at the rate of 25% annually since 1987, and over 26,000 have been publicly announced in the last ten years. Is this just a short-term aberration before we return to our senses? Or are the large number of joint venture formations a sign of greater comfort with a more cooperative style of doing business? Or, more importantly, does this trend signal a fundamental strategic shift in the very nature of what we think about business strategy itself?

(b) Changing Nature of Competition

It is clear that the nature of competition itself is changing. Companies are learning rapidly that there are great advantages to cooperation, and that joining forces with a competitor is not tantamount to collaborating with the enemy, because not every competitor is an adversary.

Relationships are blurring as the distinction between who is a competitor and who is not is becoming far more intricate. For instance, at Bell South, a $13 billion regional telecommunications company, their relationship with AT&T has become quite intricate. AT&T is their largest supplier, their largest customer, their largest competitor, and their largest alliance partner. To Bell South, this must feel like organizational schizophrenia!

But the reality is that these multiple relationships are indicative of the types of associations corporations can expect regularly in the future. Such new complexities will require a new view of the competitive landscape and a new set of rules of engagement.

(c) Driving Forces

The proliferation of joint ventures is driven by a multiplicity of forces, often with powerful and surprising results. (See Exhibit 1.2.)

EXHIBIT 1.2   Driving Forces for Joint Ventures

The best of joint ventures are powerful strategic alliances that have these strategic, structural, and operational characteristics:

Strategic Drivers	• World-class company goals • Long-term competitive positioning • Create more profitable lines of business
Resource Drivers	• Management resources • Technology resources • Financial resources
Technology Drivers	• Hybridization of technology • Development of new technology • Commercialization of technology
Market Drivers	• Globalization of markets • Access to markets • Closeness to customer • Speed to market
Risk Drivers	• Share uncertainty and unpredictability • Share operational risks • Share technology development risks
Cost Drivers	• Economies of scale • Lower capital expenses • Utilize partners' lower operating costs
Regulatory Drivers	• Government prohibitions • Legal requirements • Taxation
Production Drivers	• Control and lower cost of supplies • Improved quality and reliability • Design for manufacturing and assembly
Transformation Drivers	• Change to inadequate internal culture • Shift to new industries • Reengineer core processes

(d) Trends

(i) Global Economic and Competitive Forces.   Global economic and competitive forces have transformed the nature of some industries. In the airline industry, the liaison between United Airlines and Lufthansa has meant that Delta had to abandon its routes to Frankfurt. In an attempt to fortify its strategic arsenal, Delta linked with Swissair and drove American Airlines out of its Zurich route.

(ii) Converging Technologies and Markets.   Converging technologies and markets have been the primary factor in some of the mammoth joint ventures in the telecommunications industry. The future of wireless telecommunications has emerged as a multibillion dollar competitive battle, with companies such as Motorola, Sprint, Microsoft, and Loral creating joint ventures for the control of satellite-based cellular telephone systems. (See Exhibit 1.3.)

EXHIBIT 1.3   Galactic Joint Venture Satellite Battle of the Skies

Iridium Cellular Communications and Its Competition	
Strategy	Iridium is a telecommunications joint venture designed to enable cellular telephone users to have full and complete access to global communications. By launching 60 Low Earth Orbit (LEO) satellites, Iridium will give cellular subscribers the opportunity to call anywhere worldwide by accessing a nearby satellite.
Cost and Financing Factors	The start-up costs before reaching breakeven are estimated at over $3 billion. The joint venture raised an initial $1.6 billion in cash to get started. LEOs, because of their low height, are destined to last only 60 months. Therefore, every month a satellite will fall out of orbit, requiring replacement—a very heavy monthly operating cost.
Joint Venturers	Iridium is led by Motorola, a $15 billion technology company with core capabilities in telecommunications, chip design, and computer systems.

EXHIBIT 1.3 (*Continued*)

Joint Ventures (*continued*)	Other members include Sprint (itself a joint venture between GTE and the French and German telecos), Bell Canada, and Stet (Italian Telephone), plus financial investors, and international aerospace companies with satellite-launching capabilities, marketing communications products and services, customer billing, and the political savvy to navigate through their region's regulatory process and long-distance tariff issues.
Competitive Alliances	The winner of the global wireless telecommunications race will most probably go to the swiftest alliance that achieves global access first. Other joint ventures are competing heavily for the first position in the marketplace. Among the competitors are:

- *Inmarsat*: Spin-out from an already existing shipboard satellite communications joint venture. Led by Comsate, the Norwegian teleco, and a Japanese telecommunications ministry, the alliance expects to rush to market using the existing Inmarsat relationships with a large number of internationally connected telecommunications companies.
- *Odessey*: A joint venture led primarily by Loral (a defense contractor) and Qualcomm (a high-speed data communications research and development company) and others that will utilize developing super-high frequencies (PCD) where the broader bandwidth will enable higher levels of data communications as well as voice communications.
- *Teledesic*: A network of over 120 satellites designed to become a fundamental element in Microsoft's strategy to link telecommunications and computer systems. It is designed to leverage McCaw's large cellular presence with Microsoft's superior software abilities.

(iii) Systems Integration. Systems integration has spurred the creation of numerous joint ventures as increasingly sophisticated technologies have required closer coordination of their research, development, and customer application. In the biotech industry alone, over $2 billion is invested annually in joint ventures of this sort. In the financial services industry, ventures are proliferating to better link the customer electronically with investment services, benefits processing, bundled services, and cash access.

(iv) Value Migration. Value migration within an industry has caused numerous joint ventures in the oil industry as the profitability and risk profile of the industry has changed. Twenty year ago, oil companies tended only to form joint ventures to reduce the high risks involved in exploration and drilling of new wells. Then, as the profitability was driven out of their refining operations, more and more oil companies, such as Shell and Mobil, formed joint ventures to operate their refining plants and then jointly distribute its output. As the next decade unfolds, these companies are forming new joint ventures with their petrochemicals divisions to find new value-added possibilities together from their downstream derivative products.

(v) Globalization. Globalization has compelled many companies to engage in joint ventures to enable them to gain a position in emerging markets. In countries like Brazil and China, General Motors has established large-scale ventures to create new breeds of economy cars for developing nation markets.

(vi) Innovative Technologies. Innovative technologies have spawned numerous joint ventures. Today, 40% of all breakthrough technology development is done through collaborative ventures. IBM and Toshiba, two fierce competitors, teamed up to create a joint venture to develop and produce active-matrix lap-top computer screens. In the automotive industry, General Motors, Chrysler, and Ford collaborate regularly on new technologies, such as electric cars, batteries, brakes, and headlights.

1.3   TRANSFORMATIONAL ADVANTAGES OF JOINT VENTURES

The aspect of joint ventures with the most impact is their ability to change the very nature of the corporation itself. In 1982, General Motors and Toyota formed a joint venture called New United Motor Manufacturing, Inc. (NUMMI) that today produces Geo Prisms, Toyota Corollas, and Toyota trucks. NUMMI has paid off dramatically for General Motors by showing it how to improve its own quality. In addition, the General Motors-Toyota joint venture provided much of the organizational learning that was necessary to establish the highly effective Saturn division, now the hallmark of General Motors' future.

Similarly, Chrysler gained extensively from its joint ventures. When Chrysler purchased AMC-Jeep, it acquired the learning of AMC's joint venture with Renault, which gave AMC new methods for lean production. And with Chrysler's joint venture with Mitsubishi, it gained core knowledge about using platform teams and taking advantage of the capabilities of its vendors by forming supplier alliances. Fortunately, these new capabilities were transferred into Chrysler just at the same time the automotive recession hit in 1989. As a result of what it had learned, Chrysler transformed itself, going from the brink of bankruptcy to what is now the most profitable car company in the United States on a profit-per-car basis.

Transformations like these are not isolated to the automotive industry. Between 1970 and 1979, Xerox had experienced massive erosion of its market share due to intense competition from Japanese copy machine companies such as Ricoh, Sharp, and Canon. Turning to Fuji, their joint venture partner in Japan, Xerox learned how to adopt new methods of production, how to benchmark themselves against the competition, how to utilize suppliers more powerfully through strategic alliances, and how to accelerate production schedules. As a consequence, Xerox was able to recast itself and rebuild its business.

Smaller businesses have used the joint venture with equally striking results. In 1974, ten small Holstein milk farms in Canada linked together to form Semex, a joint venture intended to export genetic material from prize bulls. When they began, the export venture added only 5% to their revenues. Now, Semex has catalyzed a $50 million joint venture business, which provides 50% of the farms' total revenues.

1.4   FREESTANDING, SPIN-OUT AND PREACQUISITION JOINT VENTURES

(a) Freestanding Joint Ventures

The freestanding joint venture is intended to be independent and support itself as a fully self-sustaining business entity. Corning uses this approach in its joint ventures, and has been tremendously successful in doing so with partners such as Ceba-Geigy, Dow, and Samsung. Similarly, Merck, in its joint venture with Sweden's Astra, created Astra-Merck as an independent company in 1994 which now does over $4 billion in sales.

(b) Spin-out and Preacquisition Joint Ventures

Often the joint venture is used to provide a smooth transition to a new strategic position in the marketplace. For example, when Dupont recognized the need to focus on its core competencies in petrochemicals, it made the decision to spin-out its $1.2 billion pharmaceuticals division to Merck through a 50–50 joint venture. This enabled Dupont to remain competitive in the pharmaceuticals business and retain future options for expansion in this direction without having to develop a competency that could have been very elusive and extremely costly, with little return on investment for years to come.

Others use the joint venture as a preacquisition mechanism to provide a longer and less traumatic period of transition, thus enabling far better integration than an outright acquisition as the business unit shifts between the old and new business cultures. When IBM decided to divest itself of its Rolm Communications Division, rather than selling it outright, it spun it off into a 50–50 joint venture with Siemens, who then eventually bought the entire division after assimilating Rolm into a new culture.

Unlike a merger or acquisition, the joint venture is seldom intended to be a permanent, stand-alone organization—more often than not, its purpose is as an interim/bridging structure designed to enable the partners to have flexible options for the future. In fact, 80% of joint ventures are eventually bought out by one of the partners, with the average joint venture lasting seven years.

1.5   KEY FACTORS FOR JOINT VENTURE SUCCESS

(a) Reasons for Success or Failure

Successful joint ventures follow a very specific pattern that distinguishes them from unsuccessful joint ventures. In studies of hundreds of alliance successes and failures, and examining the results of CEOs, a number of key factors for success clearly distinguish the winners from the losers. (See Exhibits 1.4 and 1.5.)

EXHIBIT 1.4   Reasons for Joint Venture Success

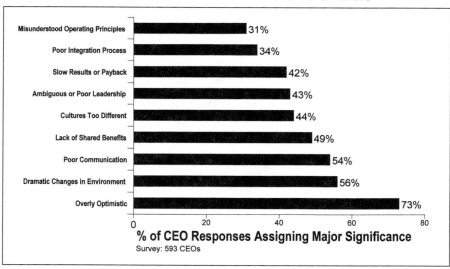

Partner Selection	75%
Senior Management Commitment	73%
Clearly Understood Roles	49%
Communications Between Partners	48%
Clearly Defined Objectives	44%
Relationship Building	36%
Thorough Planning	30%
Close Senior Management Ties	27%
Frequent Performance Feedback	16%
Day-to-Day Attention	16%
Sharing Risks & Resources	15%
Clear Payback Time Line	14%
Alignment of Culture	11%
Previous Alliance Experience	6%
Information System Integration	2%

% of CEO Responses Assigning Major Significance
Survey: 455 CEOs of Electronics Companies

Source: Data Quest, 1992.

EXHIBIT 1.5   Reasons for Joint Venture Failure

Misunderstood Operating Principles	31%
Poor Integration Process	34%
Slow Results or Payback	42%
Ambiguous or Poor Leadership	43%
Cultures Too Different	44%
Lack of Shared Benefits	49%
Poor Communication	54%
Dramatic Changes in Environment	56%
Overly Optimistic	73%

% of CEO Responses Assigning Major Significance
Survey: 593 CEOs

Source: Data Quest, 1992, & Conference Bd. Survey of CEOs, 1995.

In case after case, *before* initiating the deal, corporate executive officers (CEOs) were most concerned about: control, control, and control, followed by ownership/deal structure, oversight/board representation, valuation, and prevention of interference. However, what's important to note from the success and failure reasons analysis (Exhibits 1.4 and 1.5) is that, *from hindsight, not a single experienced CEO ever cited control, quality of the legal agreements, or deal structure* as a factor that led to the success of the venture. This does not imply that these issues are unimportant (e.g., the quality of the legal agreements will be very important in the event the alliance fails), but they may have only marginal significance on the ultimate success of the venture.

Instead, in study after study, what senior management should have been concerned about was their own personal *commitment* to the venture, their *vision* for its future, their *relationship* with the top management of the other company, the venture's operational *performance*, the "skin in the game" to ensure a fair *spread of the risks*, maintaining a high level of *communications*, and *flexibility* as the conditions that originally catalyzed the venture in the first place begin to change.

(b) Lessons from the Old Masters

(i) General.   Many joint ventures have lasted several decades or more, such as those created by Corning, Hewlett Packard, Xerox, and Union Carbide. When senior executives from these firms are queried about additional factors that lead to the success of ventures over 20 years old, they mention several additional distinguishing factors, which are discussed in the following subsections.

(ii) Long-term Synergy.   Don't confuse rationalization, cost cutting, and economies of scale with "synergy." True synergy is an "architected" process; it happens through careful strategic design and attention to the details of integrating the interactions between the two cultures to create a superordinate culture that is more than just a blend of the best elements of both parents.

This is how Fuji-Xerox has grown to be a $7 billion company and has won innumerable quality awards in Japan.

(iii) Aligned Vision.   Successful integration requires forging relationships based on an "aligned vision," constantly looking beyond the near term to create new competitive advantages over and over again. Those ventures that are

willing to recreate bold new futures for themselves have a far greater likelihood of success.

(iv) Multiple Points of Contact.   High-performance joint ventures achieve powerful results not because of their deal structures, but because of their strategic and operational capabilities. These require frequent interactions at both the top echelons and at the middle-management level. When these interactions begin to fade, trust begins to erode, and the success of the venture is surely ready to wane.

(v) Retention of Your Champion.   In case after case, the quality and longevity of the champions on each side has been a very strong indicator of success or failure.

In a recent study conducted of 462 joint ventures that received antitrust approval by the U.S. Department of Justice, the authors found the correlation of success with champions was astounding. If there were no champions in place after five years, the success rate was a dismal 20%. However, even if only one champion was in place five years later, the success rate leaped to 60%! Successful Japanese joint ventures make the champion a lifetime appointment for this reason.

When seeking a champion, look for several defining characteristics: *a passionate crusader, an entrepreneurial risk-taker, a person with a powerful and clear vision for the future, with demonstrated leadership and a successful track record, who puts his or her commitment to the greater good of their organization above personal gain or fame.* Powerful champions must be admired not only by their own organization, but also by the other partner's. Truly effective champions *must* have access to both their own top management, as well as the top management of the other side, so that they may take rapid action to keep the alliance on the right course as it navigates the rocks of corporate lethargy and the shoals of conflicting demands.

(vi) Careful Definition of the Boundaries.   The future will seldom be a reflection of the past. What looks reasonable today will often look foolish ten years from now.

For example, companies that formed alliances with the Japanese in the 1960s never thought about China as a potentially lucrative marketplace. Naturally, as China emerged from its isolationist shell and became a desirable market, the joint ventures in Japan saw the Chinese markets as their natural birthright—so did both their Japanese and American parents. A battle like this can tear an alliance apart.

(vii) Making Structure Changes As Needed.   Times change, the competitive landscape shifts, CEOs retire, technology accelerates, champions are promoted, and people move in and out of organizations.

As a case in point, these situations all happened within eighteen months to one joint venture that had been successful in the insurance industry for ten years. It is no wonder the companies were locking horns and ready to take each other to court. Once they recognized the magnitude and multiplicity of the shifts they had experienced, they were ready to shift the framework of the alliance to make it adapt to the new conditions.

(viii) Reaping Rewards from Innovations.   As a proving ground for designing bold new futures and taking risks for technology development, the joint venture has an admirable track record.

Ford, for example, has used its joint venture with Mazda to gain a formidable competitive advantage by reengineering processes to cut costs, increase quality, shorten design cycle times, and improve labor relations.

The best companies, such as Hewlett Packard, Xerox, and Corning have established sophisticated mechanisms for migrating the innovations from their alliances back into and throughout their organizations. But they don't stop simply at migration; they have developed *capability building* initiatives that enable them to form alliances faster, manage them better, and coordinate them more effectively, thus achieving a much higher level of success and performance than their competitors.

(c) Importance of Building Trust

In every successful alliance, experienced practitioners cite "high levels of trust and integrity" as critical factors in their venture. This trust did not come easily or by accident, but rather from a number of factors, including: working together closely, intense face-to-face communications, a commitment to a win-win relationship, an aligned vision for the future, and an in-depth understanding of the other company's culture, pressures, and requirements.

Often joint ventures build and accelerate trust by using team-building exercises, careful use of negotiations techniques that will regenerate trust in the future, and spending ample time on the issues of operational integration. The accomplished veterans of numerous alliance formations quickly learn that the relationships between key executives and managers are, ultimately, more important than the structure of the deal and who has control.

European, Japanese, and Canadian companies are generally more adept at building trust than their American counterparts because they understand the value of assigning people to the alliance who have *both character and competence*. Job rotational cycles for foreign firms are far less frequent than with American firms (who tend to have a revolving-door approach to job rotation), seldom giving their executives time to build trust before shipping them off to new assignments.

One technique used to create integration of personnel, seldom used in the United States but often employed elsewhere, is "secondment"—the assignment of personnel on a temporary basis to the other organization in order to supplement resources, learn new cultural patterns, establish personal relationships, build trust, and to better understand the needs and concerns of the other side.

Trust, however, must not be viewed as simply a nice thing to have in an alliance. More importantly, trust must be considered an essential ingredient to the success of the venture. High levels of trust enable much higher levels of performance, significantly greater innovation and creativity, enhanced problem resolution, expansion of possibilities, and much faster implementation. These all translate directly to the top and bottom lines of the venture, because they represent lower transaction costs between alliance partners. As one financial executive at British Petroleum exclaimed: "We thought we were lean and mean after doing our own internal reengineering; then we found we still could get another 30% in savings by a strategic alliance."

1.6 BEST PRACTICES AND ALLIANCE ARCHITECTURE

(a) General

Recently, the author's firm conducted a benchmark study of the alliance managers representing the top corporations throughout America that were the most prolific in forming joint ventures and strategic alliances. The corporations that participated (AT&T, Boeing, Dupont, General Electric, IBM, Motorola, Texas Instruments, and Xerox, among others) represented well over 1,000 alliance formations. The experienced managers identified vital "best practices" that led to their abilities to repeat success time after time, which are discussed in the following subsections.

(b) Alliance Architecture

The best companies learned that they needed an "architecture" — a set of processes, practices, frameworks, and methodologies that would yield success on a regular basis. (See Exhibit 1.6.)

Fundamentally, they learned that deal making alone was insufficient to achieve success. The best alliance architectures always put the development of a strategically sound approach first, and, crucially, the structure of the deal was never finalized until the details of operational integration were worked out ("form follows function"). As one executive proclaimed: During negotiations, "spend 80% of the time on goals and alliance management, and only 20% of the time on how to structure the deal." The best companies ensured that sufficient time was spent on understanding the other company and their own needs before entering into negotiations.

EXHIBIT 1.6 Alliance Architecture

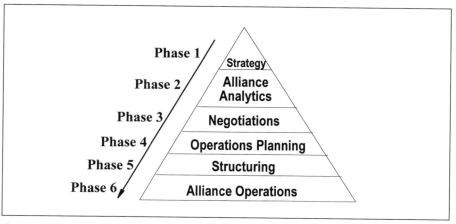

Source: The Warren Company © 1996.

17

(c) Alliances and Acquisitions

Companies that had effective joint ventures saw both alliances and acquisitions as important tools in their strategic growth arsenal, and knew how and when to use each for the most powerful impact. However, many noted using a more *formalized "cookbook" approach to the acquisition/ divestiture process*, while *alliances used a more customized architecture*, which applies key principles, checklists, core questions, and development processes, much like an architect uses core principles to customize a building.

(d) Top Management Involvement

Virtually all companies linked alliance effectiveness to top management involvement. As one executive said *"Our partners are extensions of ourselves."* There must also be a very clear, concise, and rapid method of approval of alliances so that they do not wither before birth from bureaucratic indecision.

(e) Internal Teamwork

All executives pointed out the need for exquisite teamwork between the internal business development staff and the operational units which would ultimately be responsible for the venture's success or failure. This requires seamless integration between the "front end" and the "back end" of deals, close integration between strategic planning, business development, finance, legal, and human resources, and coordination between the business development and operating groups regarding each other's respective roles, capabilities, and functions before forming the alliance.

In particular, the best companies had built a clear role for the business development staff. Typically the staff is tasked with identifying and screening candidates, conducting business analyses, linking strategic action to the operational units, providing negotiations support, and designing a system to measure the effectiveness of the venture and get it back on track when necessary.

(f) Finding the Right Partner

(i) General. Selecting the right partner may be the most important factor in creating a successful joint venture. The best companies have very specific and unique selection criteria, such as a combination of market presence, strategic fit, money, technology, etc. Generally, the more sophisticated the criteria, the greater the need for complementary critical core competencies. The factors discussed below stood out.

(ii) Partner Searches. The best companies engage in extended, proactive searches. These companies tended to indicate a higher success with alliances than companies who reactively responded to the first suitor who called.

(iii) Due Diligence. As one executive said: "You must do good due diligence to find out the real strategic direction and position of the company and make sure that they have a strong desire for growth within the markets that you would be addressing."

(iv) Screening Factors. Throughout the survey was the critical impact of both strategic fit and good chemistry as primary screening factors. These became essential "gating" factors at the front end of partner identification.

(v) Trust and Ethics. Tied closely to the chemistry issue was the factor of business ethics. This is more than just a platitude, and far stronger than an admonition. As many managers indicated, in an international deal, litigation is a highly undesirable option, and usually futile. Alliances thrive on high levels of trust. The absence of a good reputation indicated poor potential trust and was a first-level "deal-stopper" for international ventures.

(g) Staffing and Human Resources

Highly successful globalized companies make a clear and direct effort to proactively link their human resources programs to their alliance formation efforts. Career paths are carefully chosen, and individuals with the right language skills and cultural sensitivities are placed in alliance positions where their managerial and cultural capabilities will greatly increase the venture's chances of success.

(h) Cultural Issues

There was a clear relationship between those companies who had internalized an international culture and their ease at bridging the cultural gap in their ventures. Noteworthy was their observation that in the truly global company, the cultural issues involved in managing international alliances tended to focus more on the commonality of corporate culture than on the differences between their original national cultures. For the truly global company, the issue of national culture tended to have less impact on alliance management and success, except in the way the partner's political system affected the legal structure of the deal. Executives from global companies tended to agree that if companies could bond on the issue of an overarching corporate culture for the joint venture, they could generally overcome the sociopolitical cultural issues.

(i) Developing a Core Competency in Alliances

For companies that place significant reliance on a large number of alliances for the global growth, it is vital to develop a core competency in forming and managing developing alliances. This requires a certain proficiency and depth in several areas, including:

- Best practices and best processes
- Understanding alliance architecture
- Transfer of learning capacity
- Database of existing alliances
- Organizational education (clarity)
- Performance evaluation system
- Commitment to continuous improvement
- Maintaining best-in-class standards

(j) Venture Management and Control

Managing and controlling an alliance is a very critical and delicate issue in alliance formation and a clear concern for most companies. The respondents were articulate about the subject, as one experienced practitioner commented: "We try to keep 'control' from getting in the way of collaborative effort. But at times, because of capabilities of the organization—for instance if they are weak in specific technologies—you have to have control of certain parts of the process." Another experienced executive states clearly: "In order to achieve your goals, the structure and control has to be natural. You cannot really enforce control. You must set up the natural dynamics of the alliance so that controls are natural parts of the management process."

Several companies believed an ounce of prevention was worth a pound of cure and sought to use the due diligence process to determine the realm of mutual influence possible. Other companies saw the negotiations process not as bargaining, but much more as a planning process: "We want one unified plan for the venture—we create a joint marketing plan and a joint presentation given to both executive approval committees."

Financial controls still tended to dominate the mechanisms for keeping (internal) stakeholders informed. However, a variety of mechanisms were used to keep problems at a minimum, including contingency planning, conflict resolution techniques, careful operational planning and integration, team-building, project management, personnel selection, and the training of critical skills in alliance management.

1.7   WHAT THE FUTURE WILL BRING

For many companies, joint ventures will be the beginning of a new set of adventures and a powerful part of their growth strategy.

But for others with a long, futuristic view, the joint venture will be neither an end in itself nor simply part of a globalization strategy. The most advanced companies see that another massive shift is just over the horizon: the shift to a new type of organization—the networked enterprise—highly networked, focused on delivering sophisticated, fast time results. Some companies—such as Boeing, Chrysler, Xerox, Hewlett Packard, Intel, and Microsoft—are in the midst of the shift now. For others, the transition is not far away.

The networked enterprise (see Exhibit 1.7) is a highly integrated, total-solution based entity made up of alliances between suppliers, distributors, technology development companies, information systems coordinators, and, at the hub, a systems integrator that puts all the pieces together in a way that the customer gets a complete package without having to deal with a multitude of vendors, incompatible technologies, conflicting information, and confusing or interfering methods of customer application.

EXHIBIT 1.7 Organizational Shift

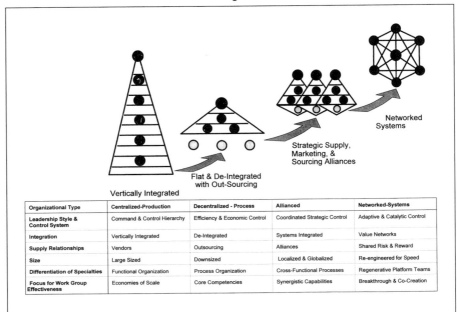

Organizational Type	Centralized-Production	Decentralized - Process	Allianced	Networked-Systems
Leadership Style & Control System	Command & Control Hierarchy	Efficiency & Economic Control	Coordinated Strategic Control	Adaptive & Catalytic Control
Integration	Vertically Integrated	De-Integrated	Systems Integrated	Value Networks
Supply Relationships	Vendors	Outsourcing	Alliances	Shared Risk & Reward
Size	Large Sized	Downsized	Localized & Globalized	Re-engineered for Speed
Differentiation of Specialties	Functional Organization	Process Organization	Cross-Functional Processes	Regenerative Platform Teams
Focus for Work Group Effectiveness	Economies of Scale	Core Competencies	Synergistic Capabilities	Breakthrough & Co-Creation

Source: The Warren Company © 1997.

The primary driving forces behind the shift to the networked enterprise are the explosive amounts of new information today, the hybridization of technologies, rapid innovation, implosive time compression, and profusive multi-/cross-functionality needed to produce outstanding products and services in today's fast-changing marketplace. This organizational shift will require the participants to master the ability to create and successfully operate multiple alliances, which will form the new enterprise's backbone.

Most importantly, the emergence of the networked enterprise is the most revolutionary and complex shift in organizational functioning and structure in the history of commerce. This shift will radically transform the nature of work, organizational interaction, leadership, and the very way we will think of business itself. Strategic alliances and joint ventures are one of the fundamental competitive building blocks needed to build these bold new futures.

CHAPTER TWO

Alternative Business Alliances

Francis J. O'Brien
ICU Medical, Inc.

2.4   Considerations in Choosing the Business Alliance Vehicle
 (a) General
 (b) Overall Cost of the Vehicle
 (c) Equity Dilution — Obligatory
 (d) Equity Dilution — Contingent
 (e) Continuing Obligation
 (f) Formation Costs
 (g) Administration Costs
 (h) Availability
 (i) Loss of Control
 (j) Installment Obligation
 (k) Expense "Off-Balance-Sheet"
 (l) Structure Flexibility
 (m) Employee Incentive
 (n) Access to Technology
 (o) Access to Markets
2.5   Conclusion

2.1   BACKGROUND

Entering into a business alliance has been likened to getting married. Both are preceded by a seduction. Both should be done only after extensive and thoughtful consideration, but are often done hastily. Both require significant sustaining effort, and both can be very expensive to terminate. But the analogy fails to capture the complexity of the business alliance. The marriage contract is fairly straightforward, and prenuptial agreements and termination provisions are often not considered or even necessary. In contrast, the business alliance can range from a remote acquaintance to an indissoluble union, and the exact terms of the alliance, operations while it is in effect, and how it can be terminated, must be carefully drawn. While some may believe that marriages may benefit from similar attention to details before they happen, we seem to plan affairs of commerce more deliberately than affairs of the heart.

Business alliances can be found throughout recorded history. While they have been brought to new levels of sophistication in the past half century, and even more recently with the "virtual corporation," there are basic elements that change little over time even if some fall into disuse at times. And, lest we think they are all complex, some are quite familiar: borrowing from a bank, renting an office, or hiring an employee. After all, an alliance is a union or connection of interests. Thus, alliances, broadly construed, cover all business relationships that are intended to continue over a period of time.

2.2 PURPOSE OF BUSINESS ALLIANCES

(a) Definition of Objectives

The first question one must ask before entering into an alliance is: What is my objective? Then the follow-up questions: What am I willing to pay and what do I expect to have when the alliance is over? As those questions are being considered, one must ask the same questions from the perspective of the counter-party — the party with whom one intends to form the alliance. One may not be able to fully answer the question from the counter-party's perspective, but the better one can determine the answers, the more likely it is that one will realize its own objectives in the alliance.

Why do parties enter into business alliances? The answer is as varied as the business transactions that they enter into, and can generally be categorized as the desire to buy or sell something. What is being acquired by one party and sold by another is generally the following:

- Funding
- Technology or "know-how"
- Personnel resources
- Products or product lines
- A business or an entire company
- Manufacturing capability
- Distribution of products or services
- Space for office or production facilities
- Services, such as construction or communication

Of course, there need not be an outright purchase and sale, and if the parties will have a continuing relationship, it can be thought of as an alliance. It may range from an employer/employee relationship or a landlord/tenant relationship to a complex arrangement to develop a technology or a market.

A common element of an alliance is that neither party has exclusive owner-ship and control of the assets that are subject to the alliance. The alliance, and therefore the counter-party, will have some right to control or use the assets that are subject to the alliance, even if legal ownership rests outside the alliance. The transfer of that control must be considered carefully. For example, if all rights to use a specific technology are put into an alliance, whether by license or a joint venture or other type of alliance, the owner of the technology may find that he or she has given up the ability to exploit the technology beyond what his or her co-venturer will tolerate. This problem is often dealt with by limiting the trans-fer of rights to technology very narrowly to the specific product application or market objective of the alliance, thereby reserving all other rights.

Even the vendor in a product-supply arrangement is giving up some con-trol over its assets. Specifically, it is ceding the productivity of some of its as-sets to the purchaser. If it agrees to a fixed price, it gives up the ability to charge more to the same or another purchaser.

While the objectives of the parties are frequently obvious and mirror each other, this is not always the case. For example, in a distribution agreement, a manufacturer is usually seeking distribution of its product, and the distribu-tor is usually seeking to earn a profit on the distribution. But what if the dis-tributor views the transaction as a precursor to acquiring the manufacturer, and further has little interest in distributing the product if it cannot acquire the manufacturer? And further, what if the manufacturer has no interest in being acquired? If the manufacturer fails to anticipate the distributor's motivation, it is likely to have a problem in the future.

(b) Basic Structure Considerations

The structure of the alliance will vary with the objective. In some cases, the appropriate structure is obvious, but in others there may be a number of work-able structures. For example, a real estate developer may need funding, and the lender may be seeking only a return on its capital, and eventually the re-turn of its capital. That transaction would typically be structured as a secured loan. But what if the lender also is seeking a part of the profits on the devel-opment? Then the alliance might be structured as a loan with a participation in the sales proceeds or operating results of the property, as a joint venture, or as an equity investment, among other alternatives. The economics to the par-ties will generally differ with each structure.

There are several basic common denominators to all structures that might be considered in structuring an alliance. Depending on objectives and results of negotiations, they will be used singly or in combination. They are:

- Equity: fixed (e.g., common stock) or contingent (e.g., warrants)
- Non-equity participations (e.g., variable royalties and profit sharing)
- Debt
- Purchase/sales of goods or services

Combinations of those elements can lead to some interesting structures. For example, a company may grant customers warrants if they purchase certain quantities of product. Or a funding party may receive convertible debt, which is a combination of debt and contingent equity. Or it may receive a royalty interest plus warrants in the entity benefiting from product development funding, which is a combination of a non-equity and contingent equity element.

2.3   BUSINESS ALLIANCE VEHICLES

(a) General

A complete inventory of potential alliance vehicles would be exhaustive, but the common elements are the following. Some may be used in combination with others and some are mutually exclusive.

(b) Common Stock

This refers to ordinary, single-class common stocks. Variations include shares with limited voting rights, or junior or senior dividend rights.

(c) Preferred Stock

Preferred stock contains one or more rights superior to common as to liquidation, voting, dividends, or redemption. These stocks may be convertible to common at holder's option. If issued by a nonpublic entity, they generally convert to common at the time of an initial public offering; if the company is public, they are often callable (in order to trigger conversion). The conversion rights are in substance an "equity kicker" and not an essential feature of the instrument.

(d) Debt

These are obligations of a company to pay that are not convertible into another class of stock. The debt may be secured or unsecured, senior or subordinated, or under a lease. It may vote on default with common, pay interest "in kind," and be callable at a declining premium. Similar to preferred stock, it may have conversion rights; these are equity "kickers" and not essential features of the instrument.

(e) Equity "Kickers"

Equity "kickers" are contingent rights to obtain equity securities of the issuer in the future. They usually have value only if the issuer's equity securities appreciate in value, although they can be priced to be "in-the-money" at issuance. They may be freestanding (e.g., options or warrants) or embedded in another security (e.g., convertible debt or convertible preferred stock).

(f) Development Funding

Development funding refers to funds raised for a specific development purpose, such as developing technology or a product, or developing a market for a product. Investor return depends solely upon success of the development (other sources of investor return tend to make the funding resemble a loan). The investor may have an active interest in the results of the development (e.g., it may intend to market a product developed), or may be a passive investor. Investor return depends solely upon development success. Research and development (R&D) partnerships and certain motion picture investments are relatively common examples of these types of arrangements; they are usually done through a special purpose corporate or partnership entity, and often include one or more series of sponsor's warrants.

(g) Joint Venture

A joint venture is two or more parties combining technology, manufacturing, marketing, and/or funding resources. A joint venture can be an operating entity or exist only on paper. They are very flexible as to purpose and provisions and can be in a corporate or non-corporate form. True joint ventures are equally owned by each party, but usage of the term extends to entities with non-equal ownership.

(h) Royalty/Revenue Participation

This involves sale to a funding party of a percentage of future revenues from a designated product in a designated area. Funding may be outright or contingent on R&D spending by the company. The funding party's return is contingent on sales.

(i) Profit Participation

Profit participation is similar to sale of revenue participation, but based on a defined calculation of profits.

(j) Sale of License to Use

This refers to a sale of the right to use a product or technology in either a defined or an unlimited manner. Payment by the funding party may be fixed, variable based on sales, and/or contingent upon R&D spending by the company.

(k) Partially Owned Subsidiary

A specific operation of a company, which may be development of a specific product, is placed in a subsidiary, and an interest (minority or majority) in the subsidiary sold to an investor or employee group. The subsidiary is flexible as to provisions and exit strategy. This structure can be functionally similar to a corporate joint venture.

(l) Distribution Agreement

This refers to an agreement for the counter-party to distribute the company's product. In its most basic form, the company product sells to the counter-party for a fixed price. Features can be added to make the distribution rights exclusive, require minimum volumes, grant the company a sharing in the counter-party's revenue or profits, and other variations. The more complex distribution arrangements can substantially resemble joint ventures.

(m) Product Purchase Agreement

This is an agreement by a company to purchase a product from a counter-party, and is often accompanied by an agreement by the counter-party to supply the product. It may be tied to a distribution agreement, or it may be for product that will not be distributed by the purchaser, but consumed internally or used in production. Features can be added to make the agreement the sole source for the purchaser, require minimum volumes, grant price incentives based on purchase volume, and other variations.

2.4 CONSIDERATIONS IN CHOOSING THE BUSINESS ALLIANCE VEHICLE

(a) General

The choice of the type of alliance can range from the results of a dispassionate analysis to something as subjective as the structure that worked in the last alliance. Cost and feasibility must be considered, and specific transactions can have very different cost and feasibility characteristics. Some of the more common factors to consider are described in this chapter. Exhibit 2.1 summarizes the interplay of some of the considerations and various structures (see Exhibit 2.1). Of course, it is general, and specific transactions may not be within the general cost and feasibility considerations.

VEHICLE	COST						FEASIBILITY							
CONSIDERATION	Overall cost of vehicle	Equity dilution-obligatory	Equity dilution-contingent	Continuing obligation	Formation costs	Administration costs	Availability	Loss of control	Repayment obligation	Expense "off-balance sheet"	Structure flexibility	Employee incentive	Access to technology	Access to markets
TRADITIONAL														
Common stock	Low to mid	Mid to high	None	None	Low	Low	Mid to high	Mid	None	No	Low	High	None	None
Preferred stock	Low to Mid	Low	None	None to low	Low	Low	High	Mid	None to high	No	Mid	Low	None	None
Debt	Low	None	None	Mid	Low	Low	Low to high	Low	High	No	Mid	No	None	None
NON-TRADITIONAL														
Equity "kickers"	Low to mid	Mid to high	None	None	Low	Low	High	Low to mid	None	No	High	High	None	None
Development funding	High	None	High	None	Mid	Mid	Low to mid	None	None	Yes	Mid	Low	None	None
Joint venture	Low to mid	Low to mid	Low to mid	Low to high	High	Mid	Mid to high	Low	None	Yes / no	High	No	Low to high	Low to high
Royalty / revenue participation	Mid to high	None	None	None	Mid	Low	Low to mid	None	None	Yes / no	Mid	No	None	None
Profit participation	Mid to high	None	None	None	High	Mid	Low	None	None	Yes / no	Mid	Low	None	None
Sale of license to use	Low	None	None	None	Mid	Low	Low to mid	None	None	Yes / no	Mid	No	None	Mid
Partially-owned subsidiary	Mid	Low to mid	Mid to high	None to low	Mid	Mid	Mid	Mid	None	Yes / no	Mid	High	Low	Mid
Distribution agreement	Low	None	None	Mid	Low to mid	Low to mid	Mid to high	None	None	No	Mid	No	None	High
Product purchase agreement	Low	None	None	Mid	Low to mid	Low to mid	Mid to high	None	None	No	Mid	No	Low	None

(b) Overall Cost of the Vehicle

This is the ultimate aggregate financial cost if the arrangement is successful. For credit-worthy entities, debt usually has a low overall cost — basically interest. In contrast, the cost of development funding is usually very high because the investor's return depends solely on the success of the development.

(c) Equity Dilution — Obligatory

Obligatory equity dilution is the fixed dilution of common equity based on terms at inception of the arrangement. Inclusion of equity "kickers" such as warrants raises dilution. Equity dilution exists only if equity securities are issued or issuable. The extent of dilution tends to vary based on specific terms. Sales of common stock tend to be the most dilutive, whereas the dilution caused by granting an interest in certain assets, such as through a joint venture or partially owned subsidiary, tends to be smaller.

(d) Equity Dilution — Contingent

Contingent equity dilution is the future dilution that arises if the counter-party may ultimately exchange its interest in the alliance for common equity of the company. For example, passive investors in development arrangements may have the right to exchange their interests in the alliance for the company's common equity, or may acquire the right pursuant to a buy-out offer by the company. Contingent equity dilution is part of an exit strategy. It can be used in almost any type of vehicle, but is found principally in development funding arrangements, joint ventures, and partially owned subsidiaries.

(e) Continuing Obligation

This refers to the obligation to incur continuing costs independent of the overall success of the arrangement. For example, common dividends are not mandatory, but interest on debt is mandatory, and payment of certain preferred dividends is practically unavoidable. There are often ongoing financial commitments to joint ventures and partially owned subsidiaries.

(f) Formation Costs

Formation costs are the initial costs of forming the arrangement (e.g., investment bankers, lawyers, accountants, executive time). Costs vary widely, depending on the complexity of the alliance. Also, public sales that must be registered with the Securities and Exchange Commission for non-traditional vehicles, or the initial public sale of traditional vehicles, typically have a high cost.

(g) Administration Costs

These are continuing administrative costs throughout the life of the arrangement. The more complex types of alliances tend to have higher administration costs.

(h) Availability

Availability means the general willingness of investors or counter-parties to enter into the type of arrangement. Traditional vehicles typically have good availability, although high-risk situations, such as poor creditworthiness or a depressed market for a company's equity securities, may make the traditional vehicles unavailable or very expensive. Non-traditional vehicles tend to be less available than traditional vehicles because there are typically fewer counter-parties that would consider them.

(i) Loss of Control

Loss of control relates to the ability of the counter-party to exercise influence over the company, by share vote or board membership, means a loss of control for the original company.

(j) Installment Obligation

This refers to a fixed obligation of the company to repay funds received from the counter-party is an installment obligation. Such an obligation exists only with debt and preferred stock with redemption provisions.

(k) Expense "Off-Balance-Sheet"

An accounting consideration of whether the funding arrangement enables a company to avoid reporting certain costs as expenses in its statement of operations is an "off-balance-sheet" expense. Properly structured development funding arrangements offer "off-balance-sheet" treatment as a major advantage. Less than majority-owned joint ventures and subsidiaries can achieve "off-balance-sheet" treatment by their exclusion from the consolidated operating results. Other non-traditional arrangements can achieve "off-balance-sheet" treatment for certain costs if they are combined with a development funding arrangement.

(l) Structure Flexibility

Structure flexibility is the practical ability of the parties to customize the terms of the arrangement to meet their specific needs. Traditional vehicles tend to have less flexibility than nontraditional vehicles, although a great deal of customization can be done to preferred stocks and debt, particularly if they are not offered publicly. Nontraditional structures are often negotiated directly with the counter-party, thereby allowing more flexibility.

(m) Employee Incentive

It may be desirable to have targeted employee incentives as part of the structure of the alliance. Common stock is the most widely used vehicle, through stock options and direct grants of stock may be used. Non-traditional vehicles can be used by permitting employees to participate as counter-parties. Employees may be granted interests in development funding arrangements, or shares in a partially owned subsidiary. A common use of a nontraditional vehicle in the past was the grant or sale of a general partnership interest in a real estate development to corporate officers of the company.

(n) Access to Technology

This refers to a company's ability to use a vehicle to receive technology from a counter-party to the arrangement. Care should be taken to carefully define the extent to which the parties to an alliance desire to transfer technology, and to guard against unexpected transfers. While technology can be transferred under almost any type of arrangement, the most common vehicles used are jointly owned entities, licenses, and development funding arrangements.

(o) Access to Markets

This is the ability to use a vehicle to obtain market access through the counter-party to the arrangement. The most common vehicles are jointly owned entities, licenses, and distribution agreements.

2.5 CONCLUSION

While the book in which this chapter appears is focused on joint ventures, suffice it to say that before parties go into a joint venture, they must first examine what the optimal structure for the alliance really is.

CHAPTER THREE

Joint Venture Financing

Daniel T. May
Coopers & Lybrand L.L.P.

3.1 INTRODUCTION AND OVERVIEW

(a) General

Financing a joint venture is similar to financing any business. The key difference is that there are two or more venturers involved in a joint venture and, therefore, financing may depend on their financial situation in addition to the joint venture's. Furthermore, the ability of the venturers to provide additional funding themselves or through existing lender and investment banking relationships can relieve a lot of financing headaches.

In addition to the advantage of venturer involvement, the financing environment is favorable for companies seeking capital at the present time. Interest rates have remained low for several years and there is also plenty of available capital for projects of any size. Large financings are of particular interest to lenders because of the ability to place capital more efficiently without the time and effort of closing many smaller transactions. Public equity markets also continue to remain at all-time highs and can be a viable source

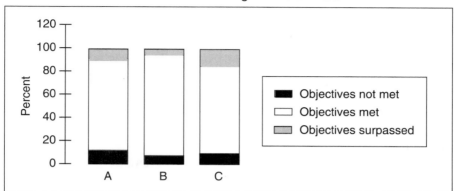

EXHIBIT 3.1 Sharing Financial Risks

A: Total Sample

B: Joint ventures created between 1993 and 1995

C: Joint ventures created before 1990

Source: Coopers & Lybrand: *Corporate Finance and Joint Ventures: an international survey* (1995).

of capital. The recent capital market growth has created an extended window of opportunity for companies, but whether this situation will continue is uncertain. For the period that these conditions exist, however, the opportunity exists to both raise capital and control the resulting capital structure.

Another advantage of using a joint venture structure is the ability for the venturers to share in the financial risks of a project. In a recent Coopers & Lybrand survey (see Exhibit 3.1), over 94% of joint venturers believed they met or exceeded their financial risk-sharing goals.

(b) Overview

The usual first step in obtaining financing is to build projections for the business and estimate the capital structure needed to make the venture a financial success. Once the projections have been created, a return on investment calculation should be performed to ensure the venture makes economic sense for all venturers. In addition, a valuation should be performed to assist the venturers in deciding their relative percentage ownership, as well as the anticipated ownership for any external investors.

After building the projections and valuing the business, the venturers must decide on the preferred capital structure. The structure should take into account any tax implications for the venturers and the joint venture. It is also important to ensure that if debt is a significant portion of the venture's capitalization, the cash flows will comfortably cover any debt repayments. A basic rule of thumb for the capital structure is: if the project is high-risk with little or no current cash flows, then it should be financed primarily with equity; if the project is low-risk with high cash flows, then it will be able to handle more debt. Additionally, if the project has a strong asset base, then debt may still be a viable choice. In general, debt is less costly than equity and, therefore, debt may often be a preferred financing method, if available.

In addition to the debt or equity decision, it is necessary to decide whether the venture should be financed internally by the venturers or from external sources. In some cases, the venture may not require any outside financing and can be entirely financed by the venturers. But if the capital is to be received from outside sources, then the projections will provide investors with a basis for their evaluation.

A good relationship with an investment banker with expertise in joint ventures can be a good way to find both debt and equity investors. Investment bankers can also be of assistance in the negotiation process.

3.2   PREPARING FINANCIAL PROJECTIONS

(a) General

Having reasonable, believable, and achievable projections is an integral part of the financing process. The projections for the venture provide the foundation for internal and external financing decisions. Once projections are complete, the venturers can decide more effectively on the best financial structure. Each venturer first should try to build summary projections independently and then compare their results with those of other venturers. Any differences should be discussed in detail. Once these issues have been resolved, the venturers should collaborate on creating agreed-to detailed financial projections.

(b) Sales Projections

Sales of the venture for at least the next five years should be estimated. These sales figures should be generated using a specific set of assumptions including: market size, market growth, the venture's anticipated market share, as well as any contracts from buyers to purchase the output of the venture. It is important to ensure the assumptions are as specific as possible. In order to create an effective sales analysis, the venture should generate three different sets of projections that are based on the high, low, and best estimates.

(c) Operating Expenses

After sales estimates have been developed, the estimated operating expenses associated with these sales should be computed. These costs include production and other direct costs, marketing, sales, administrative, research and development, and preproduction ramp-up expenses. It is important to include all expenses and to ensure that the collaboration between the venturers will generate synergies that will reduce the expenses.

(d) Capital Expenditures

Required capital expenditures should be estimated to effectively anticipate total cash flows. Typical capital expenditures include equipment, machinery, buildings, land, and other capital items.

3.3 ANALYSIS AND VALUATION

(a) General

Once the projections have been analyzed by the venturers, the next phase is to analyze in detail the return on investment (ROI) and the value of the business. This stage of the financing process determines whether the venture makes sense internally as well as externally for investors. Internally, the ROI calculation is the most effective method. For external purposes, the valuation of the business is a preferred analytical basis.

(b) Return on Investment

The primary tool for the analysis of joint venture investment is the ROI calculation. The ROI calculation is very useful in deciding whether the investment makes financial sense for the venturers. In general, if the rate of return achieved by the venture is greater than the company's weighted average cost of capital, then the project is viable. The greater the difference, the better chance the project has to be a success.

Exhibit 3.2 illustrates a potential joint venture investment. Cash flow is defined as adjusted debt-free, after-tax net cash flow. The following table shows

EXHIBIT 3.2   Illustration of Return on Investment Analysis
(Dollars in Thousands)

	1997	1998	1999	2000	2001
					(Terminal year)
Earnings before interest and taxes (EBIT)	$4,249	4,589	4,956	5,353	5,781
Income taxes (40%)	1,700	1,836	1,983	2,141	2,312
Debt-free net income	2,550	2,753	2,974	3,212	3,469
Plus depreciation	587	429	482	537	594
Debt-free cash flow	3,136	3,182	3,456	3,749	4,063
Less capital expenditures	(364)	(378)	(392)	(406)	(420)
Debt free net cash flow	2,772	2,804	3,064	3,343	3,643
Terminal value (1)					18,215
Initial investment $15,000					
Return on investment					22.9%

Notes:

(1) Terminal value was estimated using an exit multiple of five times cash flow.

(2) Changes in working capital were assumed to be zero.

(3) Potential double tax implications for a corporation were not taken into consideration.

that on a $15 million investment in this joint venture, a 22.9% return on investment is expected. When this is compared to the Weighted Average Cost of Capital (WACC) for the company, a determination can be made as to whether this is a good investment.

(c) Valuation Calculation

(i) General. In order to calculate the percentage of equity that it may make sense to relinquish to external investors in a financing, a valuation of the business is extremely useful. Three traditional methods for valuing a business are

1. The income or discounted cash flow approach

2. The cost approach

3. The market approach

The above approaches are discussed in the following sections. It should be noted that these valuation methods are for evaluation purposes only and do not generally relate to the accounting procedures with regards to reporting investments for tax and generally accepted auditing procedures (GAAP) purposes.

The process of valuing the company is also a useful exercise because it allows the venturers to see when additional funding may be needed, whether it should be debt or equity, and how much capital will be needed to continue the venture.

(ii) The Income Approach. The income approach uses a discounted cash flow (DCF) technique to value the business. This method values the venture based on the estimated future cash flows that can be taken out of the business without impairing operations and profitability. These cash flows, plus a terminal value, meaning the estimated value of the business at the end of the projection period, are discounted at an appropriate discount rate (usually the WACC) to arrive at a present value. This approach resembles the previous ROI calculation except that the unknown is the value of the business rather than the rate of return.

The WACC is calculated based on the required return based on the risk associated with an investment in the subject industry and the stage of development. The value derived by discounting these cash flows calculates the value of the assets and this value is then reduced by any anticipated debt to calculate the estimated equity value.

(iii) The Cost Approach. The cost approach is based on the notion that a prudent investor would pay no more than the cost of constructing a similar asset at prevailing prices. Under the cost approach the value is based on the subject company's assets, both tangible and intangible (i.e., patents), not of the company's liabilities. The cost approach is typically not used to value an income-generating asset because it does not consider the future economic benefits of the asset.

(iv) The Market Approach. The market approach compares recent similar private company sales information and public company market multiples with the joint venture's financial situation. This method allows the venturers to apply appropriate comparable market multiples to the projected venture financials and then adjust the calculated value by the appropriate discounts or premiums. For instance, public companies usually trade at higher multiples than private companies and, therefore, a private company discount should be applied for a private joint venture. Other discounts include minority discounts, which are useful when valuing a minority ownership position.

3.4   THE STRUCTURING DECISION

(a) General

After projections and calculations regarding value have been completed, a decision should be made about the financial structure of the venture. If the venture is going to be a cash generator, the use of the excess funds needs to be determined, such as whether the funds should be reinvested or distributed. If the business is a cash consumer, then the structure needs to provide access to the most economical source of funds. The legal structure of the organization also has a bearing on the financial structure. For example, the corporate shell protection is lost when using a partnership structure, but a partnership structure has certain tax advantages. Ideally, the perfect financial structure will generate the highest potential returns for the equity investors while maintaining the ability to repay any debt according to schedule.

(b) Asset Analysis

The first step in determining the amount and type of financing needed is to analyze the cash flow characteristics of the assets. For instance, are the cash flows cyclical or are they generated by specified contracts guaranteeing a defined cash flow? The maturity of the asset to be pledged as collateral for a loan is also important. For instance, buildings have a much longer life than most equipment. Working capital is usually considered a short-term asset, although if there is no requirement from a lender to pay down the working capital line of credit every year, then it can be considered a long-term asset. Furthermore, the interest rate sensitivity of the assets is also important. For example, if the company has low margins or a government cost-plus contract that denies the pass-through of interest costs, then interest rate increases will have a direct detrimental effect on cash flows. Finally, the current overall risk of the balance sheet needs to be considered. For instance, what is the liquidity of the assets to be used as collateral?

(c) Capital Market Analysis

The lending and financing environment may also drive the structuring decision. The window of opportunity for financing ventures may drive this decision as much as the ideal desired structure. An investigation of which financial products are currently "hot" will have an effect on the financial structure. The venturers' existing relationships with lenders and other sources of capital will also drive the structuring decision. Try to give the capital markets instruments for which they are currently paying a premium (i.e., requires a low risk-adjusted return).

(d) Dividend Policy

Dividend policy will also have an effect on the financial structure. If the joint venturers intend to distribute a significant portion of the cash flows from the venture rather than reinvesting them, then a financing may be required.

(e) Structuring Strategy

A general financial strategy for calculating the capital structure is as follows. First, establish reliable projections, calculate the ROI, and ensure that it is above a target rate of return, regardless of the availability of funds. Second, determine the optimal leverage for the venture, which is often tied to the likely bond rating. Third, try to capitalize the venture with debt up to the target ratio. Any residual debt capacity over the immediate need can be used to finance dividends or recapitalizations. Fourth, issue equity to fund the cash deficit if the shares are fairly valued. It is important not to focus on the potential dilutive effect. In a situation where the equity is undervalued, then preferred equity may be an option. In general, convertible debt is expensive and should be avoided.

(f) Determining Optimal Capital Structure

Exhibit 3.3 is a table that provides a general basis for discerning the optimal capital structure. It should be noted, however, that the venturer's risk tolerance outweighs this analysis. The debt/equity ratio that a potential lender is willing to accept is also a factor. The following table calculates the WACC based on the cost of debt and equity to the company and the ratio of debt and equity in the capital structure.

The table indicates that a structure with approximately 60% debt to total capitalization has the lowest cost of capital. The cost of equity rises significantly when the debt reaches the 80% level due to the significant additional risk of default or bankruptcy.

EXHIBIT 3.3 Determination of Optimal Capital Structure

Debt/total capitalization	20.0%	40.0%	60.0%	80.0%
Pre-tax cost of debt	8.0%	9.0%	10.0%	12.0%
Cost of debt after tax	4.8%	5.4%	6.0%	7.2%
Cost of equity	15.0%	16.0%	17.0%	25.0%
WACC	13.0%	11.8%	10.4%	10.8%

(g) Debt/Equity Decision Matrix

When designing a financial structure, the different characteristics of debt and equity drive the decision. Exhibit 3.4 is a table that describes the general differences between debt and equity for financing purposes.

EXHIBIT 3.4   Debt/Equity Decision Matrix

Characteristics	DEBT		EQUITY	
	Senior	Subordinated	Preferred	Common
Tax-deductible finance costs	X	X		
Covenants/ Restrictions	X	X		
No required fixed payments			X^a	X
Can be used in a tax-free exchange			X	X
Common equity convertibility		X	X	X
Not subject to redemption			X^a	X
Cost of financing	Low	Higher	Higher	Highest
Dilution of ownership		X^b	X	X
EPS dilution of shares		X^b	X	X

Notes:

[a] Preferred stock may have a fixed interest rate and a mandatory redemption provision.

[b] Subordinated debt can be convertible into equity or have warrants attached which may cause equity dilution.

(h) Financial Debt Reporting Structure

From a financial reporting perspective, joint venture arrangements are often appealing because the debt on the venture's balance sheet may not have to be consolidated (i.e., one line equity method reporting is allowed for the parent). In addition, a gain may be avoided with the transfer of assets to the venture when they are made at book value (with pooling-like results). The off-balance sheet treatment of a joint venture may also be useful when a weak credit company donates a pool of assets to the venture that is more creditworthy than the parent company. Other situations for off-balance sheet financings include: when the direct assumption of risk on the balance sheet would cause the company to suffer an overall diminution of its credit standing; or when the company would like to subject itself to less risk by agreeing to lesser credit support or maybe even totally non-recourse financing. It should be noted, however, that the cheaper source of financing for most creditworthy companies is on-balance sheet financing using the full direct corporate credit.

The key structuring issue for avoiding consolidation is how disproportionate a share of the risks and rewards of the venture a venturer can assume. Although there must be true joint control over the venture, a certain degree of structuring flexibility exists. However, there are some factors that can exist that may show that unilateral control is present. These include:[1]

- Throughput or take-or-pay arrangements between the venture and one of the venturers
- One venturer provides additional capital through preferred stock and therefore gains a disproportionate share of the earnings
- The ability for one venturer to gain control with techniques such as: (i) call options at a very low strike price or (ii) convertible securities that allow a venturer to gain control
- One of the venturers (i.e., the strategic venturer) guarantees the financial venturer a rate of return

If one or more of the above situations is present, then disproportionate control may exist. Typically, if disproportionate control does exist, then the joint venture is really a parent–subsidiary relationship, with one or more other

---

[1] *Accounting and Tax Planning for Joint Ventures and Partial Business Combinations.* Coopers & Lybrand L.L.P., 1995, pp. 10–11.

companies owning a minority interest in the subsidiary. The true test for unilateral control is decision-making power over the major decisions such as financial structure, mergers and acquisitions, and other major operating and strategic areas. An example of joint control would be a situation where Company A has 70% voting control, but Company B has veto power over the above major decisions. In this case, joint control exists, even though the percentage ownership interests are disproportionate. When analyzing control, care should be exercised when a company has significantly disproportionate economic interests while maintaining equal voting interests. For accounting purposes, it is unclear what level of economic interests creates a control issue but, in general, a company that is taking a significant portion of the economic risks is unwilling to share control.

3.5 INTERNAL/VENTURER FINANCING

(a) General

If a small company forms a joint venture with a strong financial venturer to raise capital, there are some advantages over raising capital in the public or private equity markets. However, it should be remembered that a joint venture should not be formed if obtaining financing is the only objective. The advantages of financing through a joint venture for a venturer in need of capital include:

Less Volatility   Financing by a strategic venturer in a joint venture is subject to less volatility than public market financing. The venturer is usually less concerned with swings in the public market and can provide a more stable financing environment (although they might be subject to their own stock fluctuations).

Access to Funding   For some small companies, accessing the public markets can be difficult, especially if it is an early stage of development or has an unproven product. By joining with a strategic venturer that has a better understanding of the product and has internal circumstances that can mitigate some of the potential risk, the venturer may be more willing to provide financing.

Ease of Financing	Forming a joint venture to finance a project with a venturer can be much quicker and less costly than other forms of financing. There are no underwriting costs, fees, and so on. In addition, the venturer understands the risks and is usually a more sophisticated investor and will, therefore, be able to make an evaluation quickly.
Valuation	A strategic venturer might be able to understand the risks and rewards of the venture and, therefore, be able to place a higher valuation on the business (and, therefore, allow the smaller company to retain more of the equity).
Ability to Finance a Particular Project	For the financial venturer, financing a joint venture can provide them with the ability to finance a particular project without having to take an equity stake in the other venturer.

(b) Venturer Equity Financing

The percentage ownership created in the joint venture is decided by the venturers at the creation of the joint venture. This ownership structure can change throughout the life of the joint venture, depending on present and future contributions and performance-based equity participation. Based on the performance of the joint venture, for instance, one venturer may have options or warrants to purchase more stock if certain benchmarks are achieved. This provides that venturer with extra incentive to make the venture succeed. Future capital contributions should be discussed before they are actually needed to ensure that the process is defined and understood. This will alleviate any future potential disagreements between venturers. Additional future funding is usually treated in three ways:

1. Half the additional cash provided is a loan from the financial party to the smaller party, which can be repaid in a defined fashion.

2. The patent or intangible asset donated by the smaller party is re-evaluated to equate to the additional extra cash infused by the money party.

3. The financial party now owns a greater percentage of the venture.

In order to ensure that a venture succeeds, the larger venturer might make an equity investment in the smaller company. This will ensure that the smaller company can remain solvent during the ramp-up phase of the joint venture. This investment may also provide the larger company with the opportunity to acquire, or make additional investments in the smaller company if the venture becomes very successful. These investments usually come with the option to purchase a majority position in the company. In this fashion, the joint venture can be a precursor to a merger or acquisition. The joint venture can serve as an extended due diligence period for the venturers to become more comfortable that their relationship can work on a long-term basis.

(c) Venturer Debt Financing

If a venturer lends capital to the joint venture, it is usually on different terms than an external lender providing the funds in an arm's-length transaction. An ordinary lender requires the repayment of principal and interest in a defined time frame with the appropriate collateral and guarantees to mitigate any potential risk. A venturer lender has more long-term strategic goals and is more interested in the success of the joint venture than immediate and complete repayment of principal and interest. However, care should be taken to make sure that there is a defined repayment plan or the investment may be considered equity. Other characteristics of venturer loans include:

Future Fundings	Funds may be available more easily for future financing rounds.
Lower Interest Rates	Typically a venturer loan carries a lower interest rate than the prevailing market rates. This is primarily due to the venturer's primary objective — to see the venture succeed, not to achieve the highest rate of return on its loan.
Repayment Schedules	The timely payments of principal and interest are less defined than an outside lender might require.
Timing/Covenants	The required covenants are less stringent and the time required to provide the funding is shorter.

3.6 EXTERNAL FINANCING

(a) External Equity Financing

For most private and public equity investors, the most important single issue in a joint venture investment is: who are the venturers? The investor's comfort level will increase dramatically if the venturers are well-respected, profitable, and successful in their own businesses. Large joint ventures can raise equity in the public markets, while smaller ventures may have to seek private equity investors to raise capital. In most respects, raising equity capital for a joint venture is the same as raising capital for other businesses.

(b) External Debt Financing

External investors/lenders evaluate several factors in addition to the regular criteria when considering a loan to a joint venture. For instance, the parent's creditworthiness is a significant contributing factor, as well as the venturer's previous history with similar ventures. Quite often, a full guarantee is required from the major venturer, which has to be reported as a contingent liability in their financial statements. A lender may also try to insert a joint and several liability clauses in the venture's loan document to best ensure probability of repayment.

In addition to venturer guarantees, lenders will also evaluate existing joint ventures in the same business to calculate their success and compare the returns for investors to their own return requirements. If the proposed venture is a project financing, the length of the contract and profitability for purchasing the output of the venture (i.e., electricity) will be evaluated. Included in this evaluation will be an analysis of the buyer of the project's output to calculate their ability to complete the purchase contract.

In order to increase the chances of receiving a loan, it is important to understand what the potential lender will ask. In general, the questions asked by the lender are: who, what, why, where, and when? Other questions may include:

Deal Structure	• What are the terms of the requested financing: term, interest, amount, repayment schedule, etc.?

- What are the financing alternatives/structure including the mix of debt, equity, options, and warrants?
- What additional products might the lender be able to provide or sell to the venture or the venturers if the fundings were to occur?
- Compare to industry standards for similar financings: is the structure legitimate?

Joint Venture Structure

- Who are the venturers? What are their backgrounds and abilities to complete the contemplated project?
- What is the rationale behind the ownership structure? Have the venturers worked together before and what is their ability to work together?
- What is the project? Is the project realistic and viable? What has been the success of other similar projects?
- What are the motives behind the creation of the joint venture (i.e., resource-driven, market-driven, or risk-driven)? What are the motives of the individual venturers?
- Where is the venture going to take place? What is the location, what is the country, risk, employment base, local tax incentives, community's desire for the project, rationale for the location?
- What is the timing for the project? Does it fit with the economic cycle, trends, and seasonality?
- Can the venturers clearly demonstrate why the project makes sense at the current time?

Credit Quality

- What is the financial strength of the venturers? What are the available cash flows from the venturers to finance the growth of the company?
- What access to the public markets do the venturers and the venture have?
- What is the strength of the venturer guarantees?

Projected Financial Performance

- Using the projections generated by the venturers in forecasting the future cash flows of the business, can the venture be considered realistic?

Industry Risk	• New industry or existing? • Experience of the venturers in the industry—do they understand the industry or is it still being pioneered? • What is the venture performance compared to industry standards? What obstacles may exist?
Political/Government Risk	• What is the risk of political/government upheaval, repossession of assets, coups, etc.?
Management Team	• Who is the management team? What is their expertise and track record for this business? • Will the management and venturers be able to work together?
Collateral	• What is the collateral being pledged by the venture? What is its quality compared to the risk? • What is the salvage value of the project at any time from the beginning to the end of the project?
Exit Strategies	• What are the exit strategies for the investors and for the bank? • What is the time frame for exit? • Are there any contingency plans?

(c) Negotiating with a Lender

If external debt financing has been decided upon, then the following tips on negotiating with a lender will ensure that some of the pertinent issues have been evaluated.[2]

• Raise all the concerns you may have, because it is better to understand and discover potential problems at this stage of the process than to find out later. All the terms of an agreement are negotiable until the document is signed.

---

[2] *Financing Source Guide.* Coopers & Lybrand L.L.P., 1992, pp. 65–84.

- Try to put a cap on the interest rate. The extra interest payments may become unattainable if there is no ceiling.
- Try to maximize the available funding:
    - Tie the amount of available financings to the growth rate of your company to allow for increases on a go-forward basis.
    - Try to negotiate periodic over-advances.
- Maximize the advance rate for the line of credit by focusing on the quality of the underlying assets.
- Realize that there are many lenders available and try to get the best terms possible.
- Try to evaluate all the fees (i.e., underwriting fee, unused line fee, and so on) involved in the financing because they can become significant. All these fees are negotiable.
- Try to delay repayment of the debt for as long as possible.
- Try to avoid large prepayment penalties.
- If possible, try to avoid personal or venturer company guarantees. This will include the exclusion of a joint and several guarantee. If there is such a guarantee, then an additional agreement between the venturers may need to be crafted to ensure that the financial venturer is reimbursed for any disproportionate payments they need to make.
- Focus on restrictions and covenants. Restrictions that may not seem onerous today may end up being extremely difficult to meet in the future. Some examples are: unusual required financial ratios, restrictions on management practices, limits on dividend payments, capital expenditure restrictions, controls on raising additional debt, and the prevention of the sale of parts of the business.

3.7 EXTERNAL FINANCING SOURCES

(a) Commercial Banks

Commercial banks are the major source of unsecured debt, and will lend up to 80% of working capital and 100% of the equity in a business on an unsecured basis. Commercial banks are also a source of secured debt based on machinery, equipment, accounts receivable, and inventory. They usually charge loan origination fees and points based on a percentage of the loan value. These fees can range from one to three percent of the loan value.

(b) Commercial Finance Companies

Commercial finance companies are a good source of financing for joint ventures. The large finance companies usually have a dedicated project/joint venture finance group. These groups usually require collateral and will lend against receivables, inventory, and other assets. Obviously, it may be some time before receivables are generated and, therefore, these lenders may look at the contracts to purchase the joint venture's output to discern whether there is future value. The interest rates are usually floating and linked to the prime rate, federal funds rate, or London InterBank Offering Rate (LIBOR). The amount of the loan will increase and decrease as the collateral rises and falls. Therefore, the finance companies watch the collateral very closely and might require a daily report of the asset base. Fees for these types of loans vary but usually include an origination fee and an annual fee based on the outstanding loan balance.

(c) Insurance Companies

Insurance companies have become a premier source of funds due to their large capital bases. Traditionally, they have been conservative in their lending practices, but they will currently lend different risk profiles of debt and even take equity positions. In order to increase their returns, they have also begun to invest in subordinated debt with equity conversion rights or preferred stock with warrants. Most loans from insurance companies have terms between 7 and 15 years and the interest rates are matched to the corresponding treasury rate (i.e., 7-year loan, 7-year treasury rate), plus a risk premium. Insurance companies are forbidden to charge fees for their financings.

(d) Pension Funds

Pension funds have similar investment profiles to the insurance companies. They are also prohibited from charging fees. This source of financing is relatively new.

(e) Venture Capital Firms

Venture capital firms (VCs) require an extremely high rate of return, in the order of 35–50%. Generally, this type of return is achieved through equity investment in high risk-reward ventures. Sometimes the VCs will invest in subordinated debt or preferred equity with equity "kickers" to boost their return. Some venture capitalists will invest in R&D limited ventures which fit their risk profile. They may also require voting control of the venture.

(f) Public Markets

In some cases, a joint venture may need to go to the public markets and raise equity or debt. This process is usually handled by an investment banker who is knowledgeable in this area. This method of financing may also be useful for large project financings which require huge amounts of capital and have well-regarded parents.

CHAPTER FOUR

Accounting and Reporting by Joint Ventures

4.1   GENERAL

This chapter addresses various considerations related to accounting and financial statements of joint ventures. Partnership accounting, which applies to many joint ventures, is covered separately in Chapter 8. Accounting by joint ventures is illustrated as part of the cases in Chapter 7.

4.2 CORPORATE JOINT VENTURES

If the formation of a corporate joint venture does not include the contribution of monetary assets, accounting for the formation is usually relatively simple. For example, if two participants form a corporate joint venture and contribute equal amounts of cash in exchange for the issuance of stock, these transactions are simply recorded in a new general ledger set up for the joint venture corporation.

However, if nonmonetary assets such as stock of an existing corporation or the net assets of an existing business are contributed by one or more of the participants, the accounting and financial reporting becomes more complex. In many cases, purchase accounting is used to revalue the net assets or net assets underlying the stock of the corporation that were contributed. In other cases, the assets are not revalued and predecessor cost is used as the accounting basis by the joint venture. If the fair market value of nonmonetary assets contributed is not readily determinable, predecessor cost would ordinarily be used as the joint venture's basis. This issue can arise especially if all participants contribute nonmonetary assets.

The Securities and Exchange Commission (SEC) has allowed the step-up of basis of contributed assets to corporate joint ventures with publicly traded stock, provided that certain conditions are met.

If revaluation is used for financial reporting by the joint venture, two basic approaches for the recordkeeping aspects of the revaluations required by purchase accounting are:

- The accounting records of the contributed company or business operations continue on a historical basis as prior to the formation of the joint venture, and the revaluations and related effects on future income and expenses are recorded as consolidation adjustments.
- The revaluations are recorded directly in the accounts of the acquired company, creating a new basis of accounting.

The term "push-down" accounting refers to the practice of preparing separate financial statements of an entity that includes purchase accounting adjustments arising from a change in ownership. The first approach described above can be used if separate financial statements of the contributed corporation are to be prepared using historical amounts. However, additional financial statements for the contributed corporation could also be prepared on a push-down accounting basis by adjusting, on a worksheet basis, the historical amounts to reflect purchase accounting adjustments.

The second approach described above would set up the primary books of account of the contributed corporation to include amounts after purchase accounting adjustments. Using this approach may make sense only if historical financial statements of the contributed corporation are not needed in the future. Before deciding to push the purchase accounting adjustments into the primary books of account, one should consider whether historical amounts will be necessary, for example, for preparation of tax returns in the future. If the joint venture formation has not resulted in changes to the inside basis for tax purposes of the contributed corporation, or if there is a continuing minority interest, the author believes that the most effective approach is to leave the historical books intact and to make worksheet adjustments in preparing separate financial statements of the joint venture.

See Section 7.3, which includes illustrations of accounting and financial reporting by a corporate joint venture with contributions of nonmonetary assets that are revalued. The illustrations in Section 7.3 present accounting for both approaches of: (a) maintaining historical books of a contributed corporation and making purchase accounting adjustments in consolidation, and (b) adjusting the books of the contributed corporation for the purchase accounting adjustments.

4.3 JOINT ACTIVITIES WITH NO SEPARATE JOINT VENTURE ENTITY

The author has seen cases in which separate books and financial statements are prepared for joint activities where there is no separate joint venture entity. Such books and financial statements may be prepared following principles analogous to generally accepted accounting principles (GAAP) or may be prepared in accordance with recordkeeping and reporting requirements specified in the agreements for the joint activity.

4.4   MISCELLANEOUS

(a) Title Transfer Dates

Sometimes regulatory or other causes delay the legal transfer of stock, other interests, or assets contributed to a joint venture until a date later than the date of joint venture formation. In practice, it has been accepted to include those in the joint venture's financial statements from the date of joint venture formation if a definitive agreement states that the transfer is to be made, the joint venture has control of the assets, and there are no significant contingencies regarding the ability to make the legal transfer. Any such situations should be discussed in the notes to the financial statements of the joint venture.

(b) Accounting Policies

Accounting policies are set at inception of the joint venture. If the policies differ from those of a contributed existing entity, this is not considered to be a change in accounting policy.

4.5   FOOTNOTE DISCLOSURES IN FINANCIAL STATEMENTS OF A JOINT VENTURE

The author believes that if a joint venture formation includes the contribution of an existing business, the notes to the financial statements of the joint venture should include, to the extent applicable, the disclosures specified in paragraph 95 of Accounting Principles Board (APB) Opinion No. 16, *Business Combinations*. While these requirements apply directly to corporate joint ventures, the author believes they should be provided for any structure of joint ventures to the extent that they are applicable and informative. These are listed as follows in the context of a joint venture formation:

- Name and a brief description of the contributed company or business
- Method of accounting for the joint venture formation—that is, by the purchase method, with revaluation of contributed nonmonetary assets

- Period for which results of operations of the contributed company or business are included in the income statement of the joint venture
- Value assigned to the contributed company or business and, if applicable, the number of shares of stock issued or issuable and the amount assigned to the issued and issuable shares
- Description of the plan for amortization of acquired goodwill, the amortization method, and period
- Contingent payments, options or commitments specified in the joint venture formation agreement, and their proposed accounting treatment

Opinion 16, paragraph 96, as amended by the Financial Accounting Standards Board (FASB) Statement No. 79, *Elimination of Certain Disclosures for Business Combinations Accounted for by the Purchase Method*, requires that if a joint venture is a publicly held company, notes to the financial statements for the period in which a purchase method joint venture formation takes place should include as supplemental information the following on a pro forma basis:

- Results of operations for the current period as though the companies had combined at the beginning of the period, unless the acquisition was at or near the beginning of the period
- Results of operations for the immediately preceding period as though the companies had combined at the beginning of that period if comparable financial statements are presented

The pro forma data need only be presented for the period of combination and the immediately preceding period. The minimum information to be disclosed in the pro forma information includes revenues, income before extraordinary items, net income, and earnings per share. In computing the pro forma results, the purchase accounting adjustments should be assumed to have taken place at the beginning of the period prior to the acquisition. The adjustments to actual data necessary to present the data on a pro forma basis will include any required changes to income taxes, preferred stock dividends, depreciation, and amortization. With respect to a joint venture formation, the only applicable disclosures may be to present the prior period pro forma data for an existing company or business that was contributed.

4.6 FASB NEW BASIS OF ACCOUNTING PROJECT

One phase of the Financial Accounting Standards Board's (FASB) major project on consolidations and related matters, the "New Basis of Accounting" phase, addresses the issue of when, if ever, an entity should recognize a new basis of accounting. A new basis of accounting would change the carrying amounts of assets (including goodwill) and liabilities to their current fair values. The project explores a series of transactions or events that may lead to preferability of revaluation, rather than continuing to carry historical amounts forward. The work in this area led to the issuance of an FASB Discussion Memorandum, *New Basis of Accounting*, in July 1992. While serving as an FASB project manager, the author participated in the research and discussions on this phase of the project.

The Discussion Memorandum discusses and illustrates various circumstances, including formations of and sales of interests in corporate joint ventures. Practice varies with respect to how a joint venture entity reports assets contributed by joint venturers. Most accounting literature focuses on how joint venturers report their share of a joint venture's financial position and operations, rather than how such are reported in the separate financial statements of the joint venture. The Discussion Memorandum explores the accounting alternatives in the following situations:

- Formation of a 50–50 corporate joint venture with initial investment of cash and property
- Formation of a 50–50 corporate joint venture with initial investment of property
- Formation of a 50–50 corporate joint venture with initial investment of property preceded by a cash transaction
- Formation of a 50–50 corporate joint venture by sale of 50% interest in an existing subsidiary
- Cash sale of a 50% interest by an investor in a corporate joint venture
- Acquisition of a 50% interest in a corporate joint venture by issuance of new shares

This section of the Discussion Memorandum discusses various views about why or why not a new basis should be recognized in financial reporting by a joint venture. Further work in this and other phases of the consolidation project may lead to future accounting principles that apply specifically to external financial reporting by joint venture entities.

CHAPTER FIVE

Accounting for Investments in Joint Ventures — General

5.1 CHARACTERISTICS OF JOINT VENTURES

The Financial Accounting Standards Board's (FASB) Issues Paper, *Joint Venture Accounting*, which was issued in July 1979, includes two descriptions that essentially provide boundaries within which entities or business activities are considered joint ventures for accounting purposes. The first description is from Section 3055 of the Canadian Institute of Chartered Accountants (CICA) Handbook:

> A joint venture is an arrangement whereby two or more parties (the venturers) jointly control a specific business undertaking and contribute resources towards its accomplishment. The life of the joint venture is limited to that of the undertaking which may be of short or long-term duration depending on the circumstances. A distinctive feature of a joint venture is that the relationship between the venturers is governed by an agreement (usually in writing) which establishes joint control. Decisions in all areas essential to the accomplishment of a joint venture require the consent of the venturers, as provided by the agreement;

none of the individual venturers is in a position to unilaterally control the venture. This feature of joint control distinguishes investments in joint ventures from investments in other enterprises where control of decisions is related to the proportion of voting interest held.

The 1979 FASB Issues Paper recommended that the substance of the CICA definition be used as the definition of a joint venture for accounting purposes. The 1979 FASB Issues Paper also included the following description of a joint venture taken from an unpublished draft of an Accounting Research Study authorized by the Accounting Principles Board (APB) on the subject of intercorporate investments:

An entity owned by a limited number of investors who have entered into operating agreements and contracts under with the "joint owners" assume all the characteristics and obligations of venturers. The "joint owners" may consist of two or more investors who may or may not have equal interests in the corporation. One of the "joint owners" may even own a majority interest. The joint venture corporation itself may either (1) pass on the costs and expenses of its product or services to the "joint owners" or (2) operate as a profit-making corporation, in which case the "joint owners" share in the net income generated.

Other joint-endeavor entities that should be included in any discussion of the problem, whether cost-sharing or profit-making, are the joint venture, the partnership, and various joint operating agreements. . . . Each constitutes a business entity or a business component. The assets used in the operation may be the property of the entity of itself or of one or more of the "joint owners" who agree that such assets are merely to be used by the entity. In the latter case, the entity comprises only the operations conducted under the joint-operating agreement. The term "joint-venture entity" refers then to both corporate and non-corporate joint-ownership ventures, whether they are distinct business entities or components of a business entity.

APB Opinion No. 18, *The Equity Method of Accounting for Investments in Common Stock*, defines *corporate joint venture* as follows:

"Corporate joint venture" refers to a corporation owned and operated by a small group of businesses [the "joint venturers"] as a separate and specific business or project for the mutual benefit of the members of the group. Government may also be a member of the group. The purpose of a corporate joint venture frequently is to share risks and rewards in developing a new market, product, or technology; to combine complementary technological knowledge; or to pool resources in developing production or other facilities. A corporate joint venture also usually provides an arrangement under which each joint venturer may participate, directly or indirectly, in the overall management of the joint venture. Joint venturers thus have an interest or relationship other than as passive investors. An entity which is a subsidiary of one of the "joint venturers" is not a corporate joint venture. The ownership of a corporate joint venture seldom changes, and its stock is usually not traded publicly. A minority public ownership, however, does not preclude a corporation from being a corporate joint venture. [APB Opinion No. 18, paragraph 3d]

The author suggests that the following efficiently describes the key characteristics of a joint venture: A joint venture is an arrangement that involves the cooperative efforts and resources of two or more participants working together to achieve agreed-upon goals. A joint venture may operate using a separate joint venture entity or may operate by agreement without a separate legal entity, is operated for the benefit of its participants, is jointly controlled by its participants, and is not controlled by a single party.

In the business community, the term "joint venture" is sometimes used to refer to a situation in which one of the participants owns a majority interest of an entity. For example, two companies might use the term of joint venture in reference to an entity that is 60% owned by one of the companies and 40% by the other, with each substantially participating in management and business activities of the investee entity. However, one participant has ultimate control. For accounting purposes, this would not be a joint venture. The 60% owner will almost always be required to consolidate the investee's accounts as a subsidiary and report the 40% owner's interest as a minority interest.

5.2 METHODS OF ACCOUNTING FOR INVESTMENTS IN JOINT VENTURES

(a) The Equity Method

The equity method is used to account for investments in corporate joint ventures. The characteristics in the definition of "joint venture" include an investor who has the ability to participate in the management of a joint venture and to influence its policies. This usually determines that the equity method should be used.

(b) Partnership Accounting

Investments in joint venture partnerships are accounted for by using partnership accounting. Although the equity method does not apply to unincorporated joint ventures in partnership form, generally accepted accounting principles (GAAP) for partnerships are substantially the same as those of the equity method.

(c) Accounting for Participation in Joint Activities with No Separate Joint Venture Entity

For joint ventures that are not conducted within a separate entity, such as participation in joint activities by contract, the author has observed an array of methods used in practice by the participants. In one approach, each participant accounts for its own assets, liabilities, revenue, expenses, gains, and losses as part of the totals of each in its own financial statements. Essentially, the totals for each item are consolidated with the participant's financial statements. For example, a participant would account for any assets provided for use in the joint venture activity. A participant would account for its share, or undivided interest, in financial statement items of a joint venture activity in which the participant and other participants each have an ownership interest. This approach is sometimes referred to as accounting for "undivided interests." While the FASB project manager for the FASB project on Consolidations and Related Matters, which included accounting for joint ventures, the author was called on to explain this approach numerous times. The author often used the following illustration by way of explanation.

Say that Participant A and Participant B agree to jointly operate a flower shop. Participant A has a lease on a storefront that is used. Participant B has cooler equipment and a cash register that is used. Each has a 50% interest in revenue and will pay 50% of the cash costs.

In the first month, using accrual accounting, the joint venture has sales of $10,000 and cash costs of $6,000. At the end of the period, joint venture cash totals $3,750, accounts receivable total $1,000, and accounts payable total $750. Each participant would report sales of $5,000, expenses of $3,000, cash of $1,875, accounts receivable of $500, and accounts payable of $375 in its financial statements. Participant A continues to report 100% of the rent expense that it pays for the storefront. Participant B continues to carry the equipment as part of its fixed assets and continues to report related depreciation expense.

Further, assume that on the first day of the second month, the participants use $2,200 of the cash to purchase a delivery truck, with each participant having a 50% undivided interest. Each participant would, in essence, record a reduction of cash of $1,100 and an increase to equipment of $1,100. Thereafter, each participant would report 50% of the depreciation expense related to the new equipment in which each has an ownership interest.

(d) Other Ways of Accounting for Investments in Joint Ventures

Various other approaches and variations of the above methods are seen in practice. The author has observed joint venture participants using a "one-line" approach like the equity method to account for participation in joint activities by contract where there was no separate entity. Some joint venture participants use pro rata consolidation for their proportionate share of assets, liabilities, revenue, expenses, gains, and losses of a joint venture entity. Such pro rata consolidation is an accepted practice in certain specialized industries, such as the mining industry, and is also seen occasionally in industries that do not recognize this as an industry practice.

A variation of the equity method that is sometimes used is the "expanded equity method." The principles of the equity method are used except that the participant's financial statement presentation uses a mixture of equity method one-line presentation and pro rata consolidation. Usually, the participant presents its proportionate shares of the joint venture's current assets, noncurrent assets, current liabilities, and noncurrent liabilities as separate line items in its balance sheet. A variety of summarized presentations in the financial statements such as the foregoing may be used.

5.3 PRINCIPLES OF PURCHASE ACCOUNTING

(a) General

Principles of the purchase method of accounting are often used in accounting for investments in joint ventures and for preparing the separate financial statements of joint ventures. The principles of the purchase method are similar to the general accounting principles for acquisition of assets and issuance of stock.

Following are broad principles of the purchase method that are relevant to joint venture accounting:

- The total cost is determined.
- The cost is allocated to identifiable assets in proportion to their respective fair values.
- If the total cost exceeds the fair value of the identifiable assets, the excess is allocated to goodwill; any excess of total fair value of the identifiable assets over total cost is applied as a pro rata reduction of long-term assets.
- Goodwill is amortized over a period not exceeding 40 years.

(b) Determining Cost

(i) General. The general guidance in paragraph 67 of APB Opinion No. 16, *Business Combinations*, is that the cost of assets acquired in a purchase should be determined in accordance with the general principles for accounting for acquisitions of assets.

- An asset acquired by exchanging cash or other assets is recorded at cost — that is, at the amount of cash disbursed or the fair value of other assets distributed.
- An asset acquired by incurring liabilities is recorded at cost — that is, at the present value of the amounts to be paid.
- An asset acquired by issuing shares of stock of the acquiring corporation is recorded at the fair value of the asset — that is, shares of stock issued are recorded at the fair value of the consideration received for stock.

(ii) Stock Issued in Payment of Purchase Price. Many acquisitions are made by exchanging cash or incurring liabilities for the net assets or stock of another company. Alternatively, equity securities of an acquiring company may be issued in exchange for the assets or stock of an acquired company. The cost of an acquisition paid for in stock is normally measured by the market price

of the stock exchanged at the date of acquisition. However, market prices for a reasonable period of time before and after the terms of an acquisition are agreed to and announced should be considered in establishing the value to be placed on the securities to avoid volatility of stock prices unduly affecting the recorded cost of the acquisition. If restricted securities are issued in an acquisition, an appraisal of the value of such securities by qualified professionals, such as investment bankers, may be necessary to establish value.

If fair value of securities issued in an acquisition is not readily determinable, all indicators of value should be considered, such as an estimate of the value of the assets received, including a direct estimate of goodwill. This basis of valuation will usually be more relevant to joint ventures that are formed by a joint venture acquiring assets or stock of an existing corporation.

(iii) Direct Expenses of Transaction. Acquisition costs should include directly related expenses such as finders' fees, directly related professional (for example, legal, accounting, and appraisal) fees, and incremental in-house costs that were directly caused by and related to the transaction. The normal costs of an internal acquisitions department, or officers or employees who work on acquisitions or joint ventures, are not includable in the cost of acquisitions because they are not incremental.

(iv) Premium or Discount. Purchase accounting requires recognition of present value concepts. Premium or discount on a debt security issued or assumed should be imputed to adjust the liability to present value based on current market interest or yield rates if the stated interest or yield rate varies significantly from current market rates. The procedure for assigning fair value to individual assets and liabilities (generally receivables or payables) requires discounting to present value or assigning a premium allocation. After acquisition, interest expense or income should be recorded through amortization of the premium or discount, using the interest method.

(v) Assets Exchanged. Assets conveyed to a seller as consideration in an acquisition should be included in the acquisition cost at fair value. Any deferred taxes related to the assets given up should be removed from the balance sheet and applied as a reduction of the fair value of the acquired assets.

(vi) Contingent Consideration. Contingent consideration on future earnings of an acquired operation should be added to acquisition cost when the

amounts are determinable beyond a reasonable doubt. Acquisition cost should be increased at that time and the additional cost allocated to assets acquired in accordance with the purchase method, usually resulting in an adjustment to long-term assets or goodwill. The additional cost should be depreciated or amortized prospectively over the remaining useful lives of the related assets. If stock has been given in consideration with a contingency requiring the issuance of additional shares or payments of cash dependent on fluctuation in future security prices, issuance of additional shares does not result in future adjustment of acquisition cost. The recorded value of shares previously issued is reduced by an amount equal to the fair value of the consideration (cash, stock, or other) paid upon resolution of the contingency.

Interest and dividends paid to an escrow agent on contingently issuable debt or securities should not be recorded as interest or dividends. Upon resolution of the contingency, if payment by the agent to the seller is required, the amounts should be recorded as additional acquisition costs if the contingency was based on earnings. If the contingency was based on security prices, the treatment is the same as for contingently issuable securities in that the value of securities previously issued is reduced to result in no change to total recorded acquisition cost and to the allocation of purchase price.

(vii) Preacquisition Contingencies. A negotiated adjustment to the purchase price related to the assumption of a contingency by the acquirer is properly includable in the cost of acquisition. Certain resolutions of contingencies after the acquisition can result in adjustments to acquisition costs.

(c) Allocating Cost to Assets and Liabilities

(i) General. Purchase accounting requires the allocation of total acquisition cost to assets acquired and liabilities assumed on the basis of their respective fair values. If the total acquisition cost exceeds the fair values of identifiable net assets, the excess is allocated to goodwill. If the fair value of identifiable assets and liabilities exceeds acquisition cost (referred to as "negative goodwill"), the deficiency is applied as a pro rata reduction of the assigned values of long-term assets, except for long-term investments in marketable securities. If long-term assets are eliminated by this procedure, any remaining negative goodwill is recorded as a deferred credit and amortized over a period not to exceed 40 years.

FASB Statement No. 109, *Accounting for Income Taxes*, which was issued in 1992, provides an array of accounting rules and procedures for establishing deferred taxes as part of the allocation of purchase price in both goodwill and negative goodwill situations, as well as for other income tax-related aspects of accounting for acquisitions.

If an acquisition was for less than 100% of an acquired company, adjustments to the carrying value of identifiable assets and liabilities are made only to the extent of the proportionate share acquired by the acquirer, and the portion of the acquired company attributable to the remaining minority interest continues to be accounted for on a historical basis.

(ii) Appraisals. Independent appraisals are often the primary means of determining the estimated fair values to be used in assigning costs. In the absence of evidence that other amounts are better estimates, the appraised values are often used as the fair values.

In a formal appraisal, an amount may be assigned to goodwill to reflect the estimated value of the acquired operation's going concern value. The basis for the goodwill may be the existence of an existing customer base or market share, an assembled and trained work force, or other intangibles of value. The appraiser may estimate the fair value of appraised goodwill based on guidelines, including percentages of goodwill to total acquisition cost evidenced in recent comparable acquisitions.

An appraiser may be aware of the total acquisition cost and may use this information in developing appraisals of individual items and the proportions of tangible and intangible assets. If the total appraised values of identifiable assets vary by an unusual amount from the total acquisition cost, ordinarily there should be an identifiable reason. For example, the acquisition cost of an unusually highly profitable business may include a higher than normal amount of goodwill. Conversely, the acquisition cost of an operation that has been experiencing losses or that a seller must sell under distress conditions for some reason, may be less than the fair values of the individual assets, resulting in negative goodwill.

In some cases the appraised values of individual assets must be adjusted to reflect certain accounting valuation adjustments required for purchase method acquisitions, such as an adjustment to a value indicated by additional information that is to be more indicative of fair value, such as a subsequent sale of one or more of the acquired assets at an amount differing from the appraised value.

(iii) APB 16 Guidelines for Allocations. *General.* Guidelines that are provided in paragraph 87 of Opinion 16 for allocating purchase price to assets acquired and liabilities assumed are presented below together with a discussion of some of the more significant aspects of implementing the guidelines in practice. These guidelines are discussed in the following sections.

Marketable Securities. Marketable securities should be recorded at current net realizable values.

Receivables. Receivables should be recorded at present values of amounts to be received, determined at appropriate current interest rates, less allowances for uncollectibility and collection costs, if necessary.

In practice, acquired trade accounts receivable expected to be collected in accordance with normal collection terms for most industries are not discounted to present value. However, if a receivable is expected to remain outstanding for a length of time that will result in a more significant discount factor, discounts should be reflected in the acquisition accounting.

Acquired notes receivable that bear an interest rate varying significantly from current market rates for similar notes should be adjusted for imputed discount or premium. The adjustment should result in an increase or decrease in interest income from the date of acquisition to the date of collection, to recognize an interest rate equal to current market rates on the adjusted receivable amount recorded at acquisition.

Inventories. Finished goods and merchandise should be recorded at estimated selling prices less the sum of: (a) costs of disposal and (b) a reasonable profit allowance for the selling effort of the acquiring corporation. Work in progress should be recorded at estimated selling prices of finished goods less the sum of: (a) costs to complete, (b) costs of disposal, and (c) a reasonable profit allowance for the completing and selling effort of the acquiring corporation based on profit for similar finished goods. Raw materials should be recorded at current replacement costs.

Special aspects of purchase accounting for inventories are discussed in Section 5.3(d)(i).

Plant and Equipment. Plant and equipment to be used should be recorded at current replacement costs for similar capacity unless the expected future use of the asset indicates a lower value to the acquirer. Plant and equipment to be sold or held for later sale rather than used should be recorded at current net realizable value. Plant and equipment to be used temporarily should be recorded at current net realizable value, recognizing future depreciation for the expected period of use.

If the total fair value of all identifiable assets acquired is greater than the total acquisition cost, the difference is applied as a proportionate reduction of the values assigned to long-term assets, including fixed assets. None of the difference is allocated to long-term marketable securities, nor would an allocation be appropriate to other long-term assets that have a cash equivalency with easy conversion. This allocation interacts with computing deferred taxes related to long-term assets.

Intangible Assets. Intangible assets that can be identified and named, including contracts, patents, franchises, customer and supplier lists, and favorable leases, should be recorded at appraised values.

Identifiable intangible assets should be valued before amounts are allocated to goodwill. Certain identifiable intangible assets may be amortized for tax purposes. In addition to the above, identifiable intangible assets may include customer lists, technology rights, patents and trademarks, and computer programs and software.

FASB Interpretation No. 4, *Applicability of FASB Statement No. 2 to Business Combinations Accounted for by the Purchase Method*, provides for the allocation of cost to identifiable tangible and intangible assets, including:

- Any assets acquired in the combinations that result from research and development activities of the acquired enterprise (such as patents, blueprints, formulas, and designs for new products)
- Assets acquired to be used in research and development activities of the combined enterprise (such as materials, supplies, equipment, and specific research projects in process)

Costs incurred related to research and development activities after an acquisition are accounted for in accordance with FASB Statement No. 2, *Accounting for Research and Development Costs*.

Additionally, if a purchase agreement includes a covenant that the seller will not compete with the acquirer for a specified period of time, a portion of the purchase price can be assigned to the covenant as an identifiable intangible that may be amortized for tax purposes.

Other Assets. Other assets, including land, natural resources, and nonmarketable securities, should be recorded at appraised values.

Accounts and Notes Payable. Accounts and notes payable, long-term debt, and other claims payable should be recorded at present values of amounts to be paid determined at appropriate current interest rates. The possible need to impute a premium or discount to adjust stated interest rates to current market rates should be considered.

Accrued Liabilities. Accrued liabilities, such as accruals for pension cost warranties, vacation pay, or deferred compensation should be recorded at present values of amounts to be paid determined at appropriate current interest rates.

Pension Costs. Purchase agreements often require the continuation of existing pension plans or that an acquirer otherwise continue to provide retirement benefits for the employees of an acquired company at least equal to those previously provided by the seller. The pension plan and related fund assets may be transferred intact to provide continuation of the existing plan or the employees may be integrated into a pension plan maintained by the acquirer. A purchase agreement may require adjustments to the purchase price to be made for future benefits to be provided for preacquisition service. For example, a seller may be required to make a payment to an acquirer or to a pension fund of an amount equal to any excess of vested benefits over fund assets related to pension plans as of the acquisition date. If an acquirer assumes a pension situation "as is" on the acquisition date, the acquirer should include in the acquisition cost and in the acquired balance sheet an accrual for the present value of the excess of vested benefits over pension fund assets, if any.

Vacation Pay and Compensated Absences. Purchase agreements often provide for a reduction of the purchase price by an amount equal to earned compensated absences, such as vacation pay, to be paid after the acquisition date. The liability should be included in computing the total acquisition cost and included as a liability in the acquired balance sheet. FASB Statement No. 43, *Accounting for Compensated Absences*, provides accounting standards for accounting for compensated absences. Vacation pay and other compensated absences must be recorded as balance sheet liabilities if employees have earned vested rights to such payments.

Other Liabilities. Other liabilities and commitments including unfavorable leases, contracts, and commitments and plant closing expenses, incident to the acquisition, should be recorded at present values of amounts to be paid determined at appropriate current interest rates.

(d) Purchase Accounting in Special Areas

(i) Inventories. *Allocation of Cost Including Seller's Profit.* The guidelines for recording acquired inventories are similar to the guidelines for other assets in that they are intended to result in assigning the value an acquirer would theoretically have had to pay to acquire the inventory items individually in their current state. For inventory, the price paid would include compensating a manufacturer for the normal profit factor allocable to manufacturing work performed on work-in-process and finished goods inventories. Therefore, amounts allocable to inventories can usually be expected to be greater than the historical cost book value of the inventories in the balance sheet of a seller, as a result of possibly higher replacement costs for raw materials and a profit attributable to manufacturing work performed by the seller on inventory items prior to the acquisition.

Allocating cost to inventory as discussed above often results in a lower reported profit as a percentage of sales in the income statement of an acquirer for the period following the acquisition because inventories sold in that period bear a higher-than-normal cost. The lower profit reflects that the earning process performed by an acquirer with respect to acquired finished goods (and work-in-process to a lesser extent) related only to the selling effort, and not to the manufacturing effort.

Inventory Purchased in a Separate Contract. The author has seen purchase transactions structured so that inventory is acquired pursuant to a separate contract and for a separate and distinct payment, which may be an amount equal to the book value of the inventories in the financial statements of the seller, or some other negotiated amount that may vary from the amount that would be allocated based on the above method. The substantive terms of a purchase transaction should be carefully evaluated to determine if it is justifiable to treat the inventory acquisition separately from the acquisition of the other assets, and to assign lower amounts to the acquired inventories, resulting in higher reported gross profits in the period after the acquisition. If the acquisition has been broken into pieces merely to avoid a higher allocation of purchase price to inventory, thereby increasing gross profit in the period following the acquisition, the author believes that the separate transactions should be collapsed into one, with an allocation of the entire purchase price to all the assets as required by Opinion 16.

Last-in First-out (LIFO) Inventory. If a business combination is accounted for as a purchase but is tax-free, or is accounted for by the pooling of interests method but is taxable, differences in the value assigned for accounting and tax purposes to inventory accounted for using the LIFO method can result.

In a purchase method acquisition, the acquirer is required to revalue the inventories to fair value at acquisition date, and the entire inventory is treated as a single LIFO layer acquired in the year of acquisition. If the transaction has been a tax-free exchange, the previous LIFO inventory layers and values may be carried forward for tax purposes. This would ordinarily cause the book LIFO inventory balance to be greater than the tax LIFO inventory. If a taxable transaction is accounted for as a pooling of interests, the reverse would ordinarily occur—the tax LIFO inventory amount would be greater than the book LIFO inventory amount.

The resulting differences between book and tax LIFO values and layers are carried forward from the date of acquisition. If inventory levels increase thereafter, book and tax cost of sales will generally be the same because the current year purchases or production will flow to cost of sales for both tax and accounting purposes. However, different values that may be allocated to fixed assets for tax and accounting purposes could create significant differences in depreciation charges allocated to production costs, which would be included in unit costs for cost of sales and incremental LIFO inventory layers. If these differences are significant enough to require recognition for accounting purposes, differences in addition to those created in the acquisition accounting can arise. The additional differences, however, may exist where "first-in, first-out" (FIFO) inventories, as well as LIFO inventories, are present.

(ii) Leases. *Unfavorable Leases.* Consistent with the basic principle that the values assigned to individual liabilities assumed should be based on fair value, if a lease assumed in a purchase bears a rental rate that is higher or lower than the current market rental rate for a similar lease, an intangible asset has been acquired, or an intangible liability has been assumed. Accordingly,

the difference between rentals required under the assumed lease and current market rental rates, discounted to present value, should be included as an asset acquired or liability assumed in the acquired balance sheet. The acquirer would record a liability at the acquisition date equal to the present value of the unfavorable lease commitment. As each subsequent lease payment is made, debits for appropriate amounts would be made to rent expense, to interest expense, and to the unfavorable lease obligation liability.

If an acquirer is required to assume a lease for an asset or facility that is of no use to the acquirer, the present value of the entire lease may be recorded as a cost of the acquisition. If only part of a leased facility or asset is of use to an acquirer, an unfavorable lease obligation should be established for the present value of the portion of future rent obligations attributable to the part of the facility or asset that is of no use.

Favorable Leases. If future rent on an assumed lease is below the market rate, the acquirer should record an asset, sometimes referred to as a "favorable lease," equal to the present value of the difference between the effective rental rate and the market rate at the date of acquisition. That amount should be amortized to rent expense ratably over the remaining term of the lease. As in the case of an unfavorable lease, this allocation is made to place the accounting for the lease on equal footing with leases in the current market. The concept is that the purchase price would be increased or decreased for the need to assume a lease that contains rental commitments that are lower or higher than the current market rents.

Lease Classification. A lease assumed in an acquisition, which was classified as an operating lease by the seller in accordance with FASB Statement No. 13, *Accounting for Leases*, continues to be accounted for as an operating lease by an acquirer if no changes are made to the terms of the lease. If the provisions of the lease are modified, the amended lease is considered to be a new lease and should be accounted for based on the criteria of Statement 13. A reclassification of a lease does not preclude the need to record the effects of any unfavorable or favorable lease commitments as described in the preceding two sections.

Assumption of a Leveraged Lease As Lessor. Leveraged leases involve financing provided by a long-term creditor that is nonrecourse to the general credit of the lessor. The creditor may have recourse only to the leased property and rentals on it. These transactions are considered to provide the lessor with significant leverage.

If an acquirer assumes a leveraged lease in an acquisition, the lease retains its classification. The acquirer should assign a net amount to the investment in the leveraged lease based on remaining cash flows adjusted for estimated future tax effects. The net investment should be divided into the following components: (a) net rentals receivable, (b) estimated residual value, and (c) unearned income including discount to adjust the other components to present value. Thereafter, leveraged lease accounting should be followed as described in Statement 13. This accounting is discussed and illustrated in FASB Interpretation No. 21, *Accounting for Leases in a Business Combination.*

(iii) Preacquisition Contingencies. Accounting principles for preacquisition contingencies are established by FASB Statement No. 38, *Accounting for Preacquisition Contingencies of Purchased Enterprises.* Statement 38 defines preacquisition contingencies as:

> . . . (a) contingency of an enterprise that is acquired in a business combination accounted for by the purchase method and that is in existence before the con-summation of the combination. A preacquisition contingency can be a contin-gent asset, a contingent liability, or a contingent impairment of an asset. . . .
> [FASB Statement No. 38, paragraph 4]

Preacquisition contingencies should be recorded in an amount equal to fair value. Fair value can be determined by the cost of resolution of a contingency during the allocation period or if the parties agreed in negotiation to an ad-justment of the purchase price by a specific amount as a result of the existence of the contingency. The allocation period lasts from the date of acquisition to when an acquirer is no longer waiting for information that it has arranged to obtain and that is known to be available or obtainable. The allocation period should usually not exceed one year from the date of the acquisition. Until the allocation period ends, the purchase price allocation should be adjusted for the effects of additional information regarding any contingencies. After the allo-cation period, any changes in the estimated fair values of contingencies are in-cluded in determining net income for the period in which the change is determined.

If fair value of a contingency cannot be determined during the allocation period, the contingency shall be included in the purchase allocation in an amount determined in accordance with the following criteria, contained in Statement 38:

(1) Information available prior to the end of the "allocation period" indicates that it is probable that an asset existed, a liability had been incurred, or an asset had been impaired at the consummation of the business combination. It is implicit in this condition that it must be probable that one or more future events will occur confirming the existence of the asset, liability, or impairment.

(2) The amount of the asset or liability can be reasonably estimated. [FASB Statement No. 38, paragraph 5]

If this approach must be used to value the contingency, the determination should be made in accordance with FASB Statement No. 5, *Accounting for Contingencies*, and the related FASB Interpretation No. 14, *Reasonable Estimation of the Amount of a Loss*.

(iv) Foreign Currency Translation.   In a purchase acquisition of a foreign operation, the assets acquired and liabilities assumed are adjusted to fair values at the date of acquisition and translated at the exchange rate in effect at the date of acquisition. Any difference between the total cost of the acquisition in dollars and the translated net assets is accounted for as goodwill or negative goodwill. Future balance sheets are translated by converting the fair values at acquisition date into dollars at the exchange rate at the balance sheet date. Any difference caused by fluctuations in exchange rates after the acquisition is accounted for in accordance with FASB Statement No. 52, *Foreign Currency Translation*.

(e) Income Tax Accounting

(i) General.   Accounting for the effects of income taxes in purchase acquisitions is governed by FASB Statement No. 109, *Accounting for Income Taxes*, which was issued in 1992. Prior to the issuance in 1987 of FASB Statement No. 96, *Accounting for Income Taxes*, accounting for income taxes in purchase acquisitions had been governed by Opinion 16. Statement 96, which amended Opinion 16's income tax accounting methods, drastically changed the income tax accounting methods required by Opinion 16. Statement 109 essentially continues the new methods established in Statement 96.

(ii) Deferred Taxes. *General.* Statement 109 requires that deferred taxes be established in a purchase price allocation for the tax effects of temporary differences between amounts of assets and liabilities to be used for financial reporting and their tax bases. This approach is quite different from previous accounting under Opinion 16, which required that such tax effects be recognized as an adjustment of the fair market value of the individual assets and liabilities.

Statement 109 provided that deferred taxes not be established for book–tax differences for goodwill to the extent that the goodwill is not deductible for tax purposes. Deferred taxes are also not established for goodwill that is recorded as a deferred credit to the extent it is not amortizable for tax purposes. Deferred taxes are also not established for leveraged leases acquired in a purchase acquisition.

Another new method established by Statement 109 is that deferred taxes are not discounted to present value from the date the tax effect is expected to be realized. Under Opinion 16, discounting of the tax effect was appropriate in determining the adjustment to be made to the fair market value of the applicable asset or liability.

Deferred Taxes in Goodwill Situations. If a purchase price exceeds the net fair value of identifiable assets and liabilities, Statement 109 requires use of the gross method of purchase price allocation. Under the gross method, purchase price is allocated using the following steps:

1. Determine the fair market values of identifiable assets and liabilities

2. Identify temporary differences related to identifiable assets and liabilities

3. Determine and recognize deferred tax asset and liabilities for deductible and taxable temporary differences

4. Determine and recognize a deferred tax assets for net operating loss and tax credit carryforwards

5. Determine and recognize a valuation allowance to reduce the value of deferred tax assets using the "more likely than not" criteria of Statement 109

6. Recognize goodwill for the difference between the total purchase price and the sum of net fair values of identifiable assets and liabilities and the deferred taxes that have been determined, net of valuation allowance

Computation of deferred taxes in a goodwill situation is illustrated as part of Exhibit 5.1.

Deferred Taxes in Negative Goodwill Situations. Statement 109 requires that deferred taxes be established for temporary differences related to the allocation to long-term assets of an excess of fair values of identifiable assets and liabilities over total purchase price, commonly referred to as negative goodwill. To synchronize the amounts to be assigned to the long-term assets and the deferred taxes, it is necessary to use a simultaneous equation. The tax rates used should be the rates expected to be in effect when the temporary differences are realized. While the simultaneous equation in Exhibit 5.1 will apply to most acquisitions, it may need modification if an acquiree has operations in more than one taxing jurisdiction, or if the acquirer's and acquiree's temporary differences, net operating loss carryforwards, tax credit carryforwards, and valuation allowances interact so as to require modification to the simultaneous equation approach.

(iii) Consolidated Tax Implications. If an acquired company will be included in the acquirer's consolidated tax return, deferred taxes attributable to the acquisition are determined based on the consolidated tax position of the consolidated entity after the acquisition, using the "more likely than not" criterion. The interaction of an acquirer's and acquiree's temporary differences, net operating loss carryforwards, and tax credit carryforwards, can result in the elimination of a valuation allowance for deferred tax assets that may have been required without the acquisition. Filing of a consolidated return may qualify as a tax strategy that would enable the realization of tax benefits.

EXHIBIT 5.1 Simultaneous Equation for Determining Adjustment in a Negative Goodwill Situation

$$\text{Net temporary difference} \times \frac{\text{Tax rate}}{(1 - \text{tax rate})} + \text{Adjustment to deferred tax assets and liabilities and noncurrent assets}$$

In determining whether the "more likely than not" criterion is met, consideration should be given to the rules related to separate return limitation year (SRLY) restrictions, limitations on built-in gains, and limitations on usage of net operating loss and tax credit carryforwards.

If tax benefits are recognized as a result of interaction of the tax positions of an acquirer and an acquiree, goodwill is reduced in the purchase price allocation. If goodwill is reduced to zero, then other long-term assets are reduced.

(iv) Postacquisition Recognition of Net Operating Loss and Tax Credit Carryforwards.   Some or all of the tax benefits of an acquirer's or acquiree's net operating loss or tax credit carryforwards may be recognized as a result of an acquisition if the "more likely than not" criterion is met at the acquisition date. If so, the effect is to reduce goodwill in the purchase price allocation.

If not, postacquisition recognition of the tax benefits of an acquirer's net operating loss or tax credit carryforwards results in a reduction of the provision for income taxes in the period of recognition. Postacquisition recognition of the tax benefits of an acquirer's or acquiree's net operating loss or tax credit carryforwards.

Some or all of the tax benefits of an acquiree's net operating loss or tax credit carryforwards may be recognized as a result of an acquisition if the "more likely than not" criterion is met at the acquisition date. If so, the effect is to reduce goodwill in the purchase price allocation. If not, subsequent recognition of the tax benefits of an acquiree's net operating loss or tax credit carryforwards should be recorded as follows:

- Goodwill from the acquisition is reduced
- If goodwill is completely eliminated, then other noncurrent intangible assets are reduced until fully eliminated
- Any further tax benefits are recorded as a reduction of the provision for income taxes

If tax benefits of an acquired company have been recognized at the acquisition date and, at a later date, it is determined that a valuation allowance is needed for the applicable items, the establishment of the valuation allowance is recorded as an increase in the provision for income taxes. Retroactive increases to goodwill are not appropriate.

If an acquired net operating loss or tax credit carryforward is utilized in a future period but is offset by a new temporary difference, the tax benefit of which is in turn recognized in a future period, the recognition is viewed as being attributable to the acquired net operating loss or tax credit carryforward. Accordingly, goodwill is reduced, notwithstanding the fact that there was an intervening temporary difference that delayed the ultimate tax effect of the net operating loss or tax credit carryforward.

Applicable tax law should be followed in determining the order in which net operating loss and tax credit carryforwards are utilized. This has accounting significance because postacquisition of an acquirer's net operating loss or tax credit carryforwards are recorded as a reduction of the provision for income taxes, whereas those of an acquiree are recorded as reductions of goodwill. If applicable tax laws do not provide the order of utilization, then the utilization should be prorated based on the proportion of the acquirer's and acquiree's respective shares of the carryforwards utilized.

If the tax benefit from an excess of tax basis of an acquired asset over the amount assigned to the asset (excess tax basis) in a purchase method allocation is not recognized in the purchase price accounting at acquisition date, subsequent recognition of that tax benefit is accounted for the same as a postacquisition recognition of an acquiree's net operating loss or tax credit carryforward, described above.

(v) Goodwill. In taxable acquisitions, sometimes a financial statement allocation to goodwill relates partly to amounts allocated to another asset for tax purposes that are deductible through amortization or otherwise. In this situation, the other asset is viewed as having excess tax basis, resulting in a temporary difference. Recognition of the tax benefit of the deductibility of that other asset is accounted for as a purchased excess tax basis at either the acquisition date or after the acquisition date.

Temporary differences are not recognizable related to goodwill for which deductions may not be taken for tax purposes. Likewise, temporary differences are not recognized for negative goodwill.

For taxing jurisdictions in which goodwill is deductible for taxes, the book and tax goodwill is divided into two categories: (a) the lesser of book or tax deductible goodwill and (b) the remainder of any book or tax goodwill. For category (a) goodwill, any basis difference (say, from different amortization amounts or writedowns) that arises in postacquisition periods is accounted for as a temporary difference.

For category (b), if tax deductible goodwill exceeds book goodwill, there will be no category (b) book goodwill and category (b) tax goodwill will be equal to the excess of tax deductible goodwill over book goodwill. If book goodwill exceeds tax deductible goodwill, there will be no category (b) tax goodwill and category (b) book goodwill will be equal to the excess of book goodwill over tax deductible goodwill. Deferred taxes are not recognized for category (b) goodwill. If category (b) goodwill consists of tax deductible goodwill when the benefits are realized, they are recognized as a reduction of book goodwill, then as a reduction of other acquired noncurrent intangible assets, and then as a reduction of the provision for income taxes.

(vi) Aggressive Tax Positions. Deferred taxes established at the date of an acquisition should be determined based on management's estimate of the tax basis that will be accepted by tax authorities, not withstanding the fact that more aggressive positions may be reported on tax returns. The same approach should be used in determining deferred taxes in postacquisition periods. Changes to management's estimate or final resolution by the closing of tax years should be accounted for by adjusting goodwill, then by adjusting other acquired noncurrent intangible assets, and then by adjusting the provision for income taxes.

(vii) Miscellaneous. *Identifiable Intangibles.* Deferred taxes are established for all identifiable intangible assets, both at the acquisition date and for postacquisition temporary differences.

LIFO Inventories. A difference between the book and tax bases of LIFO inventories is a temporary difference at the acquisition date and should be included in the computations of deferred taxes.

Tax Rates. Under Statement 109, enacted tax rates should be used in computing deferred taxes at the acquisition date even if rate changes are anticipated. Postacquisition rate changes would result in changes to the deferred tax balances, which would be reported as an adjustment of the provision for income taxes.

5.4 THE JOINT VENTURES PHASE OF THE FASB PROJECT ON CONSOLIDATIONS AND RELATED MATTERS

The FASB's project on Consolidations and Related Matters is divided into phases that are intended to address all aspects of accounting for affiliations between entities and situations that raise similar or related financial statement issues. One phase of the project addresses accounting for investments in entities that do not qualify for consolidation, including corporate and noncorporate joint ventures and partnerships. This phase includes a reconsideration of APB Opinion 18.

Another phase addresses the question of in what circumstances a new basis of accounting is appropriate for an entity's financial statements, such as when there is a substantial change in ownership.

Significant Authoritative Accounting Pronouncements on Business Combinations Applicable to Joint Venture Accounting

The following list is intended to provide guidance in referring to significant accounting pronouncements on business combinations that are relevant to joint ventures. It is not intended to be an all-inclusive index of professional requirements that may have a bearing on the subject.

APB OPINIONS

No.	Title and Description
16	Business Combinations (the comprehensive professional standard on accounting for business combinations)
17	Intangible Assets (accounting for goodwill and other purchased intangibles)
20	Accounting Changes (changes in the reporting entity)
21	Interest on Receivables and Payables (discounting to present value)

AICPA ACCOUNTING INTERPRETATIONS

No.	Title and Description
N/A	Unofficial Accounting Interpretations of Opinion 16 (39 interpretations issued on various dates between December 1970 and March 1933, which address various issues on business combination accounting)

N/A   Unofficial Accounting Interpretations of Opinion 17 (deals with
            goodwill in a step acquisition)

FASB STATEMENTS

No.   Title and Description

12   Accounting for Certain Marketable Securities (establishes
            accounting for allowance accounts in consolidated and separate
            company financial statements and for allowance accounts of equity
            method investees)

38   Accounting for Preacquisition Contingencies of Purchased
            Enterprises (guidelines for allocating cost of an acquisition to
            preacquisition contingencies)

109   Accounting for Income Taxes (accounting for deferred taxes, net
            operating loss and tax credit carryforwards, and other tax aspects
            of acquisitions)

FASB INTERPRETATIONS

No.   Title and Description

4   Applicability of FASB Statement No. 2 to Business Combinations
            Accounted for by the Purchase Method (establishes principles for
            assigning cost to assets resulting from research and development
            which have been acquired in a business combination accounted for
            by the purchase method)

21   Accounting for Leases in a Business Combination (accounting
            principles for leases assumed in a business combination)

CHAPTER SIX

The Equity Method of Accounting

6.1   OVERVIEW

Accounting Principles Board (APB) Opinion No. 18, *The Equity Method of Accounting for Investments in Common Stock*, issued in 1971, remains the primary authoritative accounting pronouncement on the equity method. An array of subsequent pronouncements have expanded, clarified, and interpreted Opinion 18.

As discussed in Section 5.4, the Financial Accounting Standards Board's (FASB) major project on Consolidations and Related Matters includes reconsideration of accounting for investments in unconsolidated entities, including joint ventures. Presently, it is not known whether any changes to equity method accounting will be made as a result of that project.

The equity method must be used to account for investments in corporate joint ventures and certain investments in common stock. The underlying principle is that an investor must use the equity method to account for an investment in common stock if the investor has significant influence over the operating and financial policies of an investee. It is essentially implicit that an investor has significant influence over an entity it considers to be a corporate joint venture based on the characteristics of a corporate joint venture described in Section 5.1.

Under the equity method, an investor holding 20% or more of the voting stock of an investee is presumed to have significant influence over the operating and financial policies of the investee. That presumption can be overcome only if there is compelling evidence that an investor is not able to exercise significant influence.

An equity method investor records its initial investment in the common stock of an investee at cost. That investment is reported as a one-line item in the balance sheet of the investor. Thereafter, the carrying amount of the investment is increased by (a) the cost of any additional investments by the investor in common stock of the investee and (b) the investor's proportionate share of net income, if any, of the investee. Also, the carrying amount of the investment is thereafter decreased by (a) any dividends paid by the investee to the investor and (b) the investor's proportionate share of net losses, if any, of the investee.

Differences between the carrying amount of an equity method investment and an investor's proportionate share of net assets reported in the financial statements of an investee should be attributed to individual assets and liabilities of the investee using principles of the purchase method of accounting for business combinations. Thereafter, the differences should be amortized based on useful lives of the underlying assets and liabilities to which the differences relate. The portion of a difference, if any, that cannot be related to identifiable underlying assets or liabilities, is amortized similarly to the amortization of goodwill.

Income taxes that would be payable assuming future payment of dividends of undistributed earnings of an equity method investee to an investor should be treated as temporary differences in computing the investor's provision for income taxes. Undistributed earnings of foreign corporate joint ventures that are essentially permanent in duration need not be recognized as temporary differences. This also applies to undistributed earnings of domestic corporate joint ventures that arose in fiscal years beginning on or before December 15, 1992. An excess of financial reporting amount over the tax basis of a foreign corporate joint venture need not be recognized as a temporary difference unless it is apparent that such difference will reverse in the foreseeable future.

6.2 CRITERIA FOR USE OF THE EQUITY METHOD

(a) Investments in Common Stock

(i) Ability to Exercise Significant Influence. If an investor has the ability to exercise significant influence over the operating and financial policies of an investee in which it has an investment in common stock, the equity method of accounting must be used. In the absence of compelling evidence to the contrary, it should be presumed that if an investor owns 20% or more of the voting stock of an investee, the investor has the ability to exercise significant influence, and that the equity method must be used. If an investor owns less than 20% of the voting stock of an investee, it should be presumed that the investor does not have the ability to exercise significant influence. In the case of ownership of less than 20% of voting stock, the equity method would not be used unless the ability to exercise significant influence can be demonstrated. An investor's voting stock interest is based on currently outstanding voting securities of an investee, excluding the effects of potential voting privileges of security holders that could become effective in the future.

(ii) Factors Indicating That an Investor Has the Ability to Exercise Significant Influence. Following are circumstances that usually indicate that an investor has the ability to exercise significant influence over the operating and financial policies of an investee, even if the investor owns less than 20% of the voting stock of the investee:

- If an investor has a high percentage ownership in relation to the concentration of other shareholders
- If an investor has significant representation on the board of directors of an investee and significant participation in the policy-making process
- Significant intercompany transactions between an investor and an investee
- Interchange of managerial personnel between an investor and an investee
- Technological dependency between the parties
- Extension of credit or guarantees of indebtedness by the investor
- Ownership by the investor of securities other than voting stock, such as warrants, debentures, or other securities

(iii) Factors Indicating That an Investor Does Not Have the Ability to Exercise Significant Influence. FASB Interpretation No. 35, *Criteria for Applying the Equity Method of Accounting for Investments in Common Stock*, identifies circumstances that provide compelling evidence that an investor does not have the ability to exercise significant influence. The existence of such circumstances may preclude use of the equity method, even if an investor owns 20% or more of the voting stock of an investee. Circumstances identified in Interpretation No. 35 and in other accounting pronouncements that support a conclusion that the equity method should not be used are:

- If an investee has challenged an investor's influence such as by filing a lawsuit against the investor or making complaints about an investor to government regulatory authorities
- If a small shareholder group owns a high percentage of an investee's voting stock and operates an investee without regard to an investor's views
- If an investor is unable to obtain adequate information from an investee for use of the equity method because of the investee's refusal to furnish the information — such as if an investee is not required to publicly report quarterly data and refuses to furnish quarterly data to an investor
- If an investor tries and is unable to obtain representation on an investee's board of directors
- If an investee is bankrupt or in a court-supervised reorganization
- If an investee is located in a foreign country that imposes severe restrictions on production or exchange
- If an investor's ability to exercise influence is likely to be temporary
- If an agreement is executed between an investor and investee in which the investor surrenders significant rights as a shareholder

In surrendering shareholder rights, sometimes a "stand-still" agreement is executed between an investor and an investee. A stand-still agreement may be entered into as a compromise if an investee is resisting a takeover attempt or if there is a dispute over efforts of an investor to increase its interest in an investee. In a stand-still agreement, an investor agrees not to increase its current level of ownership of the investee or to limit increases of ownership of an investor in an investee. All the terms of such agreements should be evaluated to determine if an investor's rights have been increased or decreased in comparison to those of other investors and to determine if there has been an increase or decrease to the ability to an investor to exercise influence over an investee.

(b) Corporate Joint Ventures

Opinion No. 18 requires the use of the equity method to account for investments in corporate joint ventures. Opinion 18 defines *corporate joint venture* as follows:

> "Corporate joint venture" refers to a corporation owned and operated by a small group of businesses [the "joint venturers"] as a separate and specific business or project for the mutual benefit of the members of the group. Government may also be a member of the group. The purpose of a corporate joint venture frequently is to share risks and rewards in developing a new market, product, or technology; to combine complementary technological knowledge; or to pool resources in developing production or other facilities. A corporate joint venture also usually provides an arrangement under which each joint venturer may participate, directly or indirectly, in the overall management of the joint venture. Joint venturers thus have an interest or relationship other than as passive investors. An entity which is a subsidiary of one of the "joint venturers" is not a corporate joint venture. The ownership of a corporate joint venture seldom changes, and its stock is usually not traded publicly. A minority public ownership, however, does not preclude a corporation from being a corporate joint venture. [APB Opinion No. 18, paragraph 3d]

Almost always, the equity method must be used to account for an investment in a corporate joint venture. However, the presence of factors such as those discussed in Section 6.2(a)(iii) could present compelling evidence that the equity method should not be used, in which case it may not be appropriate to consider the investee to be a corporate joint venture in the first place.

6.3 EQUITY METHOD ACCOUNTING PRINCIPLES

(a) General

The basic principles of the equity method, set forth in Opinion 18, paragraph 19, are as follows:

- Intercompany profits and losses should be eliminated until realized by the investor or investee.
- A difference between the cost of an investment and the amount of underlying equity in net assets of an investee should be considered goodwill and amortized over a period not to exceed 40 years, unless the difference can be related to specific accounts of the investee. In any event, this difference should be recognized systematically as part of the income and loss recognized by the investor.
- Investments in common stock should be shown in the balance sheet of an investor as a single amount. The investor's share of earnings or losses of investees should ordinarily be shown in the income statement as a single amount, except that the investor's share of extraordinary items and its share of prior period adjustments reported in the financial statements of an investee should be classified in a similar manner unless they are immaterial in the income statement of the investor.
- A capital transaction of an investee that affects an investor's share of stockholders' equity of the investee should be accounted for as if the investee were a consolidated subsidiary.
- An investor should ordinarily discontinue applying the equity method when the investment (and net advances) has been reduced to zero, and should not provide for any further losses unless the investor has guaranteed obligations of the investee or is otherwise committed to provide further financial support for the investee. If the investee subsequently reports net income, the investor should resume applying the equity method only after its share of that net income equals the share of net losses not recognized during the period the equity method was suspended. An investor should, however, provide for additional losses when the imminent return to profitable operations by an investee appears to be assured. For example, a material, nonrecurring loss of an isolated nature may reduce an investment below zero even though the historical profitable operations of an investee are unimpaired.
- If an investee has outstanding cumulative preferred stock, an investor should compute its share of earnings or losses after deducting the investee's preferred dividends, whether or not such dividends are declared.
- If an investment in voting stock of an investee company falls below 20% of the investee's outstanding voting stock, and the investor thereby is presumed to have lost the ability to influence the policies of the investee,

the investor should discontinue accruing its share of the earnings or losses of the investee, since the investment no longer qualifies for the equity method. The earnings or losses that relate to the stock retained by the investor and that were previously accrued should remain as a part of the carrying amount of the investment. However, dividends received by the investor in subsequent periods that exceed the investor's share of earnings for such periods should be applied as a reduction of the carrying amount of the investment.

- If an investment in common stock of an investee that was previously accounted for on other than the equity method becomes qualified for use of the equity method because of an increase in the level of ownership, the investor should adopt the equity method of accounting. The investment, results of operations (current and prior periods), and retained earnings of the investor should be adjusted retroactively in a manner consistent with the accounting for a step-by-step acquisition of a subsidiary.

The following sections discuss the preceding fundamental principles and an array of other aspects of the equity method of accounting that are either discussed elsewhere in accounting pronouncements or found in practice.

(b) Determining Cost of an Equity Method Investment

The cost of an equity method investment is essentially determined the same way as the total cost of a purchase method acquisition is determined. The principles of purchase accounting are discussed in Chapter 5. In brief, the cost of an equity method investment includes:

- Cash paid
- Fair market value of any property exchanged
- Liabilities assumed
- Costs incurred directly connected with the acquisition of the investment

Sometimes the formation of a joint venture includes the transfer of an existing operation or subsidiary to a newly formed joint venture entity. In that event, the net carrying amount of interest in the subsidiary or in the assets and liabilities of the transferred operation, including related deferred taxes, would become the original cost of the equity method investment.

(c) Differences between Cost of Investment and Proportionate Share of Net Assets

Often, there are differences between the cost of an equity method investment and an investor's proportionate share of the net assets reported in the separate financial statements of an investee. This can exist because of various reasons, including the following:

- The stock of an investee may have been purchased at current market value and the assets and liabilities of the investee are valued at historical cost in the financial statements of the investee.
- An investee may have assets that do not appear in its financial statements, such as patents, other intangibles, or the benefits of research and development expenditures, the costs of which may have been expensed under generally accepted accounting principles.
- An investee's business may have developed goodwill value that is not reflected in the investee's financial statements.
- The formation of a joint venture may have included the transfer of the net assets of a business to the investee by an investor. In the separate financial statements of the joint venture, the assets and liabilities may have been revalued to current fair market values, but the investment carried by the investor at the historical net book value of the net assets transferred.

Opinion 18, paragraph 19b required that differences between the cost of an investment and an investor's proportionate share of the net assets reported in the separate financial statements of an equity method investee be accounted for as if the investee were a consolidated subsidiary. That requires an allocation of the cost of the investment to the investor's proportionate share of the assets and liabilities reported by an investee using the purchase method. Although information necessary for a complete purchase price allocation may not be available, an investor should make its best efforts to identify assets and liabilities to which the differences should be allocated.

In practice, the author has seen a tendency to simply allocate such differences to goodwill, with amortization over an extended period of time. In some circumstances, such allocations can produce reasonable results. However, in many circumstances a more detailed allocation is necessary. An investor should attempt, to the extent possible, to attribute differences to identifiable assets and liabilities and future amortization of the difference should be based on that allocation. Exhibit 6.1 illustrates the allocation of a difference between cost of an equity method investment and an investor's proportionate share of the net assets reported in the separate financial statements of an equity method investee.

Depending on the details of individual assets and liabilities of an investee to which a difference must be allocated, the process of determining the annual amortization of the difference between cost of an equity method investment and an investor's proportionate share of the net assets reported in the separate

EXHIBIT 6.1   Allocation of Difference between Cost of an Equity Method Investment and Book Value of Underlying Net Assets

Assume that Company A acquires a 30% interest in Company B for $1 million and that the net assets reported in the balance sheet of Company B are $2 million. Company A performs a review of the balance sheet items and determines that the only significant identifiable asset or liability to which the current fair market value differs significantly from net book value is machinery and equipment. It is determined that the fair market value of the machinery and equipment exceeds their net book value by $800,000. The following computations illustrate the allocation of the difference:

Cost of investment		$1,000,000
Net assets reported on Company B balance sheet	$2,000,000	
Company A share	× 30%	600,000
Difference between cost of investment and proportionate share of net assets		400,000
Excess fair market value of machinery and equipment	$ 800,000	
Portion of difference allocated to machinery and equipment	× 30%	240,000
Remaining difference allocated to goodwill		$ 160,000

EXHIBIT 6.1 (*Continued*)

The following would be recorded by Company A for the first year of equity method reporting, assuming that company B reported net income of $500,000. The machinery and equipment has a remaining 10-year useful life and the portion of the difference allocated to goodwill will be amortized over 40 years.

	Dr.	Cr.
Investment in Company B	$150,000	
Equity in earnings of Company B (30% share of net income reported by Company B)		$150,000
Equity in earnings of Company B	$ 24,000	
Investment in Company B (annual charge for portion of difference allocated to machinery and equipment is $240,000/10)		$ 24,000
Equity in earnings of Company B	$ 4,000	
Investment in Company B (annual charge for portion of difference allocated to goodwill is $160,000/40)		$ 4,000

financial statements of an equity method investee can be much more complicated than the above illustration.

(d) Capital Transactions of an Equity Method Investee

Opinion 18, paragraph 19e, provides the following:

A transaction of an investee of a capital nature that affects the investor's share of stockholders' equity of the investee should be accounted for as if the investee were a consolidated subsidiary.

A capital transaction of an equity method investee occurs if the investee issues additional stock, such as in a public offering or a private placement. Alternatively, an investee might issue stock in adding another investor to an existing joint venture. Investors in a joint venture may change their ownership percentages in connection with additional capital investment by one or more of the investors, or they may make additional capital investments in proportion to their existing ownership percentages. Also, an investee might reacquire some of its outstanding stock if an investor withdraws from a joint venture or if the respective interests of the investors change.

If an investee issues new stock to a third party or another investor in exchange for consideration that on a per share basis is more or less than the previous per share book value, an investor that does not purchase new shares realizes an increase or decrease in its proportionate share of net assets of the investee. An increase or decrease in an investor's proportionate share of net assets of an investee also occurs if an investor purchases some of the new stock issued but in a lesser proportion than the investor's previous percentage interest.

There have long been differing opinions about whether an investor should recognize a gain or loss from an increase or decrease in its share of net assets from a capital transaction of an investee or whether such should be accounted for as an adjustment of paid-in capital. At one time, the Securities Exchange Commission (SEC) insisted that public companies account for the effects of these transactions as adjustments of paid-in capital — not as gains or losses. In 1983, the SEC changed this view in Staff Accounting Bulletin No. 51, which permits recognition of gain or loss if a transaction is not part of a broader corporate reorganization contemplated or planned by an investor. Gains resulting from capital transactions of an equity method investee or subsidiary are often called "SAB 51 gains."

Exhibit 6.2 illustrates the computation of a gain from a capital transaction of an equity method investee in a situation in which the investor's cost is equal to its proportionate share of net assets of an investee.

Exhibit 6.3 illustrates the computation of a gain from a capital transaction of an equity method investee in a situation in which the investor's cost is greater than its proportionate share of net assets of an investee.

If gain or loss recognition is the policy of an investor and an investee sells stock at less than the existing book value per share, a loss would be recognized.

Accounting for the effects of capital transactions of investees as adjustments of paid-in capital instead of as gains or losses is acceptable if applied consistently. Because of the previous SEC requirement that public companies

EXHIBIT 6.2 Gain on Capital Transaction of an Equity Method Investee if Cost Equals Proportionate Share of Net Assets

Assume that Company A owns 300,000 shares representing a 30% interest in Company B, an equity method investee, which has net assets of $10 million. The carrying value of the investment in Company B is $3 million on the books of Company A. Company B issues 500,000 additional shares to third parties for $10 million in cash. Following is a computation of Company A's gain:

Net assets of Company B prior to additional stock issuance	$10,000,000
Number of shares outstanding	$ 1,000,000
Book value per share	$ 10
Number of shares held by Company A	300,000
Percentage interest prior to additional stock issuance	30%
Number of additional shares issued	500,000
Price per share received by Company B	$ 20
Increase in net assets of Company B	$10,000,000
Net assets of Company B after additional stock issuance	$20,000,000
Percentage interest held after stock issuance (300,000/1,500,000)	20%
Company A's share of net assets after stock issuance ($20,000,000 × 30%)	$ 4,000,000
Company A's share of net assets before stock issuance ($10,000,000 × 30%)	$ 3,000,000
Gain from increase in Company A's share of net assets ($4,000,000 − 3,000,000)	$ 1,000,000

As a result of the foregoing, Company A would record the following entry:

	Dr.	Cr.
Investment in Company B	$1,000,000	
Gain on issuance of stock by Company B (gain on capital transaction of equity method investee)		$1,000,000

EXHIBIT 6.3   Gain on Capital Transaction of an Equity Method Investee if Cost is Greater than Proportionate Share of Net Assets

Assume that Company A owns 300,000 shares representing a 30% interest in Company B, an equity method investee, which has net assets of $10 million. The carrying value of the investment in Company B is $3,900,000 on the books of Company A. Company B issues 500,000 additional shares to third parties for $10 million in cash. Following is a computation of Company A's gain:

Net assets of Company B prior to additional stock issuance	$10,000,000
Number of shares outstanding	$ 1,000,000
Book value per share	$ 10
Number of shares held by Company A	300,000
Percentage interest prior to additional stock issuance	30%
Cost of Company A's investment in Company B	$ 3,900,000
Company A's proportionate share of net assets	$ 3,000,000
Excess cost over proportionate share of net assets	$ 900,000
Proportionate interest prior to stock issuance	30%
Proportionate interest after stock issuance (1,500,000/300,000)	20%
Change in Company A's interest	10%
Number of additional shares issued	500,000
Price per share received by Company B	$ 20
Increase in net assets of Company B	$10,000,000
Net assets of Company B after additional stock issuance	$20,000,000
Percentage interest held after stock issuance (300,000/1,500,000)	20%
Company A's share of net assets after stock issuance ($20,000,000 × 30%)	$ 4,000,000
Company A's share of net assets before stock issuance ($10,000,000 × 30%)	$ 3,000,000
Increase in Company A's share of net assets ($4,000,000 – 3,000,000)	$ 1,000,000
Portion of excess of cost over proportionate share of net assets to be retired ($900,000) × (10%/30%)	$ 300,000

EXHIBIT 6.3   *(Continued)*

Gain on increase in Company A's share of net assets ($4,000,000 – 3,000,000)	$ 700,000

As a result of the foregoing, Company A would record the following entry:

	Dr.	Cr.
Investment in Company B	$700,000	
Gain on issuance of stock by Company B (gain on capital transaction of equity method investee)		$ 700,000

adjust paid-in capital, public companies that have adjusted paid-in capital may want to change to gain or loss recognition. This is acceptable, and would represent a change in accounting policy. In implementing a change, prior transactions accounted for as adjustments of paid-in capital would *not* be restated. If an investor has adjusted paid-in capital as a result of a capital transaction of an investee and later disposes of its investment, the gain or loss on disposal is recognized based on the carrying amount of the investment at the time of disposal.

If an investor purchases stock of an investee in a proportion greater than its previous percentage interest, the cost of the additional investment is added to the carrying amount of the investment. Subsequently, the net assets of the investee after the stock issuance are used in determining the differences between the cost of the equity method investment and the investor's proportionate share of the net assets reported in the separate financial statements of an investee.

(e) Investee Financial Statements That Are Not Current

If financial statements of an investee are not available in time to report the investor's share of the earnings of the investee on a current basis, Opinion 18, paragraph 19g provides that an investor may ordinarily use the most recent available financial statements. Also, an investor may use other than the most recent financial statements if the fiscal year-end of the investor and investee are not the same.

A delay between the date of the financial statements of the investee used to apply the equity method and the financial statements of the investor should be consistent from year to year. An investor should disclose in its financial statements any significant events that have affected an investee since the date of the investee financial statements if the events are significant to the investor.

(f) Elimination of Intercompany Profits and Losses

(i) General. Opinion 18, paragraph 19a requires the elimination of intercompany profits and losses from transactions between an investor and an investee — as if the investee is a consolidated subsidiary. A 1971 APB equity method accounting interpretation provides that depending on certain circumstances, elimination of the entire profit or loss, only the portion related to an investor's interest in an investee may be necessary. Whether full or partial elimination is required depends on the attributes of the transaction and the relationship between the investor and investee. In joint venture situations, full elimination for both sales by investors to investees and by investees to investors is required.

(ii) Partial Elimination of Intercompany Profits. Under the equity method, it is appropriate to partially eliminate unrealized profits to the extent of an investor's interest in an investee if the following circumstances are present:

- An investor has a sufficient level of investment and ability to influence the policies of an investee to require use of the equity method, but the investor does not have effective control over the investee, and is not able to arbitrarily initiate intercompany transactions to increase reported profits.
- The transfer prices represent fair market pries equal to those that are or would be charged in similar transactions with third parties.
- The seller must be reasonably assured of realization of the proceeds from the transaction through means other than capital contributed to the investee entity by the seller.
- A proportionate share of the obligation to pay the transfer price must be substantively assumed by the other investors, and such investors must

have provided or be able and obligated to provide the necessary funds if such are not available from earnings of the purchaser.

The foregoing conditions are often characteristic of transactions between investors and equity method investees, resulting in the partial elimination procedure.

(iii) Full Elimination of Intercompany Profits. The following circumstances indicate that intercompany profits should be fully eliminated until the assets transferred have been sold to unrelated parties:

- The investor has effective control of the investee through voting interests, or other factors such as loans.
- The transfer is not at arm's length rates or terms.
- The seller must make a capital contribution or loan to the purchaser to enable realization of the entire selling price.
- The investee is a joint venture formed to supply the investors, and the investors have agreed to consume the production of the investee, perhaps in proportion to their equity interests. In substance, this is a cost-sharing agreement.

(iv) Intercompany Losses. If an intercompany transaction has produced a loss, the loss should not be eliminated if the loss should have been recognized on the basis of a net realizable value adjustment. If an intercompany transaction has produced a profit that has been partially recognized, the higher carrying value should be subjected to a net realizable value test and a loss recognized if appropriate. If an investor and an equity method investee have engaged in transactions prior to the investee qualifying for the equity method, profits on transactions occurring prior to the application of the equity method are not eliminated.

(v) Financial Statement Classification of Intercompany Profit and Loss Eliminations. In practice, equity method elimination of intercompany profits and losses are booked several ways. Sometimes the eliminations are recorded as an adjustment of the carrying amount of the investment and sometimes the eliminations are recorded as adjustments of other accounts.

Intercompany Sales by Investor to Investee. Exhibit 6.4 illustrates three alternative ways of recording an elimination of intercompany profit on sales of inventory by an investor to an equity method investee.

EXHIBIT 6.4 Alternative Ways to Record Elimination of Intercompany Profit on Sales from an Investor to an Investee

Assume that Company A has sold inventory to Company B, an equity method investee, that remains on hand at the balance sheet date, resulting in unrealized profits of $100,000 that must be eliminated. Assume an overall effective federal and state tax rate of 37%. Following are three alternatives for recording the elimination in the Company A:

Alternative 1:	Dr.	Cr.
Cost of sales	$100,000	
Investment in Company B (elimination of unrealized intercompany profit)		$100,000
Deferred taxes	$ 37,000	
Provision for income taxes (tax effect of elimination of unrealized intercompany profit)		$ 37,000

Alternative 2:	Dr.	Cr.
Cost of sales	$100,000	
Deferred income (elimination of unrealized intercompany profit)		$100,000
Deferred taxes	$ 37,000	
Provision for income taxes (tax effect of elimination of unrealized intercompany profit)		$ 37,000

Alternative 3:	Dr.	Cr.
Equity in earnings of Company B	$ 63,000	
Deferred taxes	37,000	
Deferred income (elimination of unrealized intercompany profit, net of taxes)		$100,000

EXHIBIT 6.5   Alternative Ways to Record Elimination of Intercompany Profit on Sales from an Investee to an Investor

Assume that Company A has purchased inventory from Company B, an equity method investee, which remains on hand at the balance sheet date, resulting in unrealized profits of $100,000 that must be eliminated. Assume an overall effective federal and state tax rate of 37%. Following are two alternatives for recording the elimination in Company A:

Alternative 1:	Dr.	Cr.
Equity in earnings of Company B	$63,000	
Investment in Company B	37,000	
Inventories (elimination of unrealized intercompany profit, net of taxes)		$100,000

Alternative 2:	Dr.	Cr.
Equity in earnings of Company B	$63,000	
Inventories (elimination of unrealized intercompany profit)		$ 63,000

Intercompany Sales by Investee to Investor. Exhibit 6.5 illustrates two alternatives for recording the elimination of intercompany profit on sales of inventory by an equity method investee to an investor.

Elimination entries such as illustrated in Exhibits 6.4 and 6.5 can be used for intercompany eliminations for transactions other than inventory. The accounts used should be selected based on the transactions.

(g) Losses in Excess of Cost of Investment

Opinion 18, paragraph 19i, provides that if an investor's share of an investee's losses has reduced an equity method investment to zero, further losses need not be recognized if the investor does not have legal or substantive obligations to continue to provide financial support that would, in effect, fund further losses. Following are circumstances that indicate the existence of legal or substantive obligations that require or may require an investor to recognize losses that exceed the cost of an equity method investment:

- An investor has guaranteed or is otherwise legally committed to pay the obligations of the investee.
- It is obvious that for important reasons, such as reputation, an investor would not allow an investee to default on its obligations. This situation may exist if a large company is an investor in a joint venture.
- The circumstances provide evidence that continued support of an investee by an investor is likely.

Before discontinuing recognition of an investor's share of losses of an equity method investee, in addition to recognizing losses that decrease the carrying amount of an equity method investment to zero, losses must also be recognized to decrease the carrying amount of any advances to the investee to zero.

If an investor has discontinued recognition of its share of losses of an investee because of elimination of its investment and advance accounts and the investee subsequently has income, the investor should not recognize its share of the investee's income up to the amount of its share of losses that was not recognized. The amount of income not to be recognized should include the effects, if any, of any amortization of differences between the cost of the investment and the investor's share of the net assets of the investee.

(h) Permanent Decline in Investment Value

Opinion 18, paragraph 19h provides that if an investor determines that an equity method investment has permanently declined in value, the investor should recognize a loss and reduce the carrying amount of the investment. A permanent decline in value can be indicated by a decline in the market price of shares in a publicly traded investee. Although not absolutely compelling, that circumstance is cause for a careful evaluation of whether the carrying amount of the investment should be decreased. Other indicators suggesting possible need for an evaluation of carrying amount are things like a series of loss periods, changes in the competition situation, technical changes, or unfavorable industry conditions.

If a writedown of an equity method investment consists of eliminating an excess of cost over net assets of an investee, the investment carrying amount would not be increased and the amount written down would not be reversed to income if circumstances subsequently improve. However, if a writedown reduces the investment carrying amount to less than an investor's share of an investee's net assets, the carrying amount may be increased up to the amount of the investor's share of the investee's net assets if circumstances subsequently improve.

(i) Capitalization of Interest Cost

An equity method investee should capitalize interest in its financial statements in accordance with FASB Statement No. 34, *Capitalization of Interest Cost*.

FASB Statement No. 58, *Capitalization of Interest Cost in Financial Statements That Include Investments Accounted for by the Equity Method*, indicates how investors should capitalize interest costs related to equity method investments. For the purposes of capitalization of interest costs, an investor's investment in an equity method investee is an asset qualifying for interest capitalization if the investee is engaged in activities necessary to commence its planned principal operations and if the activities of the investee include the use of funds to acquire qualifying assets for its operations. From the viewpoint of an investor, the equity method investment is a qualifying asset—not the individual qualifying assets of the investee. If an investee commences its planned operations, an investor must cease accounting for the equity method investment as an asset qualifying for capitalization of interest.

(j) Income Taxes on Undistributed Earnings

Income taxes that would be payable assuming future payment of dividends of undistributed earnings of an equity method investee to an investor should be treated as temporary differences in computing the investor's provision for income taxes. Undistributed earnings of domestic corporate joint ventures that are essentially permanent in duration need not be recognized as temporary differences if they existed as of September 15, 1992. An excess of financial reporting amount over the tax basis of a foreign corporate joint venture need not be recognized as a temporary difference unless it is apparent that such difference will reverse in the foreseeable future.

(k) Changes to and from the Equity Method

(i) Changes from the Cost Method to the Equity Method. Opinion 18, paragraph 19 requires that if an investment accounted for by the cost method subsequently meets the conditions for equity method accounting, previously issued financial statements are restated to use the equity method for all periods. Change from the cost method to the equity method usually result from an investor increasing its ownership percentage, circumstances that increase the ability of an investor to exercise significant influence, or elimination of compelling evidence that an investor did not have the ability to exercise significant influence. Restatement from the cost method to the equity method is similar to accounting for a step acquisition of a subsidiary and includes the following:

- The share of earnings to be recognized in each period is based on the percentage ownership during the period, even if an investor owned less than 20% of the voting stock of the investee.
- Differences between the cost of each stock purchase and the proportionate share of net assets of an investee at the date of each stock purchase must be amortized systematically from the date of each stock purchase.
- Dividends previously reported as income under the cost method must be restated as reductions of the carrying value of the investment.
- Intercompany transactions must be eliminated for all periods.
- Taxes on undistributed earnings should be provided, if required.

Exhibit 6.6 illustrates accounting for a change from the cost method to the equity method.

Since the equity method would be adopted effective January 1, 1998, the results for 1998 would be reported on the equity method as indicated.

(ii) Changes from Consolidation to the Equity Method. If an investor's interest in a subsidiary decreases to 50% and does not qualify for consolidation or otherwise no longer qualifies for consolidation and conditions for use of the equity method are met, financial statements for prior periods are restated to use the equity method. APB Opinion No. 20, *Accounting Changes*, paragraphs 12 and 34, indicate that a change of subsidiaries included in consolidation is a change in the reporting entity, resulting in the reporting entity consisting of a different group of companies. The restatements results in presentation of the new reporting entity for all periods presented.

EXHIBIT 6.6   Illustration of Accounting for a Change from the Cost Method to the Equity Method

Company A acquires a 15% interest in Company B on January 1, 1996, for $500,000, when the net assets reported by Company B amount to $2 million. During 1996, Company B reports a net income of $400,000 and pays dividends of $200,000. On January 1, 1997, Company A acquires another 3% of the voting stock of Company B for $150,000, at which time the net assets reported by Company B amount to $2.2 million. During 1997, Company B reports a net income of $800,000 and pays dividends of $300,000. On January 1, 1998, Company A acquires an additional 7% of the voting stock of Company B for $400,000, when the net assets of Company B amount to $2.7 million. In 1998, Company B reports a net income of $600,000 and pays dividends of $200,000.

Company A reported the following using the cost method to account for its investment in Company B through December 31, 1997:

	1996	1997
Net income reported by Company A:		
Dividend income (a)	$ 30,000	$ 54,000
Taxes on dividends (b)	(3,000)	(6,000)
Net income reported	$ 27,000	$ 48,000
Carrying value of investment:		
Balance, beginning of year	$ —	$500,000
Purchase of stock	500,000	150,000
Balance, end of year	$500,000	$650,000

Notes:

(a) Dividends paid to Company A:
   1996: $200,000 × 15% = $30,000
   1997: $300,000 × 18% = $54,000
   1998: $200,000 × 25% = $50,000

(b) Taxes on dividends after dividends received deduction and using 37% overall tax rate:
   1996: $30,000 − ($30,000 × 70%) × 37% = $3,000
   1997: $54,000 − ($54,000 × 70%) × 37% = $6,000
   1998: $50,000 − ($50,000 × 80%) × 37% = $4,000

EXHIBIT 6.6 *(Continued)*

The following would be reported by Company A using the equity method in accounting for the investment in Company B:

	1996	1997	1998
Net income reported by Company A:			
Share of Company B net income (c)	$ 60,000	$144,000	$ 150,000
Income tax provision:			
Taxes on dividends (b)	(3,000)	(6,000)	(4,000)
Taxes on undistributed earnings (d)	(3,000)	(6,000)	7,000
	(6,000)	(12,000)	(11,000)
Net income	$ 54,000	$132,000	$ 139,000
Carrying value of investment:			
Balance, beginning of year	$ —	$530,000	$ 770,000
Purchase of stock	500,000	150,000	400,000
Share of net income	60,000	144,000	150,000
Dividends received	(30,000)	(54,000)	(50,000)
Balance, end of year	$530,000	$770,000	$1,270,000

(c) Share of net income of Company B:

    1996: $400,000 × 15% = $60,000

    1997: $800,000 × 18% = $144,000

    1998: $600,000 × 25% = $150,000

(d) See following table:

	1996	1997	1998
Cumulative share of net income of Company B recognized	$ 60,000	$204,000	$ 354,000
Cumulative dividends received	(30,000)	(84,000)	(134,000)
Temporary difference	$ 30,000	$120,000	$ 220,000
Deferred tax at end of year (f):	$ 3,000	$ 9,000	$ 16,000

EXHIBIT 6.6 *(Continued)*

Less, deferred taxes at beginning of year	—	(3,000)	(9,000)
Current year deferred tax provision	$ 3,000	$ 6,000	$ 7,000

(f) Deferred tax computation:

1996: $ 30,000 – ($ 30,000 × 70%) × 37% = $ 3,000
1997: $120,000 – ($120,000 × 80%) × 37% = $ 9,000
1998: $220,000 – ($220,000 × 80%) × 37% = $16,000

The following adjustments would be made to restate the financial statements for 1996 and 1997:

1996:	Dr.	Cr.
Investment in Company B	$ 30,000	
Dividend income	30,000	
Provision for income taxes	3,000	
Share of earnings of Company B		60,000
Deferred income taxes payable		3,000

1997:	Dr.	Cr.
Investment in Company B	$120,000	
Dividend income	54,000	
Provision for income taxes	6,000	
Share of earnings of Company B		$144,000
Deferred income taxes payable		9,000
Retained earnings		27,000

The equity method generally results in the same net income for an investor as when an investee is reported in consolidation. There are a few possible exceptions to this general principle, such as differences that can be caused by computations of capitalization of interest costs in certain circumstances. Usually, only the classifications in the financial statements change. The assets, liabilities, revenues, expenses, gains, and losses previously displayed in consolidation for the investee are netted and displayed as a one-line investment in an unconsolidated equity method investee in the balance sheet. The investor's share of the investee's net income is displayed as a one-line caption in the statement of operations. Depending on significance, the one-line presentations in the balance sheet and statement of operations may be aggregated with other items. Also, the detailed cash flow increases and decreases are removed from the statement of cash flows and replaced by the presentation treating them as cash flows to and from an entity external to the consolidation.

(iii) Changes from the Equity Method to the Cost Method. If there is a change from the equity method to the cost method, no restatement occurs. The equity method carrying amount becomes the cost method basis and the investor discontinues recognizing its share of net income or loss of the investee. Dividends received in future periods are credited to income to the extent that the investee reports net income in future periods. To the extent that future dividends exceed future earnings, such amounts should be credited to the carrying amount of the investment.

(iv) Changes from the Equity Method to Consolidation. If an investor's interest in an equity method investee increases to more than 50% and qualifies for consolidation or otherwise qualifies for consolidation, that entity should be consolidated from the date conditions for consolidation were met. There is no restatement of prior periods. Purchase accounting allocations used in applying the equity method for each purchase of stock should be used in allocating purchase price and for accounting in consolidation.

6.4 EQUITY METHOD FINANCIAL REPORTING

(a) Financial Statement Disclosures

Opinion 18 requires the following disclosures for equity method investments in the financial statements of an investor:

(a) Parenthetically, in notes to financial statements or in separate statements of schedules:

  (i)   The ownership of common stock
  (ii) The accounting policies of the investor with respect to investments in common stock
  (iii) The differences, if any, between the amount at which an investment is carried and the amount of underlying equity in net assets of the investee and the accounting treatment of the difference

(b) The names of any significant investee corporations in which the investor holds _____% or more of the voting stock for which the investment is not accounted for using the equity method, with the reasons why the equity method is not considered appropriate should be disclosed.

(c) For those investments in common stock for which a quoted market price is available, the aggregate value of each identified investment based on the quoted market price. It should be noted that this disclosure is not required for investments in common stock of subsidiaries.

(d) Summarized information as to assets, liabilities, and results of operations presented in the notes to the investor's group where they are material in the aggregate with respect to the investor's financial statements. Normally summarized financial data will be presented in the notes.

(e) Material effects of possible conversions of outstanding convertible securities, exercises of outstanding options or warrants, or contingent issuances of additional shares of an investee.

Exhibit 6.7 illustrates a footnote that includes required disclosures for the equity method.

Various other financial statement disclosures relating to equity method investees other than the above requirements of Opinion 18 are discussed in the following sections.

(b) Related Party Disclosures

FASB Statement No. 57, *Related Party Disclosures*, requires disclosures about transactions between related parties, including transactions between investors and equity method investees. The disclosures are required in separate financial statements of both investors and equity method investees if significant intercompany transactions exist that could have resulted in different operating results or financial positions if the entities were not related.

Information required in disclosure includes the following, which often exists in transactions between investors and equity method investees:

- Sales, purchases, and transfers of real and personal property
- Services received or rendered, such as accounting, management, engineering, and legal services

EXHIBIT 6.7   Illustration of Equity Method Disclosures

The following table illustrates appropriate disclosures in notes to an investors financial statements for equity method investees, including summarized financial data:

Note 5. Joint Ventures

The Company is a participant in three 50% owned joint ventures that are accounted for by the equity method. Following is summarized financial information regarding the joint ventures:

	1998	1997	1996
Current assets	$3,200,000	$2,600,000	$1,800,000
Property, plant, and equipment, net	6,600,000	4,900,000	3,800,000
Other assets	500,000	400,000	300,000
Current liabilities	2,300,000	1,600,000	1,200,000
Long-term debt	3,000,000	2,500,000	2,000,000
Net assets	5,000,000	3,800,000	2,700,000
Net sales	30,000,000	20,000,000	15,000,000
Gross profit	6,000,000	4,000,000	3,000,000
Income before income taxes	3,000,000	2,000,000	1,500,000
Net income	1,500,000	1,000,000	750,000

At December 31, 1998, 1997, and 1996, the excess of the Company's proportionate share of net assets of the joint ventures over the carrying values of the investments in the joint ventures amounted to $400,000, $700,000, and $1,000,000, respectively. The differences are being amortized as reductions of the Company's share of net income of the joint ventures over periods ranging from 10 to 20 years.

- Leases
- Borrowings and lendings
- Guarantees
- Maintenance of bank accounts as compensating balances for the benefit of another
- Intercompany billings based on allocations of common costs

Transactions between an investor and an equity method investee that are not on an arm's length basis, such as an investor performing services for an investee at cost or without charge, creates only the need for disclosure — there is no requirement for an imputation or allocation of revenue or costs in amounts different from those agreed to by the parties.

For material related party transactions, the following should be disclosed in the notes to the financial statement:

- The nature of any interentity relationships and the names of the related parties, if necessary for an understanding of the effects of the relationships and transactions on the financial statements
- A description of related party transactions for each period for which an income statement is presented
- The dollar amounts, if any, of the transactions for each period for which an income statement is presented
- The effects of any changes from the preceding period in the methods of establishing the terms of the transactions
- Amounts receivable from or payable to the related parties as of the date of each balance sheet presented and, if not otherwise apparent, the terms and manner of settlement
- Any other information necessary for a proper understanding of the effects of the transactions on the financial statements

Representations should not be made in related party disclosures that transactions between related parties were on an arm's-length basis unless that representation can be substantiated. Section 11.8 discusses some specific SEC requirements on related party reporting for public companies.

(c) Disclosure of Guarantees

FASB Interpretation No. 34, *Disclosure of Indirect Guarantees of Indebtedness of Others*, has disclosure requirements that are applicable to some joint venture arrangements. Sometimes, one or more investors in a joint venture assist the joint venture in obtaining credit by guarantee of indebtedness of the joint venture, or by executing an agreement committing one or more of the investors to provide funds to the joint venture upon occurrence of specified events, such as if the working capital ratio of the joint venture falls below a specified level. Interpretation 34 requires that the existence and terms of any such guarantees or commitments be disclosed.

(d) Income Tax Disclosures

FASB Statement No. 109, *Accounting for Income Taxes*, requires disclosures related to any undistributed earnings on which taxes have not been provided, including those related to investments in foreign corporate joint ventures and to foreign equity method investments in common stock. This would also apply to any undistributed earnings of domestic corporate joint ventures arising prior to September 15, 1992, on which deferred taxes have not been provided. One of the following disclosures is required:

- A declaration of the intention to reinvest a portion or all of the undistributed earnings to support the conclusion that remittance of those earnings has been indefinitely postponed
- The cumulative amount of undistributed earnings on which an investor has not recognized income taxes

Primary Accounting Pronouncements on the Equity Method of Accounting

The following list is intended to provide assistance in referring to significant accounting pronouncements on the equity method of accounting. It should not be considered an all-inclusive index of the professional pronouncements that may be applicable.

APB OPINIONS

No.	Title
18	The Equity Method of Accounting for Investments in Common Stock
20	Accounting changes

AICPA INTERPRETATIONS

Dates	Title
11/71 and 2/72	Accounting Interpretations of APB Opinion No. 18

FASB STATEMENTS

No.	Title
58	Capitalization of Interest Cost in Financial Statements That Include Investments Accounted for by the Equity Method
109	Accounting for Income Taxes

FASB INTERPRETATIONS

No.	Title
34	Disclosure of Indirect Guarantees of Indebtedness of Others
35	Criteria for Applying the Equity Method of Accounting for Investments in Common Stock

FASB TECHNICAL BULLETINS

No.	Title
79-19	Investor's Accounting for Unrealized Losses on Marketable Securities Owned by an Equity Method Investee

Checklist of Disclosures Required in Investor Financial Statements for Equity Method Investments

(1) Name of each investee and percentage of common stock owned

(2) Accounting policies of investor with respect to investments in common stock

(3) The investments (as a single amount) in the investor's balance sheet, with earnings and losses from applying the equity method generally disclosed as a single amount in the income statement

(4) Amounts of differences, if any, between the amount at which the equity method investment is carried in the balance sheet of the investor and the investor's share of the underlying equity in the net assets reported in the separate financial statements of the investee, and the accounting treatment of the difference

(5) Aggregate value of each investment (except subsidiaries) based on quoted market price, if available

(6) An investor's share of any extraordinary items and prior period adjustments reported by an investee should receive the same classification in the financial statements of the investor unless they are immaterial to the financial statements of the investor.

(7) Material effects of any possible contingent issuances of equity securities of the investee

(8) If income taxes are not accrued on undistributed earnings of an equity method investee, the following information is required:

  (a) A statement of the investor's intention to reinvest undistributed earnings or remit them in the form of a tax-free liquidation

  (b) The cumulative amount of undistributed earnings on which the investor has not provided deferred taxes

(9) Material subsequent events and transactions, labeled as unaudited information

(10) Summarized financial information for unconsolidated subsidiaries and 50% or less owned entities, including assets, liabilities, and results of operations (may be wholly or partially combined)

(11) For investments not accounted for using the equity method in which 20% or more of voting stock is held, the names of significant investees and the reasons for not using the equity method

(12) Names of significant investees in which less than 20% of the voting stock is held, and the reason for using the equity method if the equity method is used

(13) Information required to be disclosed regarding related parties if not otherwise already disclosed.:

  (a) Nature of relationships with other entities, and names of related parties if necessary for an understanding of the effects of the relationships and transactions on the financial statements

  (b) A description of transactions for each period for which an income statement is presented

  (c) The dollar amounts, if any, of the transactions for each period for which an income statement is presented

  (d) The effects of any changes from the preceding period in methods of establishing the terms of the transactions

  (e) Amounts receivable or payable to the related parties as of the date of each balance sheet presented and, if not otherwise apparent, the terms and manner of settlement

  (f) Any other information necessary to a proper understanding of the effects of the transactions on the financial statements

(g) Representation should not be made that transactions between related parties were on an arm's-length basis unless that representation can be substantiated.

(14) Any guarantees of indebtedness of equity method investees, or any arrangements obligating an investor to transfer funds to an investee upon occurrence of specified events

CHAPTER SEVEN

Illustrations of Equity Method Accounting for Joint Ventures

          (i) Using Historical Amounts for Operating Company
         (ii) Using Revalued Amounts at Operating Company Level
  (e)   Investor Accounting by Company A
          (i) Company A Journal Entries
         (ii) Annual Adjustment Related to Depreciation
        (iii) Adjustment Related to Inventory
        (iv) Company A Provision for Income Taxes
  (f)   Investor Accounting by Company B

7.1 GENERAL

This section provides comprehensive illustrations of accounting using the equity method in accounting for investments in corporate joint ventures. The principles illustrated also apply to accounting for nonjoint venture investments in common stock accounted for by the equity method.

7.2 INVESTMENT CARRYING AMOUNT EQUAL TO INVESTOR'S SHARE OF INVESTEE'S NET ASSETS

(a) General Assumptions

If an investment equals the proportionate share of an investee's net assets and the investment was acquired for cash, application of the equity method is generally simpler than if they are not equal or if the investment was acquired for consideration other than cash, such as contributed assets or operations.

    Assume that Company A and Company B form a domestic corporate joint venture, Company C on January 1 of Year 1. Each investor contributes cash of $1 million to the joint venture and receives 50% of the stock of Company C. In addition to the capital investments, subsequent operating activity of Company C is summarized in the journal entries in Exhibit 7.1. The following sections illustrate in journal entry format the accounting by investee Company C and by investor Companies A and B.

(b) Investee Accounting

(i) Company C Journal Entries.   Exhibit 7.1 illustrates journal entries summarizing Year 1 accounting by Company C.

EXHIBIT 7.1 Company C Summary Journal Entries

	Dr.	Cr.
(a) Cash	$2,000,000	
Common stock		$ 2,000
Additional paid-in capital		
(sale of stock to investors)		1,998,000
(b) Machinery and equipment	$1,000,000	
Inventory	900,000	
Prepaid expenses	100,000	
Cash (expenditures to acquire		
operating assets)		$2,000,000
(c) Accounts receivable	$1,500,000	
Sales (to customers)		$1,500,000
(d) Cash	$1,000,000	
Accounts receivable		
(cash collections)		$1,000,000
(e) Operating expenses	$ 250,000	
Cash (operating expenses		
paid)		$ 250,000
(f) Operating expenses	$ 50,000	
Accounts payable (accrual		
of operating expenses)		$ 50,000
(g) Operating expenses	$ 50,000	
Prepaid expenses		
(amortization of prepaids)		$ 50,000
(h) Operating expenses	$ 100,000	
Accumulated depreciation		
(book depreciation)		$ 100,000
(i) Provision for income taxes	$ 124,000	
Income taxes payable		$ 102,000
Deferred income taxes		
(to record income tax expense)		20,000
(j) Retained earnings	$ 100,000	
Cash (dividends paid to		
investors)		$ 100,000

(ii) Company C Financial Statements.   Exhibit 7.2 illustrates Company C's balance sheet, statement of operations, and statements of retained earnings as of the end of the corporate joint venture's first year and for the year then ended.

(iii) Company C Provision for Income Taxes.   Exhibit 7.3 illustrates the computation of the Company C's Year 1 provision for income taxes.

(c) Investor Accounting

(i) Company A and Company B Journal Entries.   Exhibit 7.4 illustrates year 1 accounting by Company A and Company B.

(ii) Company A and Company B Provision for Income Taxes.   Exhibit 7.5 illustrates the computation of the Company's C's Year 1 provision for income taxes.

7.3   INVESTMENT CARRYING AMOUNT DIFFERENT FROM INVESTOR'S SHARE OF INVESTEE'S NET ASSETS

(a) General Assumptions

The illustration in this section is considerably more complex that the one in Section 7.2. Various circumstances can cause differences between the carrying amount of an investor's investment and the investor's share of net assets of an investee. One is the purchase of stock at a price exceeding the investor's share of the historical basis net assets of an investee, in which case the amortization of the difference reduces the investor's share of net income reported by the investee. Another is the contribution of appreciated property to a joint venture, in which case the amortization of the difference increases the investor's share of net income reported by the investee. These are the two most common causes of such differences that the author has seen in practice.

The reverse of each of the two situations described above would cause differences. The purchase of stock at a price less than the investor's share of the historical basis net assets of an investee would require amortization of a difference that would increase the investor's share of net income reported by the investee. The contribution of property that has decreased in value to a joint

EXHIBIT 7.2 Company C Financial Statements at the End of Year 1

Company C
Balance Sheet
End of Year 1

Assets:

Cash		$ 650,000
Accounts receivable		500,000
Inventory		150,000
Prepaid expenses		50,000
Machinery and equipment	$1,000,000	
Less, accumulated depreciation	100,000	900,000
		$2,250,000

Liabilities and Equity:

Accounts payable	$ 50,000
Income taxes payable	102,000
Deferred income taxes	20,000

Stockholders' Equity:

Common stock	2,000
Additional paid-in capital	1,998,000
Retained earnings	78,000
Total stockholders' equity	2,078,000
	$2,250,000

Company C
Statement of Operations
Year 1

Sales	$1,500,000
Cost of sales	750,000
Gross profit	750,000
Operating expenses	450,000
Income before income taxes	300,000
Provision for income taxes	122,000
Net income	$ 178,000

Company C
Statement of Retained Earnings
Year 1

Retained earnings, beginning	$ —
Net income	178,000
Dividends paid	(100,000)
Retained earnings, ending	$ 78,000

EXHIBIT 7.3   Company C Year 1 Provision for Income Taxes

Current Income Tax Expense:		
Pretax accounting income		$300,000
Officer life insurance premiums		5,000
Excess tax depreciation:		
Tax depreciation	$150,000	
Book depreciation	100,000	(50,000)
Taxable income		255,000
Assumed tax rate		× 40%
Current tax expense		$102,000
Deferred Income Tax Expense:		
Temporary Differences:		
Excess tax depreciation		$ 50,000
Assumed tax rate		× 40%
Deferred taxes, end of Year 1		20,000
Deferred taxes, beginning of Year 1		$ —
Deferred tax expense		20,000
Total income tax expense		$122,000

venture would require amortization of a difference that decreases the investor's share of net income reported by the investee.

The comments in the preceding two paragraphs related to contributed property assume that the joint venture accounts for the contributed property at fair value at the date of contribution.

Assume that on January 1 of Year 1, Company A and Company B form Company C, a domestic corporate joint venture, with each investor owning 50% of the joint venture. In exchange for its 50% interest, Company A contributes an existing business by transferring to Company C the stock of Company D. For tax purposes, the exchange of shares qualifies as a tax-free exchange, so there is no step up in basis for tax purposes. Company B contributes $10,000,000 cash in exchange for its 50% interest.

Exhibit 7.6 is the balance sheet of Company D on the date of joint venture formation. Assume that all the machinery and equipment has a 10-year life for book purposes and were acquired on an average of 2.5 years prior to the formation of the joint venture. Accordingly, accumulated depreciation for book purposes is equal to $750,000 ($3,000,000 × 2.5/10). For tax purposes, using the

EXHIBIT 7.4   Company A and Company B Summary Journal Entries

	Dr.	Cr.
(a) Investment in Company C	$1,000,000	
Cash		$1,000,000
(Initial 50% investment)		
(b) Investment in Company C	$ 89,000	
Share of Company C net income		89,000
(Equity method income recognition)		
(c) Cash	$ 50,000	
Investment in Company C		$ 50,000
(Dividend received from		
Company C)		
(d) Income tax expense — current	$ 4,000	
Income tax expense — deferred	3,120	
Income taxes payable		$ 4,000
Deferred income taxes		3,120
(To record income tax expense)		

EXHIBIT 7.5   Company A and Company B Year 1 Provision
for Income Taxes

Current income tax expense:	
Dividends received	$50,000
Corporate dividends received deduction (80%)	(40,000)
Current taxable income expense	10,000
Assumed tax rate	× 40%
Current tax expense	4,000
Deferred income tax expense:	
Undistributed earnings	$39,000
Corporate dividends received deduction (80%)	(31,200)
Current taxable income expense	7,800
Assumed tax rate	× 40%
Deferred taxes, end of Year 1	3,120
Deferred taxes, beginning of Year 1	—
	3,120
Total income tax expense:	$ 7,120

EXHIBIT 7.6   Company D Balance Sheet Date of Joint Venture Formation

Company D
Balance Sheet
Date of Joint Venture Formation

	Book Basis	Tax Basis
Assets:		
Cash	$ 500,000	$ 500,000
Accounts receivable	3,000,000	3,000,000
Inventory	2,000,000	2,000,000
Machinery and equipment	3,000,000	3,000,000
Less, accumulated depreciation	(750,000)	(1,688,000)
	$7,750,000	$6,812,000
Liabilities and Equity:		
Accounts payable	$2,000,000	$2,000,000
Deferred income taxes	375,000	
Stockholders' equity:		
Common stock	1,000	1,000
Additional paid-in capital	3,000,000	3,000,000
Retained earnings	2,374,000	1,811,000
Total stockholders' equity	5,375,000	4,812,000
	$7,750,000	$6,812,000

modified accelerated cost recovery system's (MACRS) 7-year double declining balance depreciation, Company D deducted depreciation totaling $1,688,000, equal to 56.27% of the total tax basis of $3,000,000. Deferred taxes of $375,000 consist of the temporary difference related to depreciation of $938,000 ($1,688,000 less $750,000) multiplied by an assumed tax rate of 40%.

Assume that Company D is the only operating company in the joint venture and that Company C functions as a holding company. During Year 1, the following transactions occur:

- Company C advances to Company D a total of $7,000,000, which is used to purchase new equipment that is placed in service six months after joint venture formation

- Sales of Company D amount to $20,000,000 at a gross margin of 75%, before the effect of the inventory revaluation reflected in the opening balance sheet
- Other operating expenses amount to $4,000,000
- Cash balances held by Company C earned interest income of $200,000

(b) Revaluation of Balance Sheet of Company D at the Date of Joint Venture Formation

The financial statements of Company C are prepared based on fair market values on the date of joint venture formation in accordance with the purchase method of accounting described in Accounting Principles Board's (APB) Opinion No. 16, *Business Combinations*. The total fair market value of each investor's contribution is determined to be equal to the $10 million cash contributed by Company B.

The fair market value of machinery and equipment is $5,500,000. Using an assumed combined federal and state tax rate of 40%, the difference between the fair market value of $5,500,000 and the tax basis of $1,312,000 (cost of $3,000,000 less accumulated tax depreciation of $1,688,000) results in a deferred tax liability of $1,675,000 to be included in the revalued balance sheet.

Under Opinion 16, the fair market value of inventory is equal to the selling price reduced for a profit factor for the selling and distribution activities to be performed after the revaluation. In this example, we have assumed that selling prices result in a 60% markup over cost, of which 20% is attributable to the manufacturing process and 40% relates to selling and distribution. Assume that the manufacturing process with respect to the subject inventory is 100% complete. Accordingly, the revalued amount of the inventory is $2,500,000, based on $2,000,000 × 120%, which represents the inventory cost marked up for the profit factor for manufacturing, which was earned prior to the revaluation. The difference of $500,000 between the revalued amount of $2,500,000 and tax basis of $2,000,000 requires a deferred tax liability of $200,000 using the 40% assumed rate.

Total deferred tax liabilities in the revalued balance sheet are $1,875,000, of which $1,675,000 is attributed to machinery and equipment and $200,000 is attributed to inventory. The details of the revaluation are illustrated in Exhibit 7.7.

EXHIBIT 7.7   Company D Revaluation Computations January 1, Year 1
(Date of Joint Venture Formation)

	Revalued Amounts	Book Value	Revaluation Adjustment Dr.	Cr.
Assets:				
Cash	$ 500	$ 500		
Accounts receivable	3,000	3,000		
Inventory	2,500	2,000	$ 500	
Machinery and equipment	5,500	3,000	2,500	
Accumulated depreciation		(750)	750	
Goodwill	2,375		2,375	
	$13,875	$7,750		
Liabilities and Equity:				
Accounts payable	$ 2,000	$2,000		
Deferred income taxes	1,875	375		$1,500
Stockholders' equity:				
Common stock	1	1		
Additional paid-in capital	9,999	3,000		6,999
Retained earnings		2,374	2,374	
Total stockholders' equity:	10,000	5,375		
	$13,875	$7,750	$8,499	$8,499

(c) Investee Accounting—Consolidation of the Joint Venture (Company C) at the Date of Formation

(i) Using Historical Amounts for Operating Company with Revaluation in Consolidation.   Exhibit 7.8 illustrates the consolidation and the computation of the Company C joint venture's balance sheet at the date of the joint venture formation. In the approach illustrated in Exhibit 7.8, the Company D historical amounts are brought into the consolidation. The consolidation adjustments include the revaluation adjustments computed in Exhibit 7.7 plus intercompany investment eliminations.

EXHIBIT 7.8   Company C (Joint Venture) Consolidation Using Historical Company D Amounts, January 1, Year 1 (Date of Joint Venture Formation)

	Company C	Company D	Consolidation Adjustments Dr. (Cr.)	Company C Consolidated
Assets:				
Cash	$10,000	$ 500		$10,500
Accounts receivable		3,000		3,000
Inventory		2,000	$ 500	2,500
Machinery and				
equipment		3,000	2,500	5,500
Accumulated				
depreciation		(750)	750	
Investment in				
Company D	10,000		(10,000)	
Goodwill			2,375	2,375
	$20,000	$7,750		$24,875
Liabilities and Equity:				
Accounts payable		$2,000		$ 2,000
Deferred income				
taxes		375	(1,500)	1,875
Stockholders' Equity:				
Common stock	1	1	1	1
Additional paid-in				
capital	19,999	3,000	3,000	19,999
Retained				
earnings		2,374	2,374	
Total stockholders'				
equity:	20,000	5,375		20,000
	$20,000	$7,750	$ 0	$23,875

(ii) Using Revalued Amounts at Operating Company Level.   Exhibit 7.9 illustrates the joint venture's consolidation at the date of formation if an alternative approach is used in which the revaluation adjustments are "pushed down" to the Company C balance sheet amounts, with those amounts then brought directly into the consolidation for Company C, instead of the historical amounts. Using this approach, only intercompany investment eliminations are required.

EXHIBIT 7.9 Company C (Joint Venture) Consolidation Using Company D Fair Market Value Amounts, January 1, Year 1 (Date of Joint Venture Formation)

	Company C	Company D	Consolidation Adjustments Dr. (Cr.)	Company C Consolidated
Assets:				
Cash	$10,000	$ 500		$10,500
Accounts receivable		2,500		2,500
Inventory		2,500		2,500
Machinery and equipment		7,500		7,500
Accumulated depreciation				
Investment in Company D	10,000		$(10,000)	
Goodwill		1,894		1,894
	$20,000	$14,894		$24,894
Liabilities and Equity:				
Accounts payable		$ 2,000		$ 2,000
Deferred income taxes		2,894		$ 2,894
Stockholders' equity:				
Common stock	$ 1	1	1	1
Additional paid-in capital	19,999	9,999	9,999	19,999
Retained earnings				
Total stockholders' equity:	20,000	10,000		20,000
	$20,000	$ 7,250	$ 0	$24,894

(d) Investee Accounting—Accounting by Joint Venture for the First Year of Operation

(i) Using Historical Amounts for Operating Company. Exhibit 7.10 illustrates the joint venture's consolidation at the end of Year 1, using the approach in which the historical Company D amounts are brought into the

EXHIBIT 7.10   Company C (Joint Venture) Consolidation Using Historical Company D Amounts, December 31, Year 1 (End of First Year of Operation)

	Company C	Company D	Consolidation Adjustments Dr. (Cr.)	Company C Consolidated
Assets:				
Cash	$ 3,200	$ 1,571		$ 4,771
Accounts receivable		4,500		4,500
Inventory		4,000	$ 0	4,000
Machinery and equipment		10,000	$ 2,500	12,500
Accumulated depreciation		(1,400)	500	(900)
Investment in Company D	10,000		(10,000)	
Advances to Company D	7,000		(7,000)	
Goodwill			2,375	2,375
Accumulated amortization			(119)	(119)
	$20,200	$18,671		$27,127
Liabilities and Equity:				
Accounts payable		$ 2,000		$ 2,000
Income taxes payable	$ 80	1,278		1,358
Deferred income taxes		665	(1,200)	1,865
Advances from Company C		7,000	7,000	
Stockholders' Equity:				
Common stock	1	1	1	1
Additional paid-in capital	19,999	3,000	3,000	19,999
Retained earnings (prior)		2,374	2,374	
Retained earnings (current)	120	2,353	569	1,904
Total Stockholders' Equity:	20,120	7,728		21,904
	$20,200	$18,671	$ 0	$27,127

EXHIBIT 7.10 *(Continued)*

Sales		$20,000		$20,000
Interest income	$ 200			200
Cost of sales		(11,429)	$ (500)	(11,929)
Depreciation expense		(650)	(250)	(900)
Operating expenses		(4,000)		(4,000)
Goodwill amortization			(119)	(119)
Tax provision — current	(80)	(1,278)		(1,358)
Tax provision — deferred		(290)	300	10
Net income	$ 120	$ 2,353	$ (569)	$ 1,904

CONSOLIDATION ENTRIES

Inventory:

Opening balance sheet revaluation	$ 500
Charge of opening balance sheet revaluation to cost of sales in Year 1	(500)
	$ 0

Machinery and Equipment:

Opening balance sheet revaluation	$2,500
Accumulated depreciation:	
Opening balance sheet revaluation	$ 750
Current depreciation expense adjustment	(250)
	$ 500

Goodwill:

Opening balance sheet revaluation	$2,375
Accumulated amortization of goodwill:	
Goodwill amortization expense	$ 119

Cost of Sales:

Charge of opening balance sheet revaluation to cost of sales in Year 1 (assumes all revalued inventory is sold in Year 1)	$ 500

Depreciation Expense:

Adjusted depreciation expense:		
Prior assets ($5,500/10)	$ 550	
Current additions ($7,000/10 × 6/12)	350	$ 900
Historical depreciation expense:		
Prior assets ($3,000/10)	300	
Current additions ($7,000/10 × 6/12)	350	650
Consolidation adjustment		$ 250

Goodwill Amortization:

Goodwill amortization expense, assuming amortization period is 20 years ($2,375/20)	$ 119

consolidation. The details of the consolidation adjustments follow the consolidation table. Exhibit 7.11 illustrates the computations of the provisions for income taxes.

EXHIBIT 7.11   Company C (Joint Venture) Provision for Income Taxes Using Historical Company D Amounts, Year 1 (End of First Year of Operation)

	Company C	Company D	Consolidation Adjustments Dr. (Cr.)	Company C Consolidated
Current income tax expense:				
Pretax accounting income	$200	$3,921	$ (869)	$3,252
Cost of sales — inventory			500	500
Depreciation — book		650	250	900
Depreciation — tax		(1,375)		(1,375)
Goodwill amortization			119	119
Taxable income	200	3,196	0	3,396
Assumed tax rate	40%	40%	40%	40%
Current income tax expense	80	1,278	0	1,358
Deferred income tax expense:				
Ending temporary differences:				
Depreciation		1,663	3,000	4,663
Assumed tax rate		40%	40%	40%
Deferred taxes — ending		665	1,200	1,865
Deferred taxes — beginning	—	375	1,500	1,875
Deferred income tax expense		290	(300)	(10)
Total income tax expense	$ 80	$1,568	$ (300)	$1,348

EXHIBIT 7.12   Company C (Joint Venture) Consolidation Using Company D Fair Market Value Amounts, December 31, Year 1 (End of First Year of Operation)

	Company C	Company D	Consolidation Adjustments Dr. (Cr.)	Company C Consolidated
Assets:				
Cash	$ 3,200	$ 1,571		$ 4,771
Accounts receivable		4,500		4,500
Inventory		4,000		4,000
Machinery and equipment		12,500		12,500
Accumulated depreciation		(900)		(900)
Investment in Company D	10,000		$(10,000)	
Advances to Company D	7,000		(7,000)	
Goodwill		2,375		2,375
Accumulated amortization		(119)		(119)
	$20,200	$23,927		$27,127
Liabilities and Equity:				
Accounts payable		$ 2,000		$ 2,000
Income taxes payable	$ 80	1,278		1,358
Deferred income taxes		1,865		1,865
Advances from Company C		7,000	7,000	
Stockholders' equity:				
Common stock	1	1	1	1
Additional paid-in capital	19,999	9,999	9,999	19,999
Retained earnings (prior)				
Retained earnings (current)	120	1,784		1,904
Total stockholders' equity:	20,120	7,728		21,904
	$20,200	$18,671	$ 0	$27,127

EXHIBIT 7.12 (*Continued*)

Sales		$20,000		$20,000
Interest income	$ 200			200
Cost of sales		(11,929)		(11,929)
Depreciation expense		(900)		(900)
Operating expenses		(4,000)		(4,000)
Goodwill amortization		(119)		(119)
Tax provision — current	(80)	(1,278)		(1,358)
Tax provision — deferred		10		10
Net income	$ 120	$ 1,784	$ 0	$ 1,904

(ii) Using Revalued Amounts at Operating Company Level. Exhibit 7.12 illustrates the joint venture's consolidation at the end of Year 1, using the approach in which the Company D fair market value amounts are brought into the consolidation. The only consolidation adjustments required are eliminations of intercompany investments and advances. Exhibit 7.13 illustrates the computations of the related provisions for income taxes.

(e) Investor Accounting by Company A

(i) Company A Journal Entries. Company A must consider in its accounting that the separate consolidated financial statements of the joint venture are affected by the revaluation of the assets and liabilities of Company D that were contributed by Company A. Results reported by the joint venture using the revalued amounts must be adjusted by Company A to give effect to the historical cost of its investment. Exhibit 7.14 illustrates journal entries summarizing Year 1 accounting by Company A.

(ii) Annual Adjustment Related to Depreciation. Since the separate financial statements of Company C include the machinery and equipment contributed by Company A at a higher revalued amount, depreciation expense reported by the joint venture is higher than depreciation expense that would apply to the

EXHIBIT 7.13 Company C (Joint Venture) Provision for Income Taxes Using Company D Fair Market Value Amounts, Year 1 (End of First Year of Operation)

	Company C	Company D	Consolidation Adjustments Dr. (Cr.)	Company C Consolidated
Current income tax expense:				
Pretax accounting income	$ 200	$3,052		$3,252
Cost of sales — inventory		500		500
Depreciation — book		900		900
Depreciation — tax		(1,375)		(1,375)
Goodwill amortization		119		119
Taxable income	200	3,196		3,396
Assumed tax rate	× 40%	× 40%		× 40%
Current income tax expense	80	1,278		1,358
Deferred income tax expense:				
Ending temporary differences:				
Depreciation		4,663		4,663
Assumed tax rate		× 40%		× 40%
Deferred taxes — ending		1,865		1,865
Deferred taxes — beginning		1,875		1,875
Deferred income tax expense		(10)		(10)
Total income tax expense	$ 80	$1,268		$1,348

EXHIBIT 7.14   Company A Year 1 Journal Entries

	Dr.	Cr.
(a) Investment in Company C	$5,375,000	
Investment in Company D		$5,375,000
(Initial 50% investment affected		
by exchange of Company D		
stock for Company C stock)		
(b) Investment in Company C	$ 952,000	
Share of Company C net income		$ 952,000
(Recognition of 50% share of		
Company C net income		
of $1,904,000)		
(c) Investment in Company C	$ 162,500	
Share of Company C net income		$ 162,500
(Annual adjustment to offset 50%		
of Company C depreciation		
expense of $250,000 attributable		
to revaluation of machinery and		
equipment)		
(d) Investment in Company C	$ 250,000	
Share of Company C net income		$ 250,000
(One-time adjustment to offset		
50% of Company C cost of sales		
of $500,000 attributable to		
revaluation of inventory)		
(e) Income tax expense — deferred	$ 109,160	
Deferred income taxes		$ 109,160
(To record income tax expense)		

historical carrying value of the machinery and equipment that now underlies Company A's investment in the joint venture. In each period for which results of Company C are reported by the equity method by Company A, Company A must adjust its share of Company C's net income for the resulting higher depreciation expense. Similarly, Company A would adjust its share of gain or loss reported by Company C on disposal of any of the revalued machinery and equipment.

Computing this adjustment illustrates a rather subtle technical accounting point. In the illustration, the amount of Company A's adjustment in journal entry (c) above is not equal to 50% of the $250,000 revaluation adjustment to historical depreciation expense reported by the joint venture on the contributed machinery and equipment illustrated in Exhibit 7.10. Company D has continued to depreciate the machinery and equipment over the original depreciation period used prior to formation of the joint venture. At the time of joint venture formation, the remaining useful life of the machinery and equipment was determined to be 10 years, resulting in an extension of the useful life used by the joint venture in financial reporting. The amount of the adjustment recorded by Company A in journal entry (c) gives effect to this extension of the useful lives of the assets recognized by the joint venture. Exhibit 7.15 illustrates computation of the adjustment.

(iii) Adjustment Related to Inventory. The revaluation of the inventory of Company D resulted in a one-time effect on the reported earnings of the joint

EXHIBIT 7.15 Computation of Adjustment to Share of Net Income Related to Depreciation Reported by Joint Venture

Revalued amount of contributed machinery and equipment	$5,500,000
Historical net book value:	
Cost	3,000,000
Accumulated depreciation	(750,000)
	$2,250,000
Additional amount being depreciated by joint venture	$3,250,000
Annual depreciation attributable to revaluation based on 10-year life	$ 325,000
Company A share of 50%	$ 162,500

EXHIBIT 7.16 Company A Provision for Income Taxes for Year 1

Share of net income of Company C	$ 952,000
Adjustments:	
Depreciation	162,500
Inventory	250,000
Adjusted share of net income of Company C	1,364,500
Corporate dividends received deduction (80%)	(1,091,600)
Temporary difference	272,900
Assumed tax rate	× 40%
Deferred taxes, end of Year 1	$ 109,160

venture in the first year of operation that is not consistent with Company A's historical carrying value. It is assumed that all the subject inventory was sold in the first year of operation, requiring an adjustment to equity method income reported by Company A. The adjustment is equal to 50% of the $500,000 inventory revaluation, or $250,000.

(iv) Company A Provision for Income Taxes. Exhibit 7.16 illustrates the Company A provision for income taxes recorded in connection with recognition of its share of joint venture income.

(f) Investor Accounting by Company B

The accounting by Company B for its investment in the joint venture is much simpler than that of Company A. From Company B's viewpoint, the carrying value of its investment is equal to its share of the net assets of the joint venture, and accordingly, the share of joint venture earnings to be recognized by Company B are based on the earnings reported by the joint venture. Exhibit 7.17 illustrates the journal entries that would be booked by Company B in accounting for its investment in the joint venture.

Company B would record the same amount of deferred taxes recorded by Company A, even though the share of joint venture earnings reported by

EXHIBIT 7.17   Company B Journal Entries

	Dr.	Cr.
(a) Investment in Company C	$10,000,000	
Cash		$10,000,000
(Initial 50% investment)		
(b) Investment in Company C	952,000	
Share of Company C net income		952,000
(Equity method income recognition)		
(c) Income tax expense — deferred	109,160	
Deferred income taxes		109,160
(To record income tax expense)		

Company A after adjustment is higher than the amount reported by Company B. This is because the deferred tax amount reported by Company A was based on the assumed dividend consistent with the permanent tax attributes of Company D.

CHAPTER EIGHT

Partnership Accounting

Barbara A. Jenkins
Jenkins & Jenkins, P.C.

      (i) Dissolution by Acts of the Parties

      (ii) Dissolution by Operation of the Law

      (iii) Dissolution by Judicial Decree

8.7   Admission of a New Partner

    (a)   General

    (b)   Acquisition of Interest by Purchase

    (c)   Acquisition of Interest by Investment

    (d)   Acquisition of Interest by Investment with Allowance of Bonus or Goodwill to Old Partners

      (i)   General

      (ii) Bonus

      (iii) Goodwill

      (iv) Comparison of Bonus and Goodwill Methods

      (v) Asset Revaluation

    (e)   Acquisition of Interest by Investment with Allowance of Bonus or Goodwill to a New Partner

      (i)   General

      (ii) Bonus

      (iii) Goodwill

      (iv) Comparison of Bonus and Goodwill Methods

      (v) Asset Revaluation

8.8   Settlement with a Withdrawing Partner

    (a)   General

    (b)   Payment to a Withdrawing Partner of an Amount That Exceeds Capital Balance

      (i)   General

      (ii) Bonus

      (iii) Goodwill

    (c)   Payment to a Withdrawing Partner of an Amount Less than the Partner's Capital Balance

      (i)   General

      (ii) Bonus

      (iii) Goodwill

    (d)   Settlement with an Estate

8.9   Liquidation of a Partnership

    (a)   General

    (b)   Gain or Loss on Sale of Assets Completed before Any Payments to Partners

      (i)   General

      (ii) Partners' Capital Accounts Are Sufficient to Absorb Loss on Realization of Assets

      (iii) Partners' Capital Accounts Are Insufficient to Absorb Loss on
            Sale of Assets
      (iv) Loss on Sale of Assets Resulting in a Deficiency in a Partner's
            Capital Account
      (v) Gain or Loss on Sale of Net Assets Insufficient to Pay Creditors

8.1   PARTNERSHIPS — DEFINITION, CHARACTERISTICS, AND TYPES

(a) Definition of Partnerships

A partnership is an association of two or more persons to operate a business for profit, with each contributing money, property, labor, or skill, and with all expecting to share in the profits and losses. The term "persons" includes individuals, partnerships, corporations, and other associations. The definition of the partnership may be written or oral but the result is a contract between parties. No formal sanction or recognition by a governmental unit is required in its formation.

(b) Characteristics of Partnerships

Characteristics of partnerships include the following:

Mutual Agency	Each partner is an agent of the partnership within the scope of the business. Because of this mutual agency feature, any partner can bind the partnership to a business agreement as long as he or she acts within the scope of the normal operations of the business. Acts of a partner that do not fall in the category of carrying on business in the usual manner would not bind the partnership without the special authorization of the co-partners.
Limited Life	Because a partnership is formed by a contract between partners, any change in the relationship of these parties terminates the contract and dissolves the partnership. Examples of an event which would

terminate a partnership contract are as follows: death of a partner, partner bankruptcy, or partnership terminated by agreement, as in the end of a major project.

Unlimited Liability   A partner's potential liability for partnership debts extends to his or her personal assets. Because creditors are doing business with an "association of individuals," they can look to these individuals for payment if partnership property is insufficient to meet partnership obligations. Therefore, a partner may be liable for 100% of the debt with subsequent recourse to the other partners.

Ownership of   When individuals invest property in a partnership,
an Interest   they give up the right to their separate use of the property. The property becomes an asset of the partnership and is owned jointly by all of the partners.

Participation in   Each member of a partnership has the right to share
Partnership Profits   in the firm's profits and the responsibility to share in its losses. The partnership agreement should delineate the method of distributing profits and losses to each partner. However, if the agreement only speaks to the method of profit distribution and does not mention losses, the losses will be distributed in the same manner as the profits.

(c) Types of Partnerships

Following are descriptions of different types of partnerships:

General Partnerships   A general partnership is one in which all partners may act on behalf of the partnership including binding of contracts, and in which each partner can be held individually liable for obligations of the partnership.

Limited Partnership   A limited partnership is one in which only one partner is required to be a general partner, assuming the risks and rewards of a general partner. The other members of the group are considered "limited partners" and are restricted in the amount of partnership activity that they can be involved in and are at risk for only a stated amount, which may be the amount actually invested.

Joint Stock Company A joint stock company is a partnership formed with a capital structure in the form of transferable shares. Ownership of shares, usually evidenced by a stock certificate, gives a party the right to participate in the management of the firm, to share in the profits, and to transfer holdings. This form of business organization is comparable to the corporate form of business except for the unlimited liability that attaches to ownership interests.

Limited Liability Partnerships A registered limited liability partnership is a general partnership that has been registered with the Secretary of State. By registering, the partners obtain a certain amount of liability protection in the form of malpractice, and errors and omissions of the other partners. However, unlike limited liability corporation statutes, under most limited liability partnership statutes, the partners are not protected against commercial or contract liability of the partnership. Some states are in the process, however, of passing legislation which will provide liability protection for commercial and contract debt of the limited liability partnerships.

8.2 PARTNERSHIP AGREEMENTS

Although a partnership agreement can be oral in nature, it is preferable that the agreement be written so that misunderstandings or disputes between partners as to the nature and terms of the contract can be avoided. The partnership agreement should address the following issues:

- Names, addresses, and social security numbers of parties entering into the business
- Location of the business
- Effective date of formation of the partnership and duration of the contract
- Nature of the business
- Rights, powers, and duties of the partners
- Investment by each of the partners and the value assigned to each investment
- The specifics of the partnership such as methods of accounting and year-end
- The profit and loss sharing percentages, special provisions for the recognition of differences in capital and personal contributions
- Guaranteed payments to partners, interest credits related to capital contributions, and any other special payments or allocations
- Partners' investments, transfers, sales, or other capital activity subsequent to formation and their accounting treatment
- Benefits that will be paid for by the partnership and their accounting treatment
- Method of handling a partner's death, disability, sale, or withdrawal
- Methods for resolving partners' disputes
- Any additional tax elections such as inventory method, cost or percentage depletion (oil and gas excluded), capitalization policy, cost recovery methods and assumptions, amortization of organizational costs and period, amortization of start-up expenditures and period, optional basis adjustments for property, immediate expensing of certain tangible personal property, etc.

8.3   ACCOUNTING FOR PARTNERS' ACCOUNTS

(a) Partners' Capital Accounts

Partners' original investments are recorded in each partner's individual account. Increases to partners' capital accounts are the result of the following:

- Investments in the partnership of cash, merchandise, or other assets
- Profit from the partnership
- Assumption or payment by the individual partner of partnership debt
- Collection by the partnership of personal claims of partners

Decreases to partners' capital account are the result of the following:

- Withdrawals from the partnership of cash, merchandise, or other assets
- Loss from the partnership
- Collection of partnership claims by individual partners
- Assumption or payment by the partnership of personal indebtedness of the partner, for example, life insurance premiums and personal income taxes

The above examples of increases and decreases are considered permanent in nature and are thus made directly to the capital account. Withdrawals by partners, commonly called draws, are advances in anticipation of partnership profits. These profits or losses are accumulated in income statement accounts and distributed at the end of the year to the individual partnership accounts on their agreed-to ratio.

When a partnership agreement requirement is that interest is charged to the partner when his or her capital account drops below the original investment or when interest is paid if the capital account is above the original investment, it may be advisable to segregate the original investment in a separate account. The partnership agreement should state clearly any interest provisions with respect to fluctuating capital balances.

(b) Partners' Drawing Accounts

As mentioned above, a partner may receive payments during the year in anticipation of partnership profits for the year. A credit balance in a draw account indicates that the partner has withdrawn less than the increases that took place in his or her account; a debit balance would indicate that the partner has withdrawn more than the increases. It is customary to close the draw account into the partners capital account at the end of the year and the resulting balance will become the partner's current equity in the partnership.

(c) Partners' Receivable and Payable Accounts

When the partner borrows partnership money with the intention to repay it at a date in the future, the result is a receivable from the partner. Such a receivable should be evidenced by a note with terms — a specific date due or on demand, interest rate, and method of repayment. An advance to the partnership by the partner with the anticipation that it will be repaid by the partnership is considered a loan payable to the individual partner. As in a receivable, the transaction should be documented by a note with specific terms — a specific due date or on demand, interest rate, and method of repayment.

8.4 RECORDING INVESTMENTS IN A PARTNERSHIP

The contribution to the partnership can be made in the form of cash or other assets as provided in the partnership agreement. When assets other than cash are contributed, a value for those assets must be established and all of the partners must agree with this value. When this procedure is completed, the assets are recorded and the partners capital accounts are credited. Because the value of the assets contributed become the original basis of the partner's investment, it is extremely important that the valuation of the assets be proper. Once these assets are contributed to the partnership, any subsequent gain or loss realized on the disposition of the asset will be distributed according to the partnership agreement. Because of this fact, original valuation should be fair market value.

8.5 DISTRIBUTION OF PARTNERSHIP PROFITS AND LOSSES

(a) General

Because partnerships are so flexible in their formation, partners can agree to distribute profits and losses in any manner they wish. The partnership agreement should be very specific and complete to avoid any misunderstandings or disputes as to intent.

The following methods can be used to allocate profits and losses, but the possibilities are many:

- Equally
- In an arbitrary ratio

- In the ratio of the partners' capital accounts
- Salaries or bonuses (guaranteed payments to partners) to be allocated to partners for their services and then distribution on an agreed-upon ratio
- Interest paid on average capital balances for the year and then an allocation based on an agreed upon ratio
- Interest paid on capital balances, guaranteed payments to partners, and the balance distributed on an agreed-upon ratio

The following subsections provide discussion and illustration of alternative profit and loss distributions based on the above methods. In the illustrations, the following assumptions are used:

Assumptions:

Partnership profit for the year	$32,000
Partner A capital contribution 1/1	20,000
Partner A capital contribution 7/1	5,000
Partner A draw amount 12/1	7,500
Partner B capital contribution 1/1	30,000
Partner B capital contribution 7/1	2,000
Partner B draw amount 12/1	$10,000

(b) Equal Division of Profits and Losses

The following illustrates activity in partners' capital account using equal division of profits and losses:

Partner A:

Original capital	$20,000
Subsequent contribution	5,000
Draw account (net withdrawals)	(7,500)
50% of profit	16,000
Capital account after the close of the year	$33,500

Partner B:

Original capital	$30,000
Subsequent contribution	2,000
Draw account (net withdrawals)	(10,000)
50% of profits	16,000
Capital account after the close of the year	38,000

(c) Profits and Losses in an Arbitrary Ratio

Because investment in a partnership may not be just monetary in nature, distributions of partnership profits may be computed in many different manners. For instance, if the above two partners have substantially different work and industry experience levels, but both partners will be working equal time in the partnership, they may determine that an equitable split of profits may be one-third and two-thirds. This arbitrary allocation is presented as follows:

Partner A:

Original capital	$20,000
Subsequent contribution	5,000
Draw account (net withdrawals)	(7,500)
One-third of profits	10,667
Capital account after the close of the year	$28,167

Partner B:

Original capital	$30,000
Subsequent contribution	2,000
Draw account (net withdrawals)	(10,000)
Two-thirds of profits	21,333
Capital account after the close of the year	$43,333

The allocation does not, however, have to be this simple. For example, the partners may agree to allocate the first $20,000 on a one-third and two-thirds basis and the remainder equally.

(d) Profits and Losses in the Ratio of Partners' Capital Accounts

When partners agree that the major contributor to the success of the partnership is the capital invested, the partners may distribute profits based on the partners' capital accounts. If this method of allocation is selected, then the partners must also agree upon which balances the allocation will be computed. The choices of allocations are as follows: capital accounts at the formation of the partnership, capital accounts at the beginning of each year or fiscal period, capital accounts at the end of each year or fiscal period, or average capital accounts for the year or fiscal period.

The following illustrates usage of *capital accounts at formation of the partnership* as the basis:

Partner A:

Original capital	$20,000
Subsequent contribution	5,000
Draw account (net withdrawals)	(7,500)
Profit share (20,000/50,000 × $32,000)	12,800
Capital account after the close of the year	$30,300

Partner B:

Original capital	$30,000
Subsequent contribution	2,000
Draw account (net withdrawals)	(10,000)
Profit share (30,000/50,000 × $32,000)	19,200
Capital account after the close of the year	$41,200

Capital accounts at the beginning of the year or fiscal period as the basis: For the first year of operations, the allocation of profits would be based on the same numbers as the above example. In subsequent years, the allocation would be based on beginning capital account balances considering any contributions, withdrawals, and profit or loss allocations for the previous year.

The following illustrates usage of capital accounts at the close of the year or fiscal period:

Partner A:

Original capital	$20,000
Subsequent contribution	5,000
Draw account (net withdrawals)	(7,500)
Profit share (17,500/39,500 × $32,000)	14,177
Capital account after the close of the year	$31,677

Partner B:

Original capital	$30,000
Subsequent contribution	2,000
Draw account (net withdrawals)	(10,000)
Profit share (22,000/39,500 × $32,000)	17,823
Capital account after the close of the year	$39,823

Exhibit 8.1 illustrates usage of *average capital accounts* as the basis.

EXHIBIT 8.1   Average Capital Accounts as the Basis for Profit Distribution

Date	Capital Balance	Months	Weighted Total	Weighted Average
Partner A:				
January 1	$20,000	6	$120,000	
July 1	25,000	5	125,000	
December 1	17,500	1	17,500	
Average		12		$262,500
Partner B:				
January 1	$30,000	6	$180,000	
July 1	32,000	5	160,000	
December 1	22,000	1	22,000	
Average		12		$362,000
All Partners' Average		12		$624,500

Partner A:

Original capital	$20,000
Subsequent contribution	5,000
Draw account (net withdrawals)	(7,500)
Profit share (262,500/624,500 × $32,000)	13,451
Capital account after the close of the year	$30,951

Partner B:

Original capital	$30,000
Subsequent contribution	2,000
Draw account (net withdrawals)	(10,000)
Profit share (362,000/624,500 × $32,000)	18,549
Capital account after the close of the year	$40,549

Because the use of an average capital allocation offers a reasonable distribution in terms of relative investment, it acts as an incentive for additional capital contributions. Specifics regarding whether all contributions and withdrawals are to be included in the averaging should be included in the partnership agreement.

(e) Interest on Capital Accounts Followed by Ratio Distribution

Partners often have an additional basis on which to distribute profits other than those discussed above. There are instances when partners may feel that, while recognition should be given to respective capital amounts, distribution of profits and losses in terms of relative capitals will fail to offer an equitable division for the following reasons:

- Investments represent only one factor contributing to the success of the business and distribution of profits in terms of this factor alone will fail to recognize all of the elements entering into the company's operations.
- In the event of a loss, the partner making the larger investment will absorb the greater part of the loss; in many instances, however, the partner

making the larger capital investment should be rewarded regardless of the amount of profit or loss.

To remedy this situation, the partners may agree to allocate a certain percent interest to the capital balance before any allocation of profit or loss is made. The partnership agreement should define the specific interest rate or the source of the interest rate computation and whether calculations are to be made on capital balances at a fixed point in time or on average balances.

As an example, the above partners agree that their "ability" contributions to the business are equal, but because Partner B has contributed more cash or tangible assets to the venture, they agree to allocate interest on the end-of-year capital balances at 7.5% with the residue to be distributed equally.

The computation would be as follows:

Partner A:

Capital account at the close of the year before profit/loss allocation	$17,500
Interest allocation	1,312
Profits — equally	14,519
Capital account after allocations	$33,331

Partner B:

Capital account at the close of the year before profit/loss allocation	$22,000
Interest allocation	1,650
Profits — equally	14,519
Capital account after allocations	$38,169

As can be noted from the above example, interest allocations are a small amount of the profit in the capital ratio. Also important is the fact that if interest allocations are a requirement of the partnership agreement, then they must be done even though operations have resulted in a profit less than the allowable interest or in a loss. This resulting loss will then be allocated to the partners accounts based on their profit and loss ratio.

Other types of interest arrangements can be incorporated into the partnership agreement. For example, an agreement may provide for fixed capital contributions from individual partners with interest allowed on amounts in excess of such fixed amounts and interest charged on any deficiencies.

Amounts loaned to a partner by the partnership or amounts loaned to the partnership by the partner are considered ordinary debtor/creditor transactions, and are recorded as such on the books of the partnership. As such, interest will be computed and paid on such amounts based on the terms of the notes. These types of transactions differ from the profit and loss allocations discussed above in that interest on notes is paid while interest on capital accounts is an allocation of partnership profit or loss.

(f) Guaranteed Payment to Partner Followed by Ratio Distribution

Because different experience or ability levels exist between partners or the availability of time to be spent in the business, partners may agree to a guaranteed payment to a partner or partners before a ratio distribution. This guaranteed payment to partner allocation is similar to a salary, compensating the partner for his or her additional personal contributions. This is, however, an allocation item only with no current payroll tax effects.

For example, the partners agree to allocate $2,000 per month to Partner A as compensation for managing the business on a full-time basis. Partner B will handle credit activity and will be compensated $500 per month. The remaining profits will be distributed equally, therefore, allocations will be as follows:

Partner A:

Original capital	$20,000
Subsequent contribution	5,000
Draw account (net withdrawals)	(7,500)
Guaranteed payment	24,000
50% of profits	1,000
Capital account after the close of the year	$42,500

Partner B:

Original capital	$30,000
Subsequent contribution	2,000
Draw account (net withdrawals)	(10,000)
Guaranteed payment	6,000
50% of profits	1,000
Capital account after the close of the year	$29,000

When an agreement provides for guaranteed payment to partners, this distribution must be made even though operations have resulted in a profit that is inadequate to cover these payments or in a partnership loss.

(g) Guaranteed Payments to Partners, Interest Allocations on Capital Accounts, Followed by Ratio Distribution

Partners may agree to both guaranteed payments to partners and interest allocations based on capital accounts as a means of dividing profits equitably. After the above allocations, then remaining profits can be allocated on a agreed-upon ratio. If operating profits are insufficient to cover the aforementioned allocations, then losses are distributed based on the agreed-upon ratio.

8.6 DISSOLUTION OF A PARTNERSHIP

(a) General

A partnership is legally dissolved when there is a change in the original association of the partners. Some common reasons for the dissolution of a partnership are the admission of a new partner, disability or death of a partner, or withdrawal of a partner. When the partnership is dissolved, the partners lose their authority to operate the business as a going concern. This does not mean that the business operation is necessarily ended or interrupted. The remaining partners can act for the partnership in winding up the affairs of the operation or in forming a new partnership.

(b) Conditions Resulting in Dissolution

(i) Dissolution by Acts of the Parties.   The following acts of the parties would dissolve a partnership:

Mutual Agreement	Partners may agree at any time to terminate their association for business purposes or to change their membership composition.
Withdrawal of a Partner	A partner may withdraw from the partnership based on the terms of the partnership agreement. If the partner chooses to disregard the agreement, he becomes liable to his co-partners for damages that the partnership may sustain through such action. To further explain, the partner has the power to withdraw from the partnership at any time, but he or she must also have the contractual right to do so if he or she is to avoid liability for damages. There are two exceptions to the above statement: (1) with unanimous consent of all of the partners, and (2) "partnership at will," where a partner may withdraw at any time without liability to his co-partners.
Termination of Time or Accomplishment of Purpose	If the partnership agreement designates a time certain for termination, or if a specific objective is achieved, such time or objective obtained fulfills the partnership contract and the partnership may dissolve. When a partnership does not have a fixed life or when it continues after the stipulated conditions have been met, it is known as a partnership at will.

(ii) Dissolution by Operation of the Law.   Certain contingencies recognized by law will terminate the partnership as follows:

- Death of a partner
- Bankruptcy of the partnership or any partner
- Any event that makes it unlawful for the business to be carried on or for individual members to carry on as a partnership

(iii) Dissolution by Judicial Decree.   A court may decree dissolution based on any of the following circumstances:

- Insanity of a partner or his or her inability to fulfill his or her part of the partnership contract
- Conduct of a partner that reflects unfavorably on the operation of the partnership
- Internal dissension among partners
- Lack of ability to maintain a going concern
- Other reasons that render dissolution equitable, such as misrepresentation in the formation of the partnership

8.7   ADMISSION OF A NEW PARTNER

(a) General

Admission of a new partner will dissolve the old partnership because a new association has been formed. However, the firm cannot admit a new partner without the consent of all of the old partners. When a new partner is admitted, a new partnership agreement should describe the new arrangement in detail. This agreement should be written to contain provisions with respect to the capital of the newly formed unit, the distribution of future profits and losses among partners, and all of the other pertinent data relative to this new venture.

Although the newly formed partnership can continue to use the books, records, and accounting procedures of the former entity, certain account balances will generally require restatement. Present market values should be determined for the assets that are to be identified with the new partnership. Inventories should be restated at present replacement values, adjusting for damaged goods and obsolescence. Adequate allowances should be established for receivables. Marketable securities should be reported at their current market values. Noncurrent assets should be listed at their present appraised values, and all liabilities should be determined and reported on the books and records. These adjustments will give rise to profit or loss which will be recorded by the original partners in their respective profit and loss ratios. Failure to give effect in the accounts to such changes will result in participation by an incoming partner in gains and losses that occurred prior to his entry into the partnership.

An individual may be admitted into a partnership in one of two ways:

- By purchasing an interest in the partnership from one or more of the original partners
- By investing cash or other assets in the business

(b) Acquisition of Interest by Purchase

When an individual is admitted to a partnership by purchasing an interest from an existing partner, all partners must agree to the change. If all of the partners agree, the admission of a new partner dissolves the old partnership and brings into existence a new partnership. If the partners do not agree to the new partner, then he or she simply acquires the profits and, upon dissolution, the interest to which the original partner would have been entitled as per the partnership agreement. The transfer of the interest does not, of itself, dissolve the firm, nor does it entitle the buyer to interfere in the management of the business. If the selling partner does not have the right to do so under the terms of the partnership agreement but transacts the sale, claims may be raised against him or her by the remaining partners for any losses that the partners may incur through his or her action.

If an individual acquires a portion of a partnership by purchase of this interest from an existing partner, the capital account of the purchasing partner is increased in the same amount by which the selling partner's capital account is decreased. The total partnership capital amount does not change because the transaction is between two individuals acting in their private capacities. For example:

Partner A:

Capital balance	$40,000
Profits — equally	

Partner B:

Capital balance	$40,000
Profits — equally	

Partner A sells half of his interest in the partnership to C for $25,000. Partner B agrees to the admission of the new partner. The original partnership books are to be maintained for the new partnership A, B, and C. The partnership will now make an entry to debit Partner A's capital for $20,000 and credit Partner C's capital for $20,000.

This entry is made regardless of the amount paid for the partnership interest by Partner C. The result of the above transaction is that Partner A now owns 25% of the partnership, as does Partner C, while Partner B retains his 50% ownership.

The fact that Partner C has acquired a 25% interest in the new partnership, A, B and C, does not necessarily mean that his participation in firm profits and losses will be equal to his percentage ownership. Upon Partner C's purchase in the new entity, the partners should agree upon the future distribution of profits and losses. In the absence of an agreement, Partners A, B, and C will share profits and losses equally.

If the partners feel that the current accounts fail to be representative of the value of the business, net assets could be restated and the revaluation gain or loss recognized in the capital accounts of the original partners in their profit and loss ratio. When the price paid by an incoming partner is considered to be evidence of goodwill identified with the business but not reflected on the books, such an intangible asset can be recorded prior to the entry for the transfer of the interest.

(c) Acquisition of Interest by Investment

When an individual purchases an interest in the partnership by investing assets in the partnership, both the assets and the equity (capital) of the partnership are increased. This is because the assets contributed by the entering partner now become partnership assets, as opposed to assets belonging to an individual partner. As an example:

Partner A:

Capital balance $40,000

Profits — equally

Partner B:

Capital balance $30,000

Profits — equally

Partner C is admitted to the partnership with a cash investment of $45,000. All assets are valued properly and liabilities are recorded. Profits and losses of the new partnership are allocated equally and the original partnership books are maintained for the new firm of A, B, and C.

The entry to record the investment would be recorded as a debit to Cash for $45,000, and a credit to Partner C's capital for $45,000.

Because the admission of a new partner requires a new partnership agreement, the terms of the agreement must be observed. Partner C's interest in the partnership is 45/115 or approximately 39%.

Assume that the agreement between Partners A, B, and C provides that Partner C is to invest a sum sufficient to give him a one-fifth or 20% interest in the new partnership. In this case, the combined capitals of the original members, $70,000, would represent 80% of the new entity, and an investment of $17,500 would be required from the incoming partner for a 1/5 (20%) interest. Capital for Partners A, B, and C then would be $40,000, $30,000, and $17,500, respectively; the interests upon Partner C's admission would be 45.7%, 34.3%, and 20%, respectively.

(d) Acquisition of Interest by Investment with Allowance of Bonus or Goodwill to Old Partners

(i) General.   When a partnership has operated with considerable success, the partners may admit a new member with the provision that part of the new partner's investment shall be allowed as a bonus to the old partners, or that firm goodwill shall be established and credited to the old partners.

(ii) Bonus.   Assume the following:

Partner A:

Capital balance $40,000

Profits — equally

Partner B:

Capital balance $30,000

Profits — equally

Assume that the business has been operated so successfully that C is willing to buy a one-quarter interest for $45,000. Note that the net assets prior to C's investment is $70,000, and after the investment will equal $115,000. Therefore a credit of $28,750 will give C a one-quarter interest in the new partnership. The amount by which the investment exceeds the interest allocated to C (one-quarter) is $16,250.

Since Partner A and Partner B share profits equally, they would each be allocated $8,125 of the $16,250 bonus. Based on the fact that the original partnership books will be used for the new partnership, the entry to record the investment of C would be as follows:

	Dr.	Cr.
Cash	$45,000	
Capital Partner A		$ 8,125
Capital Partner B		8,125
Capital Partner C		28,750

(iii) Goodwill.   Assume the same fact situation as before, except that C requires that his capital account report his total investment of $45,000, which still equates to a one-quarter interest in the business. In this instance, the valuation of C's one-quarter interest at $45,000 can be used as a basis for recording goodwill identified with the net asset contribution made by Partner A and Partner B to the new partnership. Since C's capital of $45,000 will be a 25% interest in the venture, the total of the capital will become $180,000, and the capital accounts of A and B will be $135,000. Based on these facts, the entry to record the investment of C would be as follows:

	Dr.	Cr.
Goodwill	$65,000	
Capital Partner A		$32,500
Capital Partner B		32,500
Cash	45,000	
Capital Partner C		45,000

Since a new partnership is being formed in both of the above instances, a new partnership agreement should be written delineating all of the pertinent information including profit and loss distributions. If nothing is said about the profit and loss sharing ratio, it is assumed that future profits and losses will be divided equally among Partners A, B, and C.

(iv) Comparison of Bonus and Goodwill Methods. As described above, Partner C obtains a one-quarter interest in assets and a one-third share of profits upon his admission by the use of either the bonus method or the goodwill method. Although either method can be used in achieving the required interest for the new partner, the two methods offer the same ultimate results only (1) when the incoming partner's percentage share of profit and loss is to be equal to his or her percentage interest in assets upon admission or (2) when the former partners continue to share profits and losses between themselves in the original ratio.

(v) Asset Revaluation. In the previous examples, we have assumed that the values assigned to net assets on the original books are acceptable. If Partner C's investment of $45,000 for a one-quarter interest in the partnership is based upon the fact that the net assets on the books are worth $65,000 greater than stated, appropriate entries would be required to restate assets at their present values and to raise the capitals of the original owners accordingly. This scenario would not require either a bonus or goodwill adjustment upon admitting Partner C to the venture.

(e) Acquisition of Interest by Investment with Allowance of Bonus or Goodwill to a New Partner

(i) General. If a partnership has been operating inefficiently and is in urgent need of operating capital, or the partners wish to solicit the abilities of another partner, this new member may be admitted with either of the following provisions: (1) part of the capitals of the old partners will be allowed as a bonus to the new partner, or (2) goodwill will be established and credited to the new partner.

(ii) Bonus. Assume the following:

Partner A:

Capital balance	$40,000
Profits — equally	

Partner B:

Capital balance	$30,000
Profits — equally	

If Partners A and B agree to give C a two-fifths interest in the new partnership for $45,000, the total net assets of the business become $115,000 and C's two-fifths interest is $46,000. The entry to record the investment of C would be as follows:

	Dr.	Cr.
Cash	$45,000	
Capital Partner A	500	
Capital Partner B	500	
Capital Partner C		$46,000

(iii) Goodwill. If, however, Partners A and B are not willing to have their capital accounts reduced, but they are willing to allow C a two-fifths interest in the firm for his investment to $45,000, the procedure would be as follows:

	Dr.	Cr.
Cash	$45,000	
Goodwill	1,667	
Capital Partner C		$46,667

In the above example, the capital balances of the old partners are used as the basis for determining the interest to be allowed C and the goodwill that he is considered to bring to the entity. If the sum of Partner A and Partner B's capitals, $70,000, is to equal three-fifths of the total capital, the total capital will have to be $116,667, and C's interest will have to be $46,667. Goodwill is, therefore, debited for the difference between the amount invested by C and the amount to be credited to his capital account.

(iv) Comparison of Bonus and Goodwill Methods.   As described above, Partner C receives a two-fifths interest in net assets and a one-third share of profits upon his being admitted to the new partnership by the use of either the bonus method or the goodwill method. As can be seen from the examples, either method can be used to obtain the required interest for Partner C, but the ultimate effect upon the partners' capital accounts will not be the same.

(v) Asset Revaluation.   In the previous examples, we have assumed that the values assigned to net assets on the original books are acceptable. If Partner C's investment of $45,000 for a two-fifths interest in the partnership is based upon the fact that the net assets on the books are worth less than the $70,000 stated, appropriate entries would be required to restate assets at their present values and reduce the capital balances of the original owners accordingly.

8.8   SETTLEMENT WITH A WITHDRAWING PARTNER

(a) General

A partner has the right to withdraw from a partnership whenever he or she chooses in compliance with the terms of the agreement. To avoid any controversy when a partner does decide to withdraw or retire from the firm, the partnership agreement should describe the appropriate actions to be taken under these circumstances. Some circumstances which may be delineated in the partnership agreement are as follows:

- Whether or not an audit will be performed by CPAs
- How or if the assets will be revalued
- How and if a bonus will be determined
- In what manner the withdrawing partner will be paid

If the partner exercises his or her power to withdraw in violation of the partnership agreement and without the mutual consent of all participants, he or she becomes liable to his co-partners for any damages they sustain through this action. In this situation, a withdrawing partner's claim for his or her interest may suffer impairment by the damages attributable to his or her withdrawal.

There are several ways in which a partner may withdraw from a partnership. Some examples are as follows:

- Sell the withdrawing partner's interest to another partner with the consent of the remaining partners
- Sell the withdrawing partner's interest to an outsider with the consent of the remaining partners
- Withdraw assets that are equal to the withdrawing partner's capital balance
  - Withdraw assets that are greater than the withdrawing partner's capital balance — this method results in a bonus to the withdrawing partner
  - Withdraw assets that are less than the withdrawing partner's capital balance — this method results in a bonus to the remaining partners

It should be noted at this point that the withdrawal of a member from a partnership and settlement with the entity does not relieve the withdrawing partner from personal liability on existing firm claims in the absence of an agreement with creditors to that effect.

Because the withdrawal of a partner normally requires an appraisal of partnership assets and an asset restatement, gains or losses resulting from said revaluation will be allocated to the partners' capital accounts in the profit and loss ratio. This allocation, therefore, has the effect of making adjustments to the capital balances that have taken place in asset values during the time when the withdrawing partner was participating in the business. If this revaluation of assets adjustment is made, the partners are normally willing to make the settlement with the withdrawing partner based on the amount in the withdrawing partner's capital account.

(b) Payment to a Withdrawing Partner of an Amount That Exceeds Capital Balance

(i) General. If a partnership has been extremely successful, a withdrawing partner may require an amount in settlement that exceeds his or her capital balance even after its revaluation adjustment of net assets as described above. Remaining partners may agree to this bonus rather than terminating the busi-

ness. If an excess payment is agreed upon, it can be handled with either a bonus to the withdrawing partner to be absorbed by the remaining partners or it can be used to record excess goodwill in the partnership.

(ii) Bonus.   Assume the following:

Partner A:

Capital balance	$20,000
Profit share — one-half	

Partner B:

Capital balance	$20,000
Profit share — one-quarter	

Partner C:

Capital balance	$20,000
Profit share — one-quarter	

If we assume that the assets are properly valued, and that the partners agree to pay Partner C $22,000 for his share of the partnership, the $2,000 excess would be considered a bonus and would be recorded as follows:

	Dr.	Cr.
Partner C Capital	$20,000	
Partner A Capital	1,333	
Partner B Capital	667	
Payable to Partner C		$22,000

(iii) Goodwill.   If we assume that Partner A and Partner B are unwilling to have their capital accounts reduced, even though they are willing to pay Partner C $22,000 in settlement of his interest in the partnership, the adjustment will be made to goodwill. If the $2,000 represents Partner C's 25% increase in net assets, then $8,000 would be the total partnership adjustment to be recorded as follows:

	Dr.	Cr.
Goodwill	$ 8,000	
Partner A Capital		$ 4,000
Partner B Capital		2,000
Partner C Capital		2,000
Partner C Capital	22,000	
Payable to Partner C		22,000

The recognition of $8,000 of goodwill and its distribution to all of the partners is consistent with the practice of recognizing the full change in other asset values and of carrying the effects of such changes to all of the capital balances. It is the practice of some, however, to recognize goodwill only to the extent of the amount allowed to the withdrawing partner; the books, then, will report only the goodwill that is actually purchased by the continuing partnership.

In summary, either the bonus method or the goodwill method can be used in recording the withdrawal of Partner C, but the result will be the same only when the remaining partners continue to share profits between themselves in the original ratio.

(c) Payment to a Withdrawing Partner of an Amount Less than the Partner's Capital Balance

(i) General. If a partner is anxious to terminate his or her relationship with the partnership, he or she may be willing to accept less than his or her capital interest in the entity. The withdrawing partner's willingness to accept such a reduced amount may arise from the realization that a forced sale of the firm's assets may result in a loss and a decrease in interest as great as or greater than that which can be effected through agreement. When a partner agrees to accept less than the amount in his capital account, the resulting difference can be recorded as a bonus to the remaining partners, or where goodwill already resides on the books of the partnership, it can be a reduction of the goodwill balance.

(ii) Bonus. As in the previous example, Partner C has a $20,000 capital account balance. He is willing to accept payment of $18,000 in full payment of

his $20,000 investment. Based on those assumptions, the entry to record the settlement would be as follows:

	Dr.	Cr.
Partner C Capital	$20,000	
Payable to C		$18,000
Partner A Capital		1,333
Partner B Capital		667

(iii) Goodwill. If we assume that the books of the partnership have goodwill recorded and Partner C accepts less than his capital balance, the remaining partners may view the payment to C of an amount that is less than his balance a shrinkage in goodwill rather than an increase in the continuing partners' capitals. Assuming that C is paid $18,000 for his $20,000 interest and the offsetting credit is a reduction of goodwill, the journal entry would be as follows:

	Dr.	Cr.
Partner C Capital	$20,000	
Goodwill		$ 2,000
Payable of Partner C		18,000

It could also be possible to record the entire shrinkage in goodwill with the withdrawal of Partner C. Since the shrinkage in goodwill attributable to C is 25%, then the total goodwill shrinkage would be $8,000. The resulting journal entry would be as follows:

	Dr.	Cr.
Partner A Capital	$ 4,000	
Partner B Capital	2,000	
Partner C Capital	20,000	
Goodwill		$ 8,000
Payable to Partner C		18,000

Although either the bonus or goodwill method can be used to record the withdrawal of Partner C, these two methods will offer the same results only when the continuing partners continue to share profits between themselves in the original ratio.

(d) Settlement with an Estate

Because the death of a partner dissolves the partnership, it is the normal procedure to summarize profits and losses, have the firms' assets appraised, and make any adjustments as required by the partnership agreement, thus establishing the decedent's interest in the partnership as of the date of death. Profit and loss from the date the books were last closed is determined and transferred to the capital accounts in the existing profit and loss ratio. The change in asset values arising from revaluation is likewise carried to the capital accounts in the profit and loss ratio. It is then the obligation of the remaining partners to proceed in winding up the business. Assets are sold, liabilities are paid off, and settlement is made with the partner's estate and to surviving partners.

Partners can agree to continuation of the business upon the death of a partner as long as it is a provision of the partnership agreement. Various methods can be used to settle the deceased partner's interest as follows:

- Payment from firm assets
- Payment by individual partners who would then acquire the interest
- Payment from partnership insurance proceeds with the surviving partners acquiring the deceased partner's interest

Thus the death of a partner results in the dissolution of the original partnership and the formation of a new business. The interest of the deceased partner as of the date of death should be recorded as a liability and the subsequent payment to the estate would be a relief of the liability balance.

8.9   LIQUIDATION OF A PARTNERSHIP

(a) General

Liquidation of a partnership is the process of ending a business, which entails selling enough assets to pay the liabilities and distributing any remaining assets among the partners. Unlike the case of dissolution, if a partnership is liquidated, the business will not continue.

The partnership agreement should indicate the procedures to be followed in the case of liquidation. Normally, the books will be adjusted and closed, with the income or loss being distributed to the partners. As the assets of the business are sold, any gain or loss should be distributed among the partners according to the established profit and loss ratio. The capital balances then become the basis for settlement. As cash becomes available, it must be applied first to outside creditors, then to partners' loans, and finally to the partners' capital balances.

If, in the course of liquidation, a partner's account decreases to a debit balance and the partner has a loan balance, the law permits exercise of the right of offset, that is the offset of a part or all of the loan against the capital deficiency.

(b) Gain or Loss on Sale of Assets Completed before Any Payments to Partners

(i) General.   When a partnership decides to liquidate, the composition of the balance sheet must be changed to cash to determine how the final liquidation may be handled.

Assume the partnership books are as follows prior to liquidation:

Assets

Cash	$ 25,000
Other Assets	225,000
Total Assets	250,000

Liabilities and Capital

Liabilities	$ 80,000
Loan payable A	10,000
Loan payable C	5,000
Capital A	60,000
Capital B	50,000
Capital C	45,000
Total Liabilities and Capital	$250,000

Partners share profits and losses 40%, 30%, and 30%, respectively.

(ii) Partners' Capital Accounts Are Sufficient to Absorb Loss on Realization of Assets.

Assume that assets are sold and $200,000 is realized from their sale. The journal entries would be as follows:

	Dr.	Cr.
Cash	$200,000	
Capital A	10,000	
Capital B	7,500	
Capital C	7,500	
Other assets		$225,000
Liabilities	80,000	
Cash		80,000
Loan payable A	10,000	
Loan payable C	5,000	
Cash		15,000
Capital A	50,000	
Capital B	42,500	
Capital C	37,500	
Cash		130,000

As mentioned above, assets are sold and cash is first applied to outside creditors, then to partners' loans, and then to partners' capital balances. As you can see, all balance sheet accounts are now zero, all are liquidated.

(iii) Partners' Capital Accounts Are Insufficient to Absorb Loss on Sale of Assets.

Assume that assets are sold and $65,000 is realized from their sale. The journal entries would be as follows:

	Dr.	Cr.
Cash	$65,000	
Capital A	64,000	
Capital B	48,000	
Capital C	48,000	
Other assets		$225,000
Liabilities	80,000	
Cash		80,000

Loan payable A	4,000	
Capital A		4,000
Loan payable C	3,000	
Capital C		3,000
Loan Payable A	6,000	
Loan Payable C	2,000	
Cash		8,000
Capital A	0	
Capital B	2,000	
Capital C	0	
Cash		2,000

As you can see, since the Capital accounts of A and C were not large enough to absorb the loss on the sale of assets, money from their loan payable was transferred to their capital accounts.

Therefore, instead of requiring A and C to make an additional investment into the liquidating partnership in settlement of their capital deficiencies, a transfer from their loan accounts to their capital accounts satisfied the requirement.

(iv) Loss on Sale of Assets Resulting in a Deficiency in a Partner's Capital Account.
If we assume that the sale of all of the assets resulted in a loss of $170,00 and re-alized cash of only $55,000, the journal entries would be as follows:

	Dr.	Cr.
Cash	$55,000	
Capital A	68,000	
Capital B	51,000	
Capital C	51,000	
Other Assets		$225,000
Liabilities	80,000	
Cash		80,000
Loan Payable A	8,000	
Capital A		8,000
Loan Payable C	5,000	
Capital C		5,000

Because the partnership realized such a large loss on the sale of other assets, and because the application of the loan payable to C was not sufficient to cover the debit in his capital account, both Partner B and Partner C have a debit in their capital accounts of $1,000 each. If we assume that both B and C pay in the deficiencies in their capital accounts, the final journal entry would be as follows:

	Dr.	Cr.
Cash	$2,000	
Capital B		$1,000
Capital C		1,000
Loan Payable A	2,000	
Cash		2,000

At this point, all balance sheet accounts are zero, the partnership has been liquidated.

If Partner B and Partner C do not contribute their proportionate share of the loss ($1,000 each), then A must bear their share of the loss and the journal entry would be as follows:

	Dr.	Cr.
Capital A	$2,000	
Capital B		$1,000
Capital C		1,000

(v) Gain or Loss on Sale of Net Assets Insufficient to Pay Creditors. If we assume that a sale of the other assets of the partnership realize only $45,000 in cash, thus resulting in a loss of $180,000, and that all partners are personally solvent and capable of meeting any obligations to the firm that may emerge from liquidation, the journal entries would be as follows:

	Dr.	Cr.
Cash	$45,000	
Capital A	72,000	
Capital B	54,000	
Capital C	54,000	
Other Assets		$225,000

Loan Payable A	10,000	
Loan Payable C	5,000	
Capital A		10,000
Capital C		5,000
Cash	10,000	
Capital A		2,000
Capital B		4,000
Capital C		4,000
Liabilities	80,000	
Cash		80,000

As shown in the previous example, settlement with creditors was achieved through contributions to the firm made by deficient partners in full settlement of their obligations. Assume, however, that creditors, finding that firm assets are insufficient to meet firm liabilities in full, proceed against the individual partners without regard to their equities in the firm. If they are successful in collecting the balance of money owed to them from C, for example, then C's interest in the firm would go up by the amount that he paid personally. Upon ultimate payment of deficiencies by A and B, then C would be paid the amount in his capital account.

Using the above example, if a creditor went against C for the $10,000 it was owed, C paid it, and then was reimbursed by A and B, the above last two journal entries would be corrected as follows:

	Dr.	Cr.
Cash	$10,000	
Capital C		$10,000
Liabilities	80,000	
Cash		80,000
Cash	6,000	
Capital A	2,000	
Capital B		4,000
Capital C	6,000	
Cash		6,000

If we assume that certain partners are personally insolvent, the law requires a marshaling of assets that calls for the following procedure: the partnership assets must first be applied to the settlement of the partnership's own liabilities, and each partner's separate assets must first be applied to the settlement of the partner's own liabilities. Thus, creditors of an insolvent partnership may claim only that portion of a partner's separate property that is not required for the satisfaction of his or her personal obligations; such separate property in excess of personal obligations may be claimed by firm creditors regardless of the partner's status in the firm. Creditors of an insolvent partner may claim partnership property only after firm creditors have been satisfied in full. The claim of separate creditors is limited to the positive interest that the particular partner has in the firm. To summarize, if a partner becomes insolvent, the claims against his separate property will rank in the following order:

1. Liabilities to separate creditors

2. Liabilities to partnership creditors

3. Liabilities to partners by way of contribution

Therefore, a deficiency in a partner's capital account is to be met only after other personal and partnership creditors are fully satisfied.

CHAPTER NINE

Accounting for Research and Development Joint Ventures

9.1   GENERAL

(a) Research and Development Joint Ventures in Which Funds Are Provided by Others

Many different kinds of joint venture arrangements are used to structure research and development activities, sometimes involving an entity formed specifically as a vehicle to carry out the research activities. That entity may direct and perform the research and development activities. The separate research and development entity is usually granted, as part of the arrangement, rights to future economic benefits of the results of the research and development activities, such as a royalty interest, a revenue interest, or a share of profits realized from the related products. While the arrangements often involve the formation of a separate research and development entity, they are sometimes set up merely as a contract between a sponsor entity and other existing entities.

Sponsor entities often obtain funds from other parties for use in performing the research and development. Many companies do not engage in transactions in which research and development is funded by others because of difficulty in obtaining investor interest and high cost of capital. However, there are enough of these arrangements that take place in one form or another that this is an important area of accounting for joint ventures.

If a separate research and development entity is used, the funds are obtained through equity investments or loans to that entity. In other types of arrangements, funds are obtained directly from other parties. The arrangements often provide that the funds are paid to the sponsor entity for services performed in carrying out the research and development work. Some research and development arrangements obligate the sponsor entity to assume risks that would otherwise be risks of the funding parties. In some cases, a sponsor entity takes on an obligation to assure that the parties providing the funds will recover all or a portion of the funds provided, regardless of the outcome of the research and development activities.

This can be established, for example, by a sponsor entity agreeing to an obligation to purchase ownership interests or assets of the research and development entity under specified conditions or by a sponsor entity giving a guarantee that the funding parties will recover some or all of the funds provided through guaranteed minimum royalties.

If a sponsor entity assumes risks that protect funding parties from losses that would otherwise be risks of true equity participants in a research and development project, the funding is, in substance, a financing. The accounting principles that have been established for such arrangements recognize this. The accounting principles and their applications are discussed in this chapter.

9.2 ACCOUNTING PRINCIPLES FOR RESEARCH AND DEVELOPMENT ARRANGEMENTS

(a) FASB Statement No. 68

Financial Accounting Standards Board's (FASB) Statement No. 68, *Research and Development Arrangements*, is the primary accounting pronouncement on accounting for research and development arrangements, including those done through joint ventures. FASB Statement No. 68 applies to all research and development arrangements that are completely or partially funded by others. The major thrust of FASB Statement No. 68 is to define how to identify and account for research and development arrangements that should be considered financing transactions.

The following table summarizes how to account for funds provided by others in research and development arrangements:

Terms of Arrangement	*Accounting*
The sponsor entity can be required to repay the funding parties, regardless of the results of the research and development.	Funds provided by others are accounted for as a liability.
The sponsor entity has the right but not the obligation to acquire the results of the research and development.	Funds provided by others are accounted for as reimbursed costs under a contract to perform research and development for others.

If a research and development arrangement is subject to the AICPA's *Government Contractors' Audit Guide*, accounting and financial presentation may be different than under Statement No. 68 — the applicable rules for those situations are more narrow and definitive than those of Statement No. 68. The scope of this chapter does not include those situations.

(b) Arrangements Covered by Statement No. 68

A research and development arrangement as meant by Statement No. 68 is a formal or informal agreement between two or more parties to finance or engage in research and development. The arrangement may be structured as a joint venture, a limited partnership, a limited liability company, a corporation, a contract to perform research and development services for others, or otherwise. The research and development work is generally performed under contract by one of the parties to the arrangement.

FASB Statement No. 2, *Accounting for Research and Development Costs*, defines "research" as follows:

Research is planned search or critical investigation aimed at discovery of new knowledge with the hope that such knowledge will be useful in developing a new product or service . . . or a new process or technique . . . or in bringing about a significant improvement in existing products or processes. [FASB Statement No. 2, paragraph 8.a]

Statement 2 defines "development" as follows:

Development is the translation of new knowledge gained in research or other knowledge into a plan or design for new or significantly improved products or processes, whether intended for sale or internal use. It includes the conceptual formulation, design, and testing of product alternatives, construction of prototypes, and operation of pilot plants; it does not include routine or periodic alterations to existing products and processes nor market research and market testing activities. [FASB Statement No. 2, paragraph 8.b]

9.3   DETERMINING IF A LIABILITY TO REPAY EXISTS

(a) Explicit Contractual Liability to Repay

An entity participating in a research and development arrangement in which funds are provided by others must determine whether the terms of the arrangement result in a liability to repay some or all of the funds provided by the other parties. Various circumstances can result in the conclusion that there is a liability to repay. Several examples of circumstances that indicate the existence of an obligation to repay are:

(a) The enterprise guarantees, or has a contractual commitment that assures, repayment of the funds provided by the other parties regardless of the outcome of the research and development.

(b) The other parties can require the enterprise to purchase their interests in the research and development regardless of the outcome.

(c) The other parties automatically will receive debt or equity securities of the enterprise upon termination or completion of the research and development regardless of the outcome. [FASB Statement No. 68, paragraph 6]

If any of the above circumstances are present, they will usually be based on contractual terms and will be relatively easy to evaluate in making the determination of whether an obligation to repay exists.

(b) Substantive Liability to Repay

The evaluation of whether there is a liability to repay does not end with considering only explicit contractual obligations. It is also necessary to evaluate whether circumstances other than explicit contractual terms result in a substantive liability to repay. The passage of risk must be substantive and genuine. Following are examples of conditions indicative of the existence of a substantive obligation to repay:

(a) The enterprise has indicated an intent to repay all or a portion of the funds provided, regardless of the outcome of the research and development.

(b) The enterprise would suffer a severe economic penalty if it failed to repay any of the funds provided to it regardless of the outcome of the research and development. An economic penalty is considered severe if, in the normal course of business, an enterprise would probably choose to pay the other parties rather than incur the penalty. For example, an enterprise might purchase the partnership's interest in the research and development if the enterprise had provided the partnership with proprietary basic technology necessary for the enterprise's ongoing operations without retaining a way to recover that technology or prevent it from being transferred to another party, except by purchasing the partnership's interest.

(c) A significant related party relationship between the enterprise and the parties funding the research and development exists at the time the enterprise enters into the arrangement.

(d) The enterprise has essentially completed the project before entering into the arrangement. [FASB Statement No. 68, paragraph 6]

If one of the above conditions is present, there is a presumption that there is a liability to repay some or all of the funds provided by others if the research and development is not successful and the transactions should be accounted for as if there is a contractual obligation to repay. This presumption can be overcome only by substantial evidence that clearly establishes that the other parties have retained the risk of the loss of the funds they have provided.

(c) Related Parties in Research and Development Arrangements

If a significant related party has provided funds in a research and development arrangement, it is virtually impossible to overcome the presumption that there is an obligation to repay, regardless of the contractual arrangements. The rationale for this is that because of the significant related party relationship, the stated terms of the arrangement could be changed to benefit the funding party to the detriment of the sponsor entity, or the effect of a repayment could be achieved outside the scope of the research and development arrangement. For example, the effect of a repayment could be accomplished by additional dividend payments or adjustment of future pricing of products and services sold by one related party to another.

If a significant related party relationship exists, efforts to present substantial evidence that there is no obligation to repay are generally futile. A significant party relationship combined with significant participation of the related party in the research and development arrangement essentially cannot be overcome. No formal guidelines or requirements exist to establish a "bright line" of how large the related party's interests or how large the related party's interest in the research and development arrangement must be to make the presumption of an obligation to repay impossible to overcome. However, cases seen in practice indicate that the presumption certainly cannot be overcome if a related party ownership interest (of either party in the other) or the related party's participation in the research and development arrangement are 10% or more. The 10% level is not necessarily conclusive, but it is presumptive, requiring compelling evidence to overcome.

9.4   ACCOUNTING IF THERE IS A LIABILITY TO REPAY

Generally, sponsor entities will avoid research and development arrangements with a liability to repay because they do not achieve the often-desired effect of "off-balance-sheet" financing. However, occasionally they are seen in practice and it is important to understand the accounting implications of a liability to repay. If it has been determined that there is a liability to repay, the sponsor entity should record a liability equal to the funds provided. To illustrate, assume that a sponsor entity has incurred research and development costs of $100,000 in developing a software product. Other parties have provided 90% of the funds, totaling $90,000 in exchange for a royalty interest of 10% of gross revenue from sale of the software product. The contractual terms or other conditions lead to the conclusion that there is an obligation to repay. Exhibit 9.1 illustrates the journal entries that would be made by the sponsor entity.

EXHIBIT 9.1 Journal Entries to Record Liability to Repay

	Dr.	Cr.
Research and development expense	$100,000	
Cash		$100,000
(Expenditures)		
Cash	90,000	
Liability to repay others		90,000
(Funds received from others)		

If the sponsor entity later purchases the interests of the others, or otherwise repays them, that transaction is recorded as the payment of a liability, as illustrated in Exhibit 9.2.

If the sponsor entity is not required to repay the others after having recorded a liability, the accounting for the retirement of the liability depends on whether the research and development has been successful or unsuccessful. If the project has been unsuccessful and the related products are abandoned, and it is determined that no repayment will be made, the liability is reversed as illustrated in Exhibit 9.3.

If this results in a significant credit to current expense, adequate disclosure should be made. It might be appropriate to report the credit as a separate line item in the income statement, depending on significance. If the transaction is with a related party, the SEC may require that the credit be to capital rather than to income. The SEC has required such a capital contribution approach in similar situations involving related parties.

EXHIBIT 9.2 Journal Entry to Record Repayment

	Dr.	Cr.
Liability to repay others	$90,000	
Cash (or other consideration given)		$90,000
(Repayment of others)		

EXHIBIT 9.3   Journal Entry to Record Reversal of Liability to Income

	Dr.	Cr.
Liability to repay others	$90,000	
Other income		$90,000
(Elimination of liability to repay)		

If the project has been successful, the liability is retired as the benefits of the research and development are realized by the others (such as through royalty payments). The effect of this is that the sponsor entity would report in income all of the profits derived from the products or services until the liability has been completely retired. To illustrate, assume that others are to receive royalties of $90,000 based on 10% of first-year revenue totaling $900,000. The sponsor entity would record the entry illustrated in Exhibit 9.4.

If for the second period after project completion, the same revenue level of $900,000 was achieved, the sponsor entity would record the entry illustrated in Exhibit 9.5.

As illustrated above, initial payments to others are accounted for as repayment of the liability and subsequent payments are accounted for as an expense.

EXHIBIT 9.4   Journal Entry to Record Payments of Royalties Prior
to Elimination of Recorded Liability

	Dr.	Cr.
Cash (or accounts receivable)	$900,000	
Revenue		$900,000
(Gross revenue)		
Liability to repay others	90,000	
Cash (or accounts payable)		90,000
(Royalties due to others)		

EXHIBIT 9.5   Journal Entry to Record Payments of Royalties after Elimination of Recorded Liability

	Dr.	Cr.
Cash (or accounts receivable)	$900,000	
Revenue		$900,000
(Gross revenue)		
Royalty expense	90,000	
Cash (or accounts payable)		90,000
(Royalties due to others)		

9.5   ACCOUNTING IF THERE IS NO LIABILITY TO REPAY

If it has been determined that there is no obligation to repay funds provided by others, the sponsor entity should account for the transaction as a contract to perform research and development for others. Funds to be received should be recognized as revenue when earned and costs allocable to the portion of the project related to the interests of the other parties should be recognized as expenses. To illustrate, assume the same facts as described in Section 9.4. The accounting for funds provided by others and costs incurred would be as illustrated in Exhibit 9.6.

In the preceding entry, the credit could be recorded as a reduction of expenses. If the above accounting is used for the receipt of the funds, without the recording of a liability, the accounting illustrated in Exhibit 9.7 would result in both the first and second years after completion of the product using the assumptions described in Section 9.4.

The sponsor entity recognizes royalty expenses of $90,000 in both the first and second years. In the illustration in Section 9.4, the first-year royalties are charged to the liability, resulting in higher reported income by the sponsor entity. In the end, the only significant difference between the illustrations in Sections 9.4 and 9.5 relates to timing of income recognition. If there is a liability to repay, there is, in effect, a delay in the recognition of proceeds from the funding parties in income.

If there is no liability to repay and the sponsor entity later exercises an option to purchase the interests of the other parties, the acquisition of the others'

EXHIBIT 9.6   Accounting for Funds Received without Liability to Repay

	Dr.	Cr.
Research and development expense	$10,000	
Operating expenses	90,000	
(salaries, facilities, etc.)		
Cash		$100,000
(Expenditures)		
Cash	90,000	
Services (or consulting) revenue		90,000
(Funds received from others)		

interests should be accounted for in accordance with APB Opinion No. 17, *Intangible Assets*.

Under Opinion 17, assets acquired for use in research and development would be charged to research and development expenses unless they have an alternative future use. This accounting is discussed in FASB Interpretation No. 4, *Applicability of FASB Statement No. 2 to Business Combinations Accounted for by the Purchase Method*, and Emerging Issues Task Force Issue No. 86-14, *Purchased Research and Development Projects in a Business Combination*.

EXHIBIT 9.7   Accounting for Subsequent Payments to Providers of Funds If No Liability Has Been Recorded

	Dr.	Cr.
Cash (or accounts receivable)	$900,000	
Revenue		$900,000
(Gross revenue)		
Royalty expense	90,000	
Cash (or accounts payable)		90,000
(Royalties due to others)		

9.6 LIABILITY TO REPAY A PORTION OF FUNDS PROVIDED

The terms of some research and development arrangements result in a sponsor entity having an obligation to repay only a portion of funds provided by others.

This can be caused by a contractual obligation to purchase only a portion of the others' interests or by a contractual limitation that the sponsor entity can be required to repay, which is less than the total funds provided. An obligation to repay a portion of funds provided should be accounted for (a) partly as an obligation to repay and (b) partly as a contract to perform research and development for others.

For the portion of the arrangement accounted for as an obligation to repay, a liability should be recorded based on the contractual terms of the arrangement. Generally, such "partial obligation to repay" will arise either as the initial funds are provided or on a pro rata basis as the funds are provided.

To illustrate, assume that a sponsor entity guarantees minimum return of the interests of others for an amount equal to 50% of funds provided to date by others. Total funds of $200,000 have been provided to date by others and used for expenditures on the project. The sponsor entity would account for the funds provided as illustrated in Exhibit 9.8.

As mentioned in Section 9.5, the credit to revenue could alternatively be recorded as a reduction of software development expenses.

EXHIBIT 9.8   Accounting for Partial Liability to Repay

	Dr.	Cr.
Cash (or accounts receivable)	$200,000	
Services (or consulting) revenue		$100,000
Liability to repay others		100,000
(Funds received from others)		

9.7   SPECIAL CONSIDERATIONS FOR ISSUANCE OF SECURITIES IN CONNECTION WITH A RESEARCH AND DEVELOPMENT ARRANGEMENT

(a) General

Sometimes a sponsor entity has an obligation to acquire the results of research and development or an obligation to repay funds provided by others by issuing securities, such as common stock of the sponsor entity. Alternatively, a sponsor entity may not have an obligation, but may elect to purchase the results of research and development by issuing securities pursuant to an option or otherwise. Accounting for these situations is discussed in FASB Technical Bulletin No. 84-1, *Accounting for Stock Issued to Acquire the Results of a Research and Development Arrangement.* However, the value to be assigned to the securities needs special consideration.

Also, most research and development arrangements include the issuance of stock purchase warrants to funding parties. If warrants are issued in connection with a research and development arrangement, a portion of the proceeds received from the funding parties, equal to the fair market value of the warrants, should be allocated to paid-in capital. This reduces the amount of proceeds available to recognize as revenue or as a credit to expense.

Stock issued in connection with a research and development arrangement, including stock issued pursuant to the exercise of warrants or similar instruments, should be accounted for at the fair market value of the stock issued or the consideration received, whichever is more clearly evident. Generally, the fair market value of the stock issued will be more clearly evident. However, the determination of fair market value of securities can be other than straightforward in some situations, even if a sponsor entity's stock is traded publicly. For example, stock to be issued may not be registered and freely tradable, leading to a value less than the price of publicly traded shares. Other restrictions placed on the stock should also be considered for possible effects on fair market value. In some circumstances, it may be necessary to obtain an appraisal of fair market value of securities from a qualified expert, such as an investment banker.

(b) If There Is an Obligation to Repay

If the accounting is based on an obligation to repay, the sponsor entity should record a liability when the funds are provided by others, as illustrated in Section 9.4. Thereafter, to the extent that the fair market value of the securities that would be issued exceeds the recorded liability, the liability should be increased and additional interest expense recognized.

To illustrate, assume that others provide to a sponsor entity $200,000 for research and development and the sponsor entity is obligated to acquire the results by issuing 10,000 shares of common stock to the funding parties at the conclusion of a research and development project, regardless of its outcome. The fair market value of the stock is $20 per share at the inception of the arrangement. In performing the research and development, the sponsor entity incurs costs of $175,000. At the end of the project, the market value of the stock has increased to $30 per share for a total of $300,000 (10,000 shares × $30) and the stock is issued. The sponsor entity would record the entries illustrated in Exhibit 9.9.

EXHIBIT 9.9   Accounting for Liability to Repay by Issuance of Securities

	Dr.	Cr.
Cash	$200,000	
Liability to repay others		$200,000
(Funds received from others)		
Research and development expense	175,000	
Cash (or accounts payable)		175,000
(Expenditures)		
Interest expense	100,000	
Liability to repay others		100,000
(Increase liability to market value		
of stock)		
Liability to repay others	300,000	
Common stock and additional		
paid-in capital		300,000
(Issuance of stock)		

(c) If There Is No Obligation to Repay

If the accounting is based on no obligation to repay, the sponsor entity should account for the arrangement as a contract to perform research and development for others, as illustrated in Section 9.5. If the sponsor entity has an option to acquire the results of the research and development in exchange for securities, a later acquisition of the results of the research and development should be accounted for based on the following:

- If the project consists of incomplete research and development, the fair market value of the securities issued should be recognized as research and development expenses.
- If the project consists of complete research and development, but the fair market value of the securities issued exceeds the amount that can be supported as the fair market value of the assets acquired, the supportable value of the acquired assets is recorded to assets and the excess of the value of the securities over the value of the assets is recognized as research and development expenses. It is unlikely that a company would do this because the economics do not make sense.
- If the project consists of complete research and development and the fair market value of the securities is less than the supportable value of the assets acquired, the assets are recorded at the value of the securities issued.

If both complete and incomplete research and development are acquired as a package, which frequently happens, an allocation should be made to each based on discounted cash flow expected to be received from the software products.

9.8   FINANCIAL REPORTING FOR RESEARCH AND DEVELOPMENT ARRANGEMENTS

(a) If There Is an Obligation to Repay

There are no special financial statement disclosure requirements for a research and development arrangement accounted for as an obligation to repay. However, if an arrangement is significant, it would be appropriate to describe the

EXHIBIT 9.10 Illustrative Note to Financial Statements
If There Is An Obligation to Repay

Note 5—Research and Development Arrangements

In 1994 ABC Sponsor entity ("the Company") entered into a research and development arrangement to develop Program XYZ. The arrangement was structured as a limited partnership. The partnership agreement provides that upon successful completion of the project, the Company will receive from the partnership an exclusive license to market Program XYZ and the partnership will receive royalties equal to 10% of the Company's total revenues from Program XYZ. The Company became the general partner of the partnership. The total funds contributed by all limited partners including the Company amounted to $1,000,000. The Company guaranteed minimum royalties to the other participants regardless of the outcome of the research and development activities in an amount equal to the total funds provided by the other participants. As of December 31, 1994, the Company has recorded a liability of $300,000 representing the amount of funds provided by the other participants.

arrangement and the related amounts that have been recognized in the financial statements—these disclosures are generally considered to be appropriate for any significant research and development arrangement, regardless of how it is accounted for. Exhibit 9.10 illustrates a financial statement note describing a significant research and development arrangement accounted for as an obligation to repay.

(b) If There Is an Obligation to Repay but No Repayment Is Made

If a sponsor entity accounts for an arrangement as an obligation to repay, but is not required to make a repayment of some or all of the obligation in connection with a successful project, note disclosure can be somewhat more complex. Exhibit 9.11 is an illustration of a financial statement note appropriate

EXHIBIT 9.11   Illustrative Note to Financial Statements for Partial
Payment of an Obligation to Repay

Note 5 — Research and Development Arrangements

In 1994 ABC Sponsor entity ("the Company") entered into a
research and development arrangement to develop Program XYZ.
The arrangement was structured as a limited partnership. Total capital
contributed by the partners amounted to $7,000,000. The partnership
agreement provided that the Company would perform the research
and development and that upon the successful development of Program XYZ, the Company would receive an exclusive license to market
the product in exchange for a royalty to be paid to the partnership
equal to 15% of the Company's total revenue from the product. The
Company is the general partner in the partnership. The Company
accounted for the research and development arrangement as a
financing because the partnership agreement obligated the Company
to purchase the limited partners' interests for the amount of their original investment. Accordingly, the Company recorded the receipt of
$7,000,000 from the partnership as a liability. In 1995, the Company
was required to purchase certain of the limited partner interests for
$4,000,000 and recorded the payments as reductions of the liability.
The remaining liability of $3,000,000 is being reduced as payments
are made for royalties earned by remaining limited partners other than
the Company.

---

for a sponsor entity that was required to purchase only a portion of the interests of other participants.

(c) Contracts to Perform Research and Development for Others

FASB Statement No. 68 requires the following disclosures for research and
development arrangements accounted for as contracts to perform research
and development for others. Similar arrangements may be combined in making the disclosures.

- Terms of significant arrangements as of the date of each balance sheet presented, including the terms of any royalty arrangements, purchase provisions, license agreements, and commitments to provide additional funding
- Amounts of compensation earned and costs incurred for the arrangements for each period for which an income statement is presented

9.9 ILLUSTRATION OF ACCOUNTING FOR A RESEARCH AND DEVELOPMENT JOINT VENTURE WITH A LIABILITY TO REPAY

(a) Assumptions

ABC Sponsor entity causes a research and development partnership to be formed for the purpose of developing Program XYZ. The partnership will be funded by the sale of 1,000 partnership units at $10,000 each, for a total of $10,000,000. ABC Sponsor entity will purchase 30% of the units and the remaining 70% will be sold to unrelated third parties. ABC Sponsor entity is engaged by the partnership to perform the research and development for which the partnership pays ABC Sponsor entity $10,000,000. Performing the research and development costs ABC Sponsor entity $8,000,000.

The partnership agreement provides that at the conclusion of the project, at the option of the other parties, ABC Sponsor entity can be required to purchase the partnership interests of the other parties at an amount equal to their original investment. The project is a success and the new product is licensed to ABC Sponsor entity for exclusive marketing in exchange for a royalty obligation equal to 5% of ABC Sponsor entity's gross revenue from the product. At the conclusion of the project, 50% of the partnership interests held by third parties were tendered to ABC Sponsor entity pursuant to the repayment obligation. In the first year of marketing Program XYZ, ABC Sponsor entity realized gross revenue of $12,000,000 from the product.

The following entries assume completion of all activities. As a project is in progress, various receivables and payables between ABC Sponsor entity and the partnership would be established and relieved as cash transfers and research activities take place.

EXHIBIT 9.12   Accounting by Joint Venture Partnership

	Dr.	Cr.
(1) Cash	$10,000,000	
Capital—ABC Sponsor entity		$ 3,000,000
Capital—others		7,000,000
(Capital contributions)		
(2) Research and development expense	10,000,000	
Cash		10,000,000
(Expenditures)		
(3) Capital—others	3,500,000	
Capital—ABC Sponsor entity		3,500,000
(Purchase of 350 units by ABC Sponsor entity)		
(4) Cash	600,000	
Royalty income		600,000
(5% royalty on revenue of $12,000,000)		

(b) Accounting by the Joint Venture Partnership

The partnership books would be prepared as illustrated in Exhibit 9.12.

(c) Accounting by ABC Sponsor Entity

(i) Separate Entity Books of ABC Sponsor Entity.   The separate entity books of ABC Sponsor entity would be prepared as illustrated in Exhibit 9.13.

Some sponsor entities would record the credit in entry (3) of Exhibit 9.13 to research and development expense. The approach used in this section and in the following section is to prepare the separate entity books of ABC Sponsor entity as if the research and development arrangement is accounted for on the basis of the structure of the arrangement. This results in preparation of the company's books on a statutory basis — such as how the company's records

EXHIBIT 9.13 Accounting by ABC Sponsor Entity

	Dr.	Cr.
(1) Investment in partnership	$ 3,000,000	
Cash		$ 3,000,000
(Capital contribution)		
(2) Operating expenses	8,000,000	
Cash		8,000,000
(Expenditures)		
(3) Cash	10,000,000	
Service (or consulting) revenue		10,000,000
(Payment from partnership for performing research and development services)		
(4) Research and development expense	3,000,000	
Investment in partnership (ABC Company share of partnership loss)		3,000,000
(5) Investment in partnership	3,500,000	
Cash		3,500,000
(Purchase of 350 partnership units)		
(6) Cash (or accounts receivable)	12,000,000	
Product revenue (Revenues from marketing Program XYZ)		12,000,000
(7) Royalty expense	600,000	
Cash		600,000
(Royalties due to partnership)		
(8) Investment in partnership	390,000	
Royalty income (or share of partnership income) (ABC Company share of royalties earned by partnership)		390,000

would be maintained to flow directly into the company's tax return. Using a statutory view, the company and the partnership are different entities and the accounting follows the legal and tax treatment of the arrangement. If this approach is used, adjustments to recast the structural treatment into the reporting required for generally accepted accounting principles for external reporting may be booked along with consolidation entries even if they do not relate to consolidation of entities.

EXHIBIT 9.14   ABC Sponsor Entity Consolidation Entries

	Dr.	Cr.
(a) Service (or consulting) revenue	$3,000,000	
Research and development expense		$3,000,000
(Eliminate revenue in proportion to ABC Company ownership of partnership)		
(b) Service (or consulting) revenue	7,000,000	
Liability to others		7,000,000
(To establish liability for funds provided by others)		
(c) Research and development expense	8,000,000	
Operating expenses (salaries, facilities, etc.)		8,000,000
(Reclassify expenses)		
(d) Liability to repay others	3,500,000	
Investment in partnership		3,500,000
(ABC Company share of partnership loss)		
(e) Liability to repay others	210,000	
Royalty expense		210,000
(Record share of royalties payable to others)		

EXHIBIT 9.15 ABC Sponsor Entity Consolidation

ABC SPONSOR ENTITY CONSOLIDATION
(amounts in thousands)

Account		ABC Sponsor Entity	Consolidation Entries		Consolidated
Cash	(1)	$ (3,000)			
	(2)	(8,000)			
	(3)	10,000			
	(5)	(3,500)			
	(6)	12,000			
	(7)	(600)			
		6,900			$ 6,900
Investment in partnership	(1)	3,000	(D)	$ (3,500)	
	(4)	(3,000)			
	(5)	3,500			
	(8)	390			
		3,890		(3,500)	390
Liability to others			(B)	(7,000)	
			(D)	3,500	
			(E)	210	
				(3,290)	(3,290)
Product revenue	(6)	(12,000)			(12,000)
Service revenue	(3)	(10,000)	(A)	3,000	
			(B)	7,000	
				10,000	
Operating expenses	(2)	8,000	(C)	(8,000)	
Research and development expense	(4)	3,000	(A)	(3,000)	
			(C)	8,000	
				5,000	8,000
Royalty income and expense	(7)	600	(E)	210	
	(8)	(390)			
		210			

Alternatively, and perhaps even more frequently seen, is an approach in which pro rata direct eliminations are booked in the primary books of accounts of the company to result in the accounting required for external reporting. If this approach is used, the pro rata direct eliminations would need to be "unbooked" on a worksheet basis in preparing the company's tax return to recast the data to the legal and statutory structure. This approach, which will not be illustrated, can be achieved by recording the consolidation entries illustrated in the following section, directly in the books of the company, or by recording the entries illustrated above net of the effects of the entries illustrated in the following section.

(ii) ABC Sponsor Entity Consolidation Entries.   Exhibit 9.14 illustrates entries that would be recorded in the ABC Sponsor entity consolidation.

(iii) ABC Sponsor Entity Consolidated Statements — Overall Effect.   Combining the ABC Sponsor entity separate entity books in Section 9.9(c)(i) and the consolidation entries in Section 9.9(c)(ii) results in the overall effects of the research and development arrangement in the ABC Sponsor entity consolidated financial statements that are illustrated in Exhibit 9.15. As discussed in the preceding section, these overall effects can be recorded in the primary books of the company rather than in two pieces — one for the legal and statutory treatment, and another in consolidation to recast the data to amounts for external financial reporting.

CHAPTER TEN

Public Accounting Firms' Role in Joint Ventures

Ray H. Johnson
Price Waterhouse LLP

10.1 GENERAL

Today's complex business challenges require expert and creative responses within tight time frames. More than ever, companies of all sizes rely on their independent accounting firms for services and support in numerous business areas. Public accountants provide assistance to joint ventures and their sponsors in all of the three stages of development of joint ventures — Analysis and Planning, Formation and Implementation, and Operations and Management. Services in the areas of accounting, auditing, and tax by independent accountants are well understood and expected by the management and boards of directors of companies. However, the full range of multidisciplinary service offerings in areas such as joint ventures, change integration, reengineering, information technology, and many others are not as fully understood and expected.

This chapter will provide insights into service requirements of joint ventures and their sponsors designed to enhance achievement of success. In addition, while it is not practicable to provide a complete guide for auditing the financial statements of joint ventures and the related investments by sponsors, the chapter will provide guidance in areas that are unique to joint ventures or are expected to be encountered on a frequent basis. Because an earlier chapter provides detailed information on the tax aspects of joint ventures, only passing reference will be made to taxes in the discussion of structuring alliances and joint ventures. Finally, any discussion of services by independent accountants will touch on accounting principles and financial reporting even though these are discussed in detail in Chapters 5 through 9 of this book.

10.2   SERVICES IN THE ANALYSIS AND PLANNING STAGE

During the analysis and planning stage, joint ventures may be one of several forms of organization being considered. It is during this phase that the client will determine strategic imperatives for considering a collaborative venture, risk factors, return on investment requirements, the ideal partner profile, synergy opportunities, organizational options, and integration opportunities. In each of the foregoing activities, the independent accountants can participate and in some they may take the lead.

Both by training and experience, the independent accountant is equipped to identify risks inherent in a proposed venture. By applying analytic techniques, he or she is able to identify present and prospective trends in the specific industry, emerging technological developments and techniques, and competitive forces. Through benchmarking or best practice comparisons, he or she is able to advise the client of the relative strengths and weaknesses in the operations or activities proposed to be included in a venture. Such analyses can also result in estimates of capital requirements to position the activities to compete effectively in the chosen marketplace.

Based on the analyses, the independent accountant can assist the client in formulating strategies for the designated operations. Such strategies may include considerations such as mergers or acquisitions, sales, or spin-offs, as well as joint ventures. Assuming that the optimal path to achieve the strategic objectives for the operations is through a joint venture with a partner that complements the strengths of the client, the independent accountants can assist in the formulation of criteria for a joint venture partner. Using the criteria developed with the client, a search of available databases can surface potential venture partners. Frequently, the accountants are in a position to approach one or more of the potential partners on a confidential no-names basis.

In many instances, it is possible to obtain enough operating and industry data about a prospective joint venture partner to prepare preliminary valuations and to identify synergies which may result from the proposed venture. Such analyses can narrow the choice of prospective partners, eliminate those who create unwanted consequences, and enable the client to make the initial approach from a knowledgeable position. By the same token, such analyses also can identify differences in strategy, culture, or operations which would make a joint venture with the analyzed partner inadvisable.

The analysis and planning stage provides the opportunity to compare the strategy of potential partners with strategic directions identified for the intended venture. Such analyses are usually undertaken by members of the strategic consulting staff and are designed to identify strategic fit, potential conflicts, and accommodations or redirections of plans which may be required. This process also should identify major areas for rationalization of combined operations, potential synergies, and cost savings and return on investment alternatives. An important by-product of the analysis process should be the development of risk factors and organizational options. As an expert in quantifying planned activities, the public accountant is in a unique position to provide the foregoing range of services.

10.3 SERVICES IN THE FORMATION AND IMPLEMENTATION STAGE

Partner contact and exploration are frequently undertaken by a third party to obtain an indication of interest before disclosure of the principal. This is often undertaken by the public accountants because of their standing in the business community and their reputation for integrity and confidentiality. Prospective joint venture partners also are more willing to share business objectives and financial results and expectations with the independent accountants. During exploratory meetings, it may be possible to evaluate selection criteria such as knowledge of local markets, standing with governmental authorities, compatibility of cultures, strategies and operations, and other opportunities for complementary collaboration.

Joint venture valuation is an essential process in negotiating the final structure of the alliance. The valuation services groups of large CPA firms have the capability to determine the current value of business segments which will become part of the joint venture. The group analyzes the precise nature of the assets and the reasons for the valuations. In performing these services, the group applies the latest valuation methodologies to ensure thoroughness and creativity and coordinates valuations with other aspects of the joint venture structure. Valuation services also support tax experts in establishing a basis of tangible and intangible assets in taxable transactions.

Public accountants frequently support joint venture members in the structuring of the venture and negotiating with the other venturers. The structuring considerations are heavily tax- and finance-oriented. Specific areas in which the independent accountants may make a contribution include the following:

- Form of organization (partnership, corporation, limited liability company) and jurisdiction (county, state, etc.)
- Tax considerations including taxable or nontaxable transactions
- Financing alternatives (debt, equity, specific assets, letters of credit, etc.)
- Venture governance provisions, dispute resolutions, and exit strategies
- Management contracts, supply contracts, take or pay arrangements, and information systems support
- Development and implementation of executive compensation arrangements for key joint venture management
- Asset deployment and site selection

Even though the venture may be in the preoperating stage, a detailed operation plan should be developed by the joint venture team and future management. The independent accountants can be involved in this process by evaluating the adequacy of the information processing and financial reporting systems proposed to support the planned venture. They also can be of significant value in developing transformation strategies. Transformation strategies focus on fundamental processes for integrating the separate functions of the joint venture partners in areas such as product rationalization, marketing integration, and combination or consolidation of manufacturing facilities and operations. Due consideration is given to advanced management techniques, such as "fast time to market" and "high-performance team work" to ensure that the combined operations will meet or exceed the joint venture operating plan. The independent accountants are active members of action planning work sessions held to identify integration tasks which will be undertaken immediately following formation of the venture. Change integration consultants are usually of prime importance in identifying operations and processes which are expected to yield the greatest savings and improvement.

10.4 SERVICES TO JOINT VENTURE MANAGEMENT DURING OPERATIONS STAGES

The formation of a joint venture from the operations of two previously unrelated companies provides the opportunity to examine all major business processes and activities. Through the application of process design principles and appropriate technologies, it is possible to shorten cycle times, lower costs, and improve quality and productivity.

Change integration methodology developed by large accounting and consulting firms is designed to plan for and manage large-scale corporate transformations such as the formation of a major joint venture. Large change integration projects can be grouped under three consulting disciplines:

- Strategic change. Products and services, customers and markets
- Organizational change. Structure, people, and reward systems
- Business process transformation. Processes, training, and information technology

Successful change integration projects make use of the best industry practices and advanced information technology. The performance reporting systems must be integrated with the enhanced processes and provide the measurements to drive the performance incentive systems.

10.5 PROVIDING AUDIT SERVICES TO JOINT VENTURE ENTITIES

(a) General

An accounting firm that is engaged to provide audits and other services to a joint venture entity will face a variety of situations that create unusual client relationships and business considerations. Audit engagements involving joint ventures can also present an auditor with a number of unusual technical auditing, accounting, and reporting issues. The following sections discuss a number of matters to be considered in these areas.

(b) Client Relationships

If an accounting firm serves as auditor for both a joint venture and for one of the participants, it is important for the accounting firm to establish a satisfactory relationship and line of communication with the nonclient participants. It is also important that satisfactory relationships be established with all the participants if an accounting firm audits a joint venture but does not serve as auditor for any of the participants. Furthermore, without sound working relationships and lines of communication between the accounting firm and all the participants, nonclient participants may be more inclined to interpret actions or professional advice of the accounting firm as being partial to the client participant, and even as possible detriments to nonclient participants.

The appointment of a participant's accounting firm to serve as auditor for a joint venture is sometimes a formally or informally negotiated concession on the part of other participants. The other participants might have preferred that their own accounting firms be appointed, or that the joint venture be audited by an accounting firm having no previous relationship with any of the participants.

Representatives of the accounting firm, at the partner and manager staff levels, should establish satisfactory relationships and lines of communication with management personnel in each of the participant organizations. The accounting firm's representatives should discuss the following areas with the representatives of the participant organizations as appropriate:

- The accounting firm's independence in regard to the joint venture engagement and to each of the participants
- Significant or unusual accounting, auditing, or other matters regarding the financial statements of the joint venture
- Confirmation of the details of related party arrangements and terms of transactions between the participant and the joint venture
- Relevant tax matters, including transactions between the participants and the joint venture, distributions from the joint venture, implications

of possible future participant ownership changes, or the possible future sale or liquidation of the joint venture

(c) Business Considerations

Assistance during the formation and negotiation of a joint venture can lead to an engagement to serve as auditor for the joint venture. Joint ventures rarely have the necessary in-house personnel and capabilities to support all the new financial and tax functions. Accordingly, many times a joint venture's independent accounting firm is engaged to provide ongoing services in such areas as systems development, tax planning, and tax return preparation.

Although the acquisition of a new audit client is usually considered to be favorable in that it represents growth in a firm's practice, the fees that are realized from providing professional services to joint ventures may sometimes be less than normal in relation to the number of service hours that can be required to complete an audit and to perform additional professional services. There are a variety of causes for this. The formation of many joint ventures includes the transfer by a participant to the joint venture of an existing operating division or subsidiary. Since the division or subsidiary may have represented a relatively small percentage of the participant's overall operations and financial statements, the participant may not have been committed to staffing and systems needs in the accounting area of the division or subsidiary, and easily auditable records may not have been maintained. Furthermore, because of the materiality consideration, the contributed division or subsidiary may never have been audited. The initial audit of a joint venture can be the audit of a business which has been operating for years with an underdeveloped and understaffed accounting function, compounded by the usual accounting complexities caused by the formation of a joint venture.

The participants in a joint venture are likely to focus more on the relatively small size of a joint venture entity in determining the amounts of the audit and other professional service fees that they expect to pay. This can lead to engagements that are unprofitable in terms of the usual economic measures, such as the percentage of standard rates realized and the average rate per hour. However, if in conjunction with an initial audit the accounting firm assists a joint venture in establishing sound accounting records and procedures and adequate internal controls, the relative profitability can be greatly improved.

10.6 AUDITING INVESTMENTS IN JOINT VENTURES

(a) General

AU Section 332, entitled "Long Term Investments," provides guidelines for auditing long-term investments (which would normally include investments in joint ventures). The guidance provided in this section generally deals with audit practices for three major areas:

- The amounts at which long-term investments are carried in an investor's financial statements
- The amounts reported by an investor as his or her share of the earnings, losses, or other transactions of investees
- Required financial statement disclosure

AU Section 332 indicates that in the process of ascertaining that long-term investments have been accounted for in conformity with generally accepted accounting principles that have been applied consistently, and in ensuring that financial statement disclosures are adequate, the auditor should examine sufficient competent evidential matter to support the conclusions reached. Appropriate audit procedures for this purpose include the following.

(b) Audited Financial Statements

Financial statements of the investee generally constitute sufficient evidential matter as to the equity in underlying net assets and results of operations of the investee when such statements have been audited by the investor's auditor or by another independent auditor whose report is satisfactory, for this purpose, to the investor's auditor. Audited financial statements also constitute one of the items of evidential matter that may be used with respect to investments in bonds and similar debt obligations, loans, and advances.

(c) Unaudited Financial Statements

Unaudited financial statements, reports issued on examination by regulatory bodies and taxing authorities, and similar data provide information and evidence but are not by themselves sufficient as evidential matter.

(d) Applying Audit Procedures to Financial Statements of an Investee

By application of auditing procedures to the financial statements of an investee, the auditor obtains evidential matter as to the equity in underlying net assets and results of operations of the investee. The auditor for the investor may utilize the investee's auditor for this purpose. The materiality of the investment in relation to the financial statements of the investor is a factor which should be considered in determining the extent and nature of such procedures.

(e) Market Quotations

If market quotations of security prices are based on a reasonably broad and active market, they ordinarily constitute sufficient competent evidential matter as to the current market value of unrestricted securities.

(f) Other Evidential Matter

When the carrying amount of an investment reflects (i) factors (such as mineral rights, growing timber, patents, and goodwill) which are not recognized in financial statements of the investee, or (ii) fair values of assets which are materially different from the investee's carrying amounts, evidential matter may be available in the form of current evaluations of these factors. Evaluations made by persons within the investor or within the investee may be acceptable; evaluations made by persons independent of these companies will usually provide greater assurance of reliability than evaluations made by persons within the companies.

Negotiable securities, real estate, chattels, or other property are often assigned as collateral for investments in bonds, notes, loans, or advances. If the collateral is an important factor in considering collectibility of the obligation, the auditor should satisfy himself regarding the existence and transferability of such collateral and should obtain evidential matter as to its value (such as market quotations, the amount of underlying net assets or appraisals) as may be appropriate in the circumstances.

(g) Verifying That an Appropriate Accounting Method Is Used

The auditor must ascertain that an investor in a joint venture has used an appropriate method of accounting for its investment. Since most joint ventures will be accounted for by the equity method, this usually can be accomplished by ascertaining that the percentage interest held by the investor is within the normal prescribed range (between 20% and 50%), and that there are no other circumstances precluding the use of the equity method because of limitations on the ability of the investor to exercise influence over the financial and operating policies of the investee.

Similarly, an auditor must ascertain the appropriateness of the use of an accounting method other than the equity method of accounting for its investment. Other appropriate methods may include the cost method, consolidation, proportionate consolidation, or the expanded equity method. Industry practice, the ownership percentages, SEC rules and regulations, and other facts and circumstances should be considered in concluding the appropriateness of the accounting method used.

If an investor accounts for an investment in a joint venture using a method which is contrary to the presumed applicable method (e.g., consolidation for over 50% ownership, the equity method for between 20% and 50%, and the cost method for less than 20%), sufficient competent evidential matter should be obtained and examined by the auditor to support a conclusion that the applicable presumption has been overcome.

AU Section 332.09 notes that the refusal of an investee to furnish financial data to an investor is evidence, although not necessarily conclusive, that an investor does not have the ability to exercise significant control over an investee. This may justify, or be a factor in justifying, not using the equity method. However, if these circumstances are present, one would have to question whether the investee should, in fact, be considered a joint venture.

(h) Different Financial Statement Dates

AU Sections 332.10 through 332.12 discuss what an auditor should consider if the date of an investor's financial statements does not coincide with the date of an investee's financial statements. The following situations typically exist:

- An investor and joint venture have different fiscal year ends, so audited financial statements for both entities as of the same date are not available.
- A joint venture's financial statements are not available on a timely basis, resulting in the need to adopt a time lag in the periods for which the proportionate share of the financial results of the joint venture are included in the financial statements of the investor.

Situations sometimes exist where the fiscal year ends of an investor and joint venture differ (for example, an investor's year-end may be December 31, and a joint venture's year-end may be September 30), and interim financial statements of the joint venture that coincide with the fiscal year-end of the investor are not available on a timely basis. Where an investor includes a joint venture's financial data through a "stub" period (in this example, the joint venture's financial statements for the three months ending December 31) in its financial statements on the equity method, the auditor must realize that the periods included for the joint venture (the last three quarters of the joint venture's latest complete year, and the first quarter of its current year), will constitute unaudited periods, even though the joint venture financial statements for the year ended as of September 30 were audited. In such circumstances, the auditor must apply such auditing procedures as may in his judgment be necessary to the unaudited periods, giving consideration to the significance of the financial statements of the joint venture to those of the investor.

Sometimes an investor in a joint venture, for practical reasons, will report its share of joint venture financial results on a delayed basis. Such time lags in reporting may be necessary if a joint venture's financial statements are not available on a timely basis. Another reason for adopting a time lag would be to enable an investor to base its reported share of joint venture financial results on audited joint venture financial statements. If a time lag in reporting is adopted, the time lag should be consistent from period to period and should not exceed three months.

(i) Subsequent Events Reviews

An investor's auditor has a responsibility to review events that occur after the date of an investee joint venture's financial statements up to the date of the audit report on the financial statements of the investor. The subsequent events review should include reading any available interim financial information regarding the investee and also making appropriate inquiries of the management of the investor. In doing so, the auditor should be alert for any significant events, transactions, or developments that may have taken place with regard to the joint venture. Any subsequent events that are significant to the financial statements of the investor should be recognized in the investor's financial statements if they are indicative of conditions that existed at the date of the investor's financial statements. If a subsequent event involving a joint venture that is significant to the financial statements of the investor is not indicative of conditions that existed at the date of the investor's financial statements, the event should be disclosed and labeled as unaudited information in the notes to the investor's financial statements.

AU Section 332.14 notes that events may occur after the date of an investee's financial statements and before the date of an investor's financial statements that cause a decrease in the value of the investment that should be recognized in the investor's financial statements.

(j) Elimination of Intercompany Profits and Losses

An auditor of the financial statements of an investor in a joint venture should verify the proper elimination of unrealized intercompany profits and losses related to transactions between the investor and the joint venture at the end of the period used for including results in the investor's financial statements. If such are potentially significant, the applicable accounts and transactions should be subjected to appropriate audit procedures. An investor's auditor may need to obtain documentation and information from the joint venture and its auditor to complete the procedures in this area.

(k) Reporting Where Sufficient Evidential Matter Is Not Available

If an investment in a joint venture is significant to the financial statements of an investor, and an auditor is not able to obtain sufficient competent evidential matter in regard to the investment in the joint venture, the auditor must determine whether this constitutes a limitation on the scope of the examination. AU Section 508.24 presents the examples of the auditor being unable to obtain the audited financial statements of a joint venture.

If circumstances occur that result in an auditor concluding that there has been a scope limitation, AU Section 542.25 indicates that the auditor should describe the scope limitation in an explanatory paragraph of the audit report and the explanation should be referred to in both the scope and opinion paragraphs.

(l) Considerations Where Other Auditors Are Involved

The financial statements of a joint venture are often audited by an auditor other than the auditor of the investor. AU Section 543.14 indicates that where an auditor uses another auditor's report for the purpose of reporting on an investor's equity in an investee's underlying net assets, and its share of the investee's earnings, losses, and other transactions, the auditor is a principal auditor using the work and reports of other auditors. This can apply whether an investment in a joint venture is accounted for using the equity method or another method.

AU Section 543 provides professional guidance and standards for using the work and reports of another auditor. These standards are discussed below.

(m) Determining Principal Auditor Status

The initial area for consideration by an auditor of the financial statements of an investor in a joint venture is the determination of whether the extent of the audit will enable reporting as a principal auditor. Factors to be considered in making this judgment include the following:

- The portion of the financial statements audited by other auditors
- The extent of the review of the other auditor's work

Normally, the auditor of an investor in a joint venture would not have much difficulty in qualifying for principal auditor status if only the financial statements of one or more joint ventures have been audited by other auditors. However, in some cases an investor's most significant asset is an investment in a joint venture, and based on the amounts involved, only the auditors of the joint venture can properly assume principal auditor status.

(n) Deciding Whether to Refer to the Work and Report of Another Auditor

If a principal auditor decides to assume responsibility for the work of another auditor, there should be no reference to the work or report of the other auditor in the principal auditor's report. A principal auditor should decide that it is appropriate not to refer to the work or report of another auditor only if the principal auditor is satisfied as to the independence and professional standing of the other auditor.

A decision not to refer to the work or report of another auditor is appropriate where one of the following conditions exist:

- The other auditor is an associated or correspondent accounting firm
- The other auditor was retained by the principal auditor, and the work of the other auditor was performed under the principal auditor's control and guidance
- Whether or not another auditor was selected by the principal auditor, adequate steps were taken by the principal auditor to enable her to make a conclusion as to the reasonableness of the accounts audited by the other auditor for purposes of inclusion in the financial statements being audited and reported on by the principal auditor
- The portion of the financial statements examined by the other auditor is not significant to the financial statements covered by the principal auditor's opinion

Principal auditors may determine that it is appropriate to refer in the audit report to the other auditor's work and report. This happens when:

- It is impracticable for the principal auditor to review the other auditor's work or to perform other procedures that would be necessary to satisfy her as to the sufficiency of the other auditor's examination.

- The portion of the financial statements reported on by another auditor is significant to the financial statements of the enterprise as a whole that are being reported on by the principal auditor.

The following is an example of a principal auditor's report that refers to the report of another auditor that examined the financial statements of a joint venture.

Independent Auditor's Report

We have audited the consolidated balance sheet of X Company and subsidiaries as of December 31, 19XX, and the related consolidated statements of income and retained earnings and cash flows for the year then ended. These financial statements are the responsibility of the Company's management. Our responsibility is to express an opinion on these financial statements based on our audits. We did not audit the financial statements of JV Corporation, a 50% owned joint venture accounted for using the equity method which statements reflect investments and net income constituting 20% and 22%, respectively, of consolidated assets and net income, respectively. Those statements were audited by other auditors whose report has been furnished to us, and our opinion, insofar as it relates to the amounts included for JV Company, is based solely on the report of the other auditors.

We conducted our audit in accordance with generally accepted auditing standards. Those standards require that we plan and perform the audit to obtain reasonable assurance about whether the financial statements are free of material misstatement. An audit includes examining, on a test basis, evidence supporting the amounts and disclosures in the financial statements. An audit also includes assessing the accounting principles used and significant estimates made by management, as well as evaluating the overall financial statement presentation. We believe that our audit and the report of the other auditors provide a reasonable basis for our opinion.

In our opinion, based on our audit and the report of the other auditors, the consolidated financial statements referred to above present fairly, in all material respects, the consolidated financial position of X Company and subsidiaries as of December 31, 19XX, and the consolidated results of their operations and cash flows for the year then ended in conformity with generally accepted accounting principles.

When two or more auditors in addition to the principal auditor participate in the audit, the percentages covered by the other auditors may be stated in the aggregate.

(o) Procedures Applicable Whether or Not Reference Is Made

The principal auditor should carry out the following procedures:

- Verify the professional reputation and independence of the other auditor
- Assure the coordination of audit activities
- Enable the review and audit of matters that affect the consolidated financial statements

(p) Additional Procedures Where Reference Is Not Made

AU Section 543.12 recommends that a principal auditor who has decided not to make reference to the work or report of another auditor consider performing a number of more in-depth procedures. These procedures include:

- Meeting with the other auditor to discuss the audit procedures and tests performed by the other auditor, the results of the procedures and tests, and the audit findings and conclusions of the other auditor
- Reviewing the audit programs of the other auditor and issuance of any necessary instructions to the other auditor as to the scope of audit procedures
- Reviewing the other auditor's workpapers, including the review of the client's accounting systems and the evaluation of internal control
- Participating in discussions regarding the accounts and significant accounting and auditing issues and matters with management of the entity being examined by the other auditor, and performance by the principal auditor of supplemental testing of the accounts and records if considered necessary

(q) Other Auditor's Report Departs from Standard Report

If the report of the other auditor is other than a standard report, the principal auditor should decide whether the reason for the departure from the standard report is of such a nature and significance in relation to the financial statements on which the principal auditor is reporting that it would require recognition in his report. The report of a principal auditor need not refer to the reason for departure if the reason is not material in this respect. However, AU Section 543.15 indicates that if the report of another auditor is to be presented with the financial statements of the enterprise as a whole in addition to the report of a principal auditor, a principal auditor may consider it appropriate to refer to such departure and its disposition.

(r) Communications between a Principal Auditor and Another Auditor

Certain matters should be communicated in writing between a principal auditor and another auditor. A principal auditor should initiate communication with another auditor if, in the past, there were matters known by the principal auditor that could be important to the examination of the other auditor that may not be known by the other auditor. Where another auditor considers it appropriate to make an inquiry of a principal auditor, the inquiry should usually be in writing, and should include a request for a written reply on a date near the anticipated date of the other auditor's report.

10.7   AUDITING AND REPORTING ON THE FINANCIAL STATEMENTS OF A JOINT VENTURE

(a) General

A variety of special auditing considerations is often encountered by an auditor who has been engaged to audit and report on the financial statements of a joint venture. Generally, most of these special audit matters fall into the following categories:

- Related party relationships and related party transactions
- Financial statement disclosures appropriate in the joint venture's financial statements
- Information and special representations from the joint venture participants
- Joint ventures dependent upon continued support of its participants

(b) Related Party Relationships and Transactions

Audit procedures that should be performed in the very important area of related party transactions are discussed later in this chapter. This section will discuss several related party matters of particular importance to joint venture financial statements. Of primary importance, the auditor must understand the nature and details of any related party relationships and related party transactions between the joint venture entity and the joint venture's participants or with other entities that are controlled by, or affiliated with, the joint venture participants.

In many joint venture situations, one or more of the joint venture participants provide various types of services to a joint venture, with the joint venture paying the participant for the services in agreed-upon amounts. While such arrangements often provide that the reimbursement includes the participant's direct costs plus an overhead factor, the situation may be that the joint venture could not obtain services of the same quality, supported by the sometimes considerable technical and administrative capabilities of the participant organizations, from third parties at prices comparable to the amounts of the reimbursements. Under the accounting requirements for related party transactions, such transactions negotiated between a joint venture and its participants at apparently other than arm's-length rates, present only a disclosure matter. There are no accounting rules that require adjustments for accounting purposes to the terms of related party transactions.

The following is a suggested example of note language for inclusion in a joint venture's financial statements.

Note 7. Related Party Transactions

Joint Venture Company purchases services that are provided by Participant A and Participant B in various manufacturing, technical, and administrative areas, on a cost reimbursement (based on a direct costs plus an overhead factor) basis. The statements of income for the years ended December 31, 19X8 and 19X7, include expenses of $268,000 and $212,000, respectively, for such services purchased.

(c) Other Disclosure Items

Several commonly made disclosures unique to joint venture financial statements are identification of the entity as a joint venture, discussion of the purpose for which the joint venture was formed, and naming of the joint venture participants with disclosure of each participant's ownership interest. What follows is an example of language that can be used to make these disclosures.

Note 1. Formation of the Company and Business

JVC, Inc. is a joint venture corporation formed by Participant A, Inc., and Participant B, Inc. for the purposes of developing, manufacturing, and marketing Product A. Each stockholder received 50% of the Company's outstanding stock in exchange for capital contributions consisting of $5 million cash by Participant A, and all the outstanding stock of its wholly owned subsidiary, Company SUB, Inc., by Participant B.

(d) Information and Special Representations Needed from Joint Venture Participants

Sometimes joint venture management will be unable to provide information needed to fully understand and evaluate matters that could affect the joint venture financial statements, making it necessary for the auditor to communicate with the participant organizations. Further, there may be matters or arrangements regarding questions of interpretation that are significant to the joint venture's financial statements. In such circumstances, the auditor should consider obtaining written confirmation or representation from the joint venture participants to support the conclusions reached with respect to the correctness of accounting treatments and adequacy of disclosure. Examples of matters that might require written representation from a joint venture's participants would be the agreed-upon fair market values assigned to assets contributed to a joint venture, tax attributes of contributed assets or subsidiaries, and the nature and extent of intercompany transactions, receivables, and payables.

It is advisable for the joint venture auditor to request the participants to review and approve a draft of the joint venture financial statements, including notes. The issues that joint venture participants raise upon reviewing a draft of the financial statements of a joint venture can be significant.

(e) Procedural and Systems Considerations

The joint venture accounting systems and records may present a wide variety of situations impacting an audit. The most conventional situations, and the easiest to deal with from an audit perspective, is where a joint venture has an adequate accounting system which is under the control of joint venture management. This situation can result in a normal audit process.

A more complex audit environment is encountered if a joint venture functions as a remote job entry site with the accounting system operated by the data processing department of one of the participant organizations. The appropriate audit procedures in this circumstance will depend on whether input/output controls provide adequate controls in which case the participant's data processing organization usually can be viewed as an outside service bureau, or whether the control systems exist only at the participant's data processing systems.

As a result, the auditors may conclude that the accounting internal control systems cannot be relied on to limit audit testing of account balances, resulting in a need to establish an audit scope which includes examination of all significant accounts.

These circumstances can lead to substantial audit hours and costs.

(f) Going Concern Questions

In some cases, an auditor will find that a joint venture is so financially dependent on the continued support of its participants that without the support it would be unable to continue in existence. This situation presents the auditor with some unique auditing and reporting considerations.

AU Section 341 contains a number of auditing and reporting standards that apply where questions arise about an entity's ability to continue in existence. Generally accepted auditing standards require an auditor to evaluate whether there is substantial doubt of an entity's ability to continue as a going concern for a reasonable period of time. In performing audit tests such as analytical procedures, review of subsequent events, review of debt agreements, reading of board of directors minutes and inquiry of legal counsel, the auditor may identify conditions and events raising doubts as to the going concern assumption.

Examples of conditions and events which may cast doubt on a joint venture's ability to continue as a going concern are negative trends in operations, working capital or revenues, defaults on loans or leases, arrearages in dividends, work stoppages or labor disputes, and external matters such as legal proceedings and loss of key licenses, customers, or suppliers. An auditor may, however, consider other factors that mitigate concerns regarding solvency, such as plans to dispose of assets, new borrowing arrangements, plans to reduce costs or delay expenditures, and plans to raise new equity capital.

When, after considering management's plans, the auditor concludes there is substantial doubt about the joint venture's ability to continue as a going concern for a reasonable period of time, the auditor should consider the possible effects on the financial statements including the adequacy of the related disclosure. Information that might be disclosed includes: (1) conditions and events giving rise to the assessment of substantial doubt, (2) the possible effects of such conditions and events, (3) management's plans including possible discontinuance of operations, and (4) information about the recoverability of recorded assets and classification of liabilities.

If after fully considering conditions and events and management's plans, the auditor concludes that substantial doubt remains, the audit report should include an explanatory paragraph to reflect the conclusion. The auditor's doubt should be expressed through the phrase "substantial doubt about the joint venture's ability to continue as a going concern."

10.8   AUDITING WHERE RELATED PARTIES ARE PRESENT

(a) General

Joint ventures frequently engage in transactions with the participants and other related parties which give rise to accounting and auditing considerations. The accounting rules for related party arrangements and transactions establish disclosure requirements, rather than defining special accounting principles for transactions between related parties. The primary professional auditing standards related to auditing in relating party situations are contained in AU Section 334, entitled "Related Parties." In view of the fact that joint ventures involve related party relationships and transactions, the joint venture audit should include appropriate audit procedures in the related party area.

Important factors to be considered in planning the nature and extent of the procedures include the business purpose served by each component of the entity, management responsibilities, and internal controls over management activities. The auditor should consider that related party relationships and transactions sometimes can be intentionally concealed by the manner in which a business is structured and operated.

The auditor's procedures regarding related parties are designed to achieve the following objectives:

- Determine the existence of related parties
- Identify transactions with related parties
- Examine and evaluate identified related party transactions

(b) Determining the Existence of Related Parties

While an auditor should be able to obtain the identity of related parties from management of the entity being audited, the auditor should carry out appropriate procedures to verify that the representations have been complete and accurate. In planning the nature and extent of the procedures, the auditor should be alert for the following types of transactions, cited in AU Section 334.03, that may indicate the existence of related parties:

- Borrowing or lending at an interest-free basis or at a rate of interest significantly above or below market rates prevailing at the time of the transaction
- Selling real estate at a price that differs significantly from its appraised value
- Exchanging property for similar property in a nonmonetary transaction
- Making loans with no scheduled terms for when or how the funds will be repaid

In addition to identifying obviously related party relationships, audit procedures designed to detect less apparent related party relationships are listed in AU Section 334.07:

- Evaluate the company's procedures for identifying and properly accounting for related party transactions
- Request from appropriate management personnel the names of all related parties and inquire whether there were any transactions with these parties during the period
- Review filings by the entity with the Securities and Exchange Commission and other regulatory agencies for the names of related parties and for other business in which officers and directors occupy directorships or management positions
- Determine the names of all pensions and other trusts established for the benefit of employees and the names of their officers and trustees. According to Financial Accounting Standards Board's (FASB) Statement No. 57, paragraph 24F "trusts for the benefit of employees, such as pension and profit-sharing trusts that are managed by or under trusteeship of management, are related parties."
- Review stockholder listings of closely held companies to identify principal stockholders
- Review prior years' working papers for the names of known related parties
- Inquire of predecessor, principal, or other auditors of related entities concerning their knowledge of existing relationships and the extent of management involvement in material transactions
- Review material investment transactions during the period under examination to determine whether the nature and extent of investments during the period create related parties

(c) Identifying Transactions with Related Parties

AU Section 334.06 lists the following circumstances that have been known to motivate companies to engage in transactions with related parties:

- Lack of sufficient capital or credit to continue the business
- An urgent desire for a continued favorable earnings record in the hope of supporting the price of the company's stock
- An overly optimistic earnings forecast
- Dependence on a single or relatively few products, customers, or transactions for the continuing success of the venture
- A declining industry characterized by a large number of business failures
- Excess capacity
- Significant obsolescence dangers because the company is in a high-technology industry

AU Section 334.08 lists the following procedures that are designed primarily for the purpose of identifying related party transactions.

- Provide audit personnel performing segments of the examination or examining and reporting separately on the accounts of related components of the reporting entity with the names of known related parties so that they may become aware of transactions with such parties during their examinations.
- Review the minutes of meetings of the board of directors and executive or operating committees for information about material transactions authorized or discussed at their meetings.
- Review proxy and other material filed with the SEC and comparable data filed with other regulatory agencies for information about material transactions with related parties.
- Review conflict-of-interest statements obtained by the company from its management. Conflict-of-interest statements are intended to provide the board of directors with information about the existence or nonexistence of relationships between the reporting persons and parties with whom the company transacts business.
- Review the extent and nature of business transacted with major customers, suppliers, borrowers, and lenders for indications of previously undisclosed relationships.

- Consider whether transactions are occurring, but are not being given accounting recognition, such as receiving or providing accounting, management, or other services at no charge or a major stockholder absorbing corporate expenses.
- Review accounting records for large, unusual, or nonrecurring transactions or balances, paying particular attention to transactions recognized at or near the end of the reporting period.
- Review confirmations of compensating balance arrangements for indications that balances are or were maintained for or by related parties.
- Review invoices from law firms that have performed regular or special services for the company for indications of the existence of related parties or related party transactions.
- Review confirmations of loans receivable and payable for indications of guarantees. When guarantees are indicated, determine their nature and the relationship, if any, of the guarantors to the reporting entity.

(d) Examining and Evaluating Identified Related Party Transactions

The purpose, nature, and extent of identified related party transactions and their effects on the financial statements should be evaluated. The auditor should obtain sufficient competent evidential matter to support the conclusions reached. AU Section 334.09 lists the following procedures that should be considered for performance as part of evaluating the implications of related party transactions:

- Obtain an understanding of the business purpose of the transactions
- Examine invoices, executed copies of agreements, contracts, and other pertinent documents, such as receiving reports and shipping documents
- Determine whether the transaction has been approved by the board of directors or other appropriate officials
- Test the compilation of amounts to be disclosed, or considered for disclosure, in the financial statements for reasonableness
- Arrange for the audits of intercompany account balances to be performed as of concurrent dates, even if the fiscal years differ, and for the examination of specified, important, and representative related party

transactions by the auditors for each of the parties, with appropriate exchange of relevant information
- Inspect, or confirm and obtain, satisfaction concerning the transferability and value of collateral

Furthermore, AU Section 334.10 lists a number of additional procedures that may be necessary to fully understand and verify certain related party transactions. Since AU Section 334.10 states that these additional procedures are not necessarily required to comply with generally accepted auditing standards, the auditor must exercise professional judgment in deciding whether or not to perform the following procedures:

- Confirm transaction amounts and terms, including guarantees and other significant data, with the other party or parties to the transaction.
- Inspect evidence in possession of the other party or parties to the transaction.
- Confirm or discuss significant information with intermediaries, such as banks, guarantors, agents, or attorneys, to obtain a better understanding of the transaction.
- Refer to financial publications, trade journals, credit agencies, and other information sources when there is reason to believe that unfamiliar customers, supplies, or other business enterprises with whom material amounts of business have been transacted may lack substance.
- With respect to material uncollected balances, guarantees, and other obligations, obtain information about the financial capability of the other party or parties to the transaction. Such information may be obtained from audited financial statements, unaudited financial statements, income tax returns, and reports issued by regulatory agencies. The auditor should decide on the degree of assurance required and the extent to which available information provides such assurance.

(e) Related Party Disclosures and Audit Report Implications

As set forth in Financial Accounting Standards Board's Statement No. 57, financial statements should include disclosures of material related party transactions. Disclosure of transactions that are eliminated in the preparation of consolidated or combined financial statements is not required. The required disclosures include:

- The nature of the relationship(s) involved.
- A description of the transactions, including transactions to which no amounts or only nominal amounts were ascribed, for each of the periods for which income statements are presented and such other information deemed necessary to an understanding of the effects of the transactions on the financial statements.
- The dollar amounts of transactions for each of the periods for which income statements are presented and the effects of any change in the method of establishing the terms from that used in the preceding period.
- Amounts due from or to related parties as of the date of each balance sheet presented and, if not otherwise apparent, the terms and manner of settlement.
- The nature of control relationships that could result in operating results or financial position significantly different from those that would have been obtained if the enterprises were autonomous, regardless of whether there are transactions between the related parties.

As discussed in Statement No. 57, disclosure in some cases may be accomplished by aggregating similar transactions by type of related party. Where a parent company supplies most of a subsidiary's products, or distributes or purchases substantially all of the products of a subsidiary, or where two wholly owned subsidiaries of a common parent engage in recurring transactions with each other, disclosing only the relationship itself together with a general statement regarding, or specific disclosure of, the extent of such transactions may be adequate.

If an affiliate relationship does not exist, disclosure of common ownership or management is not required unless there is a clear ability to influence the transactions between the controlled entities or such transactions are significant. The fact that a company is an affiliate of another company should be disclosed even if there are no transactions between the two entities.

If financial statements contain adequate disclosure and the auditor is satisfied through appropriate auditing procedures as to the accuracy of such disclosure, there is normally no need to modify the audit report because of related party transactions. However, the auditor may wish to emphasize the transactions in an explanatory paragraph because of their nature, materiality, or pervasive impact on the financial statements. One good test, where it can be made, of whether an explanatory paragraph should be included in the auditor's report is whether the reported financial position and results of operations are materially different from what would have been reported in the absence of the related party relationship.

An example of an explanatory paragraph emphasizing related party transactions is as follows:

Company X is a member of a group of affiliated companies and, as disclosed in the financial statements, has extensive transactions and relationships with members of the group. Because of these relationships, it is possible that the terms of these transactions are not the same as those that would result from transactions among wholly unrelated parties.

(f) Client Representation Regarding Related Parties

An important step in identifying whether related party transactions have occurred is to review with management the company's policies, formal or informal, on corporate ethics and conflict of interests. If no formal policies exist, confirmation may be desirable from officers and directors as to whether they, or entities in which they or members of their family have a financial interest, have entered into any transactions with the company or whether possible conflicts of interests exist because of their outside activities.

The client representation letter should include a representation as to related party transactions. In obtaining this representation, the auditor should be satisfied that client officials are aware of what is meant by related party transactions. Explanatory information may need to be incorporated in the letter or by appendix. Management representations alone are not sufficient competent evidential matter for reliance and should be corroborated by other documented auditing procedures to the extent necessary and practicable.

CHAPTER ELEVEN

Securities and Exchange Commission and Other Regulatory Requirements

Robert J. Puls
Price Waterhouse LLP

11.6 Summarized Financial Information Requirements
  (a) General
  (b) Minimum Disclosures
  (c) Periods Required
  (d) Need if Separate Financial Statements Included
  (e) Omission for Immaterial Entities

11.7 Separate Financial Statement Requirements
  (a) General
  (b) Periods to Be Presented
  (c) Differing Year-Ends
  (d) Foreign Joint Ventures

11.8 Related Parties
  (a) What Constitutes Related Parties
  (b) Related Party Disclosures

11.9 SEC Views on Joint Venture Specific Accounting Issues
  (a) General
  (b) Gain Recognition on Formation
  (c) Restatement
  (d) Proportionate Consolidation

11.10 Antitrust Regulations

11.1   GENERAL

The term "joint venture" has been, and continues to be, used very loosely to describe a multitude of business arrangements ranging from informal agreements between two parties to work together to majority owned and controlled corporate subsidiaries. For purposes of the remainder of this chapter, a joint venture is merely defined as an entity which is not controlled by a public company (i.e., a registrant) and therefore not consolidated. The registrant, as a joint venture partner, typically has significant influence over the venture and its activities. As such, the registrant's investment therein (whether in the form of a corporation or a partnership) is usually accounted for under the equity method as opposed to the cost method.

If for some reason a venture is consolidated, separate financial statements of the venture would not be required and disclosures in a registrant's financial statements would be limited to a discussion of the venture's business and, depending on its nature and significance, segment information as required by Statement of Financial Accounting Standards (SFAS) No. 14, *Financial Reporting for Segments of a Business Enterprise* (effective for fiscal years beginning after December 15, 1997, SFAS No. 14 has been superseded by SFAS No. 131, *Disclosures About Segments of an Enterprise and Related Information*).

11.2   OVERVIEW OF THE REGULATORY ENVIRONMENT

Different regulatory bodies have jurisdiction over the activities of joint ventures depending on various factors including, but not limited to, the following:

- The nature and business of the venture
- Its ownership
- The industry and country in which it operates
- The way in which it is financed

The structuring of a joint venture and the determination of what laws and regulations apply must be carefully evaluated by each party considering such an investment and should involve close consultation with appropriate legal counsel.

The primary objective of this chapter is to provide the reader with a general awareness of some of the major regulatory requirements which may impact financial reporting by public companies involved in significant joint ventures. It is not, however, intended to provide a comprehensive presentation of the various regulations.

11.3   PUBLIC JOINT VENTURES

(a) General

Certain joint ventures themselves may be "public" in that the entity has either issued debt or equity securities (including common stock, preferred stock, or partnership units) in U.S. public markets. In these situations, the joint venture, just like any other public entity, is a registrant subject to all of the filing rules and regulations of the Securities Act of 1933 (the 1933 Act) and the Securities Exchange Act of 1934 (the 1934 Act). Which Act is to be followed is dependent on the nature of the filing.

(b) The 1933 Act

The 1933 Act governs initial public and secondary offerings of securities (e.g., filings on Forms S-1, S-3, SB-1, F-1, etc.). The primary objectives of the 1933 Act are:

- To provide investors with material financial and other information concerning securities publicly offered for sale
- To prohibit misrepresentation, deceit, or other fraudulent practices in the sale of securities

(c) The 1934 Act

The 1934 Act governs trading of securities in secondary markets and ongoing periodic disclosures and reporting (e.g., filings on Forms 10-K, 10-Q, 8-K, 10-KSB, etc.) after an initial public offering or other distribution of securities under the 1933 Act. The 1934 Act generally deals with the following five areas:

- Regulation of national securities exchanges and of trading on the exchanges
- Regulation of trading in the over-the-counter market
- Adequacy of periodic disclosures and the prevention of abuses in proxy solicitation and insider trading
- Control of credit in the securities market
- Prohibition of market manipulation, primarily on securities exchanges

In addition, the 1934 Act created the Securities and Exchange Commission (SEC) and granted it the rule-making and enforcement powers necessary to carry out the provisions of the statute.

Under either Act, the requirements of SEC Regulation S-X (SX) must be followed with respect to financial statement presentation and disclosure and SEC Regulation S-K (SK) must be followed with respect to other nonfinancial statement disclosures such as business information, selected financial data, management's discussion and analysis, executive compensation, etc.

11.4   IMPACT OF SEC REQUIREMENTS ON A REGISTRANT'S JOINT VENTURE(S)

The rules and regulations promulgated by the SEC contain many provisions that affect the financial reporting of a public registrant and its joint venture investments. These rules and regulations are more explicit and are generally more extensive than the requirements included in generally accepted accounting principles (GAAP). The major thrust of the SEC rules is to provide a reader of a registrant's financial reports with complete disclosure of the more significant information regarding its investments in joint ventures, as well as activities which take place between a registrant and its joint ventures (related party transactions).

11.5   SIGNIFICANT SUBSIDIARY TESTS

(a) General

In public filings, the SEC requires either the disclosure of summarized financial information or the inclusion of complete separate financial statements of equity investees if certain tests are met. These tests effectively preclude the exercise of judgment by quantifying specific thresholds at which such information must be disclosed and are regarded by the SEC as an interpretation of paragraph 20(d) of Accounting Principles Board (APB) Opinion No. 18, *The Equity Method of Accounting for Investments in Common Stock*, which states that summarized financial information or separate statements may be required for equity investees.

The tests established by the SEC—commonly referred to as the "significant subsidiary" tests—are set forth in SX Rule 1-02(w). A joint venture is considered to be significant to a registrant if any of three measured amounts relating to assets and income exceed 10% of the related amounts for the registrant on a consolidated basis. If considered significant, summarized financial information of the joint venture is required to be disclosed in the notes to the financial statements of the registrant. Further, if based on the same tests, any of the measured amounts exceed 20% of the related amounts of the registrant on a consolidated basis, complete separate financial statements of the joint venture, prepared in accordance with SX, are required.

(i) An SEC Exception.   In Financial Reporting Release (FRR) No. 44, the SEC excluded the asset test discussed below from the determination of whether complete financial statements are needed for an equity investee, such as a joint venture; however, for determining whether full financial statements are required for unconsolidated majority-owned subsidiaries, the asset test is still applicable. Further, the asset test continues to be required for equity in-

vestees when assessing significance relating to footnote disclosure of summarized information.

(b) Regulation S-X Rule 1-02(w)

A joint venture is considered "significant" if it meets any of the following criteria specified by this Rule. Note that these tests are performed as of the end of each year presented in a registrant's financial statements.

- *Investment Test.* The registrant's and its other subsidiaries' investments in and advances to the joint venture exceed 10% of the registrant's consolidated total assets.
- *Asset Test.* The registrant's and its other subsidiaries' proportionate share of the total assests (after any necessary intercompany eliminations) of the joint venture exceeds 10% of the registrant's consolidated total assets.
- *Income Test.* The registrant's and its other subsidiaries' equity in income of the joint venture from continuing operations before income taxes, extraordinary items, and cumulative effect of accounting changes, exceeds 10% of such income of the registrant on a consolidated basis.

(c) Computational Interpretations

The following interpretations of the significant subsidiary test should be considered in situations involving joint ventures.

(i) Contingent Consideration.   The acquisition of a joint venture interest may provide for either the issuance of additional shares of a security or the transfer of other consideration *contingent* on specified events or transactions occurring in the future. Any such contingent consideration needs to be included as part of a registrant's total investment in the joint venture, unless its payment is considered to be remote.

(ii) Intercompany Eliminations.   The Asset Test of SX Rule 1-02(w) includes the phrase "after intercompany eliminations." The following are interpretations which attempt to clarify that phrase:

- Receivables of the joint venture from members of a registrant's consolidated group should be eliminated from its total assets.

- Receivables from the joint venture should *not* be eliminated from a registrant's consolidated assets.
- No adjustments should be made to a registrant's consolidated assets included in the denominator of the fraction since all appropriate intercompany eliminations should have already been made in the consolidation procedure.

Although the phrase "after intercompany eliminations" is not specifically used in the Income Test of SX Rule 1-02(w), adjustments to income before income taxes for intercompany profits should be made to a joint venture being tested which would be similar to those made in recording such earnings in consolidation.

(iii) Five-Year Averaging.   If the consolidated income of a registrant for the latest fiscal year is a least 10% lower than its average consolidated income for the most recent five fiscal years, that average should be used in the income test for the most recent fiscal year; loss years, however, should be excluded from this average calculation. In addition, it should be noted that the five-year averaging method is not permitted if the registrant reported a loss in its most recent year; in that case, significance should be evaluated relative to the absolute value of the most recent year's loss.

(iv) Preferred Stock Cash Dividends.   Cash dividends on preferred stock may be deducted in computing a registrant's proportionate equity in the pre-tax earnings of a joint venture. However, experience has shown that a waiver from the SEC staff will typically be required for any registrant wishing to take advantage of this interpretation.

(d) Application to Investees of Investees

As previously mentioned, SX Rule 3-09 requires the presentation of separate financial statements of joint ventures by a registrant if any of the significant subsidiary tests are met at a 20% or higher level. In practice, the question has come up as to whether the requirements for separate financial statements are also applicable to an investee accounted for by the equity method by a joint venture of a registrant.

This issue was addressed by the SEC in Staff Accounting Bulletin (SAB) No. 44 (Topic 6K) wherein the staff stated that SX Rule 3-09 applies to *all* investees that are material to the financial position or results of operations of a registrant, *regardless* of whether the investment is held by the registrant, a subsidiary, or another investee, such as a joint venture. Accordingly, separate financial statements should be provided for any lower-tier investee where such an entity is significant to a registrant's consolidated financial statements.

An example of the application of the income test of the significant subsidiary rules to such an investee situation is set forth in the following section (Exhibit 11.5).

(e) Examples of Application of the Tests

Exhibits 11.1 through 11.5 illustrate the application of the above tests and interpretations to a 50% owned joint venture investment.

11.6 SUMMARIZED FINANCIAL INFORMATION REQUIREMENTS

(a) General

As stated above, summarized financial information of a joint venture is required by SX Rule 4-08(g) to be presented in the notes to the financial statements of a registrant either, on an individual or combined basis (i.e., combined with all other equity investees), if any one of the significant subsidiary tests outlined above is met at the 10% level.

(b) Minimum Disclosures

The minimum financial information necessary to be included in the notes to a registrant's financial statement footnotes if one of the significant subsidiary tests is met at the 10% level follows [SX Rules 4-08(g) and 1-02(bb)]:

EXHIBIT 11.1 Both Registrant and Joint Venture Have Income, with Registrant's Income Being Comparable to Prior Years (i.e., Prior Years within 10% of Current Year)

	Registrant Consolidated	Joint Venture
Assumptions:		
Total assets	$750,000,000	$150,000,000
Investment in joint venture	50,000,000	N/A
Advances to joint venture	15,000,000	N/A
Intra-entity receivable (payable)	(5,000,000)	5,000,000
Income, as defined	60,000,000	15,000,000
Investment Test:		
Registrant's investment in joint venture		$ 50,000,000
Registrant's advances to joint venture		15,000,000
		65,000,000
Divided by registrant's total assets		750,000,000
Test result		8.7%
Asset Test:		
Joint venture's total assets		$150,000,000
Less intra-entity receivable		5,000,000
		145,000,000
Registrant's ownership		50%
		72,500,000
Divided by registrant's total assets		750,000,000
Test result		9.7%
Income Test:		
Joint venture's income, as defined		$ 15,000,000
Registrant's ownership		50%
		7,500,000
Divided by registrant's income, as defined		60,000,000
Test result		12.5%

Conclusion:
Since the result of the income test exceeds 10%, the joint venture is considered a significant subsidiary and summarized financial data is required to be disclosed in the financial statements of the registrant.

EXHIBIT 11.2 Registrant Has Income but Joint Venture Has a Loss, with Registrant's Income Being Comparable to Prior Years (i.e., Prior Years within 10% of Current Year)

	Registrant Consolidated	Joint Venture
Assumptions:		
Total assets	$750,000,000	$150,000,000
Investment in joint venture	50,000,000	N/A
Advances to joint venture	15,000,000	N/A
Intra-entity receivable (payable)	(5,000,000)	5,000,000
Income (loss), as defined	60,000,000	(20,000,000)
Investment Test:		
Test result identical to that shown for Exhibit 11.1 or 8.7%.		
Asset Test:		
Test result identical to that shown for Exhibit 11.1 or 9.7%.		
Income Test:		
Joint venture's loss, as defined		$ (20,000,000)
Registrant's ownership		50%
		(10,000,000)
Divided by Adjusted Registrant's Income:		
Registrant's income, as defined	$ 60,000,000	
Add registrant's share of joint venture's loss, as defined	10,000,000	70,000,000
Test result		14.3%

Conclusion:
Since the result of the income test exceeds 10%, the joint venture is considered a significant subsidiary and summarized financial data is required to be disclosed in the financial statements of the registrant.

EXHIBIT 11.3 Registrant Has a Loss but Joint Venture Has Income

	Registrant Consolidated	Joint Venture
Assumptions:		
Total assets	$750,000,000	$150,000,000
Investment in joint venture	50,000,000	N/A
Advances to joint venture	15,000,000	N/A
Intra-entity receivable (payable)	(5,000,000)	5,000,000
Income (loss), as defined	(50,000,000)	15,000,000
Investment Test:		
Test result identical to that shown for Exhibit 11.1 or 8.7%.		
Asset Test:		
Test result identical to that shown for Exhibit 11.1 or 9.7%.		
Income Test:		
Joint venture's income, as defined		$ 15,000,000
Registrant's ownership		50%
		7,500,000
Divided by Adjusted Registrant's Loss:		
Registrant's loss, as defined	$ (50,000,000)	
Add registrant's share of joint venture's income, as defined	7,500,000	(57,500,000)
Test result		13%

Conclusion:
Since the result of the income test exceeds 10%, the joint venture is considered a significant subsidiary and summarized financial data is required to be disclosed in the financial statements of the registrant.

- *Balance Sheet Information.* Current assets, noncurrent assets, current liabilities, noncurrent liabilities, and, where applicable, redeemable preferred stock and minority interests
- *Income Statement Information.* Net sales or gross revenues, gross profit (or cost and expenses applicable to net sales or gross revenues), income or loss from continuing operations (before extraordinary items and cumulative effect of accounting changes), and net income or loss

EXHIBIT 11.4   Both Registrant and Joint Venture Have Income, with Registrant's Income *Not* Being Comparable to Prior Years (i.e., Prior Years *Not* Within 10% of Current Year)

	Registrant Consolidated	Joint Venture
Assumptions:		
Total assets	$750,000,000	$150,000,000
Investment in joint venture	50,000,000	N/A
Advances to joint venture	15,000,000	N/A
Intra-entity receivable (payable)	(5,000,000)	5,000,000
Income (loss), as defined:		
Most recent year	60,000,000	15,000,000
Second most recent year	90,000,000	N/A
Third most recent year	(50,000,000)	N/A
Fourth most recent year	80,000,000	N/A
Fifth most recent year	75,000,000	N/A

Investment Test:

Test result identical to that shown
   for Exhibit 11.1 or 8.7%.

Asset Test:

Test result identical to that shown
   for Example 11.1 or 9.7%.

Income Test:

Because the registrant's most recent year's income may have fluctuated greater than 10% over the past five years, this test becomes a two-step process. Step 1 is to determine if the most recent year's income is at least 10% less than (or 90% of) the average income of the registrant over the past five years. If it is, then in Step 2, the registrant's most recent year's income is replaced with that average for purposes of comparing it to the joint venture. If not, then the result will be identical to that shown in Exhibit 11.1.

EXHIBIT 11.4   (*Continued*)

Step 1:

Total registrant income, as defined, for past 5 years, excluding any loss years	$305,000,000
Divided by number of years included	4
Average income per year	76,250,000
Factor for comparison	90%
Alternate income	$ 68,625,000

Since the alternate income exceeds the most recent year's income of $60,000,000, the average income needs to be utilized in Step 2.

Step 2:

Joint venture's income, as defined	$ 15,000,000
Registrant's ownership	50%
	7,500,000
Divided by registrant's average income	76,250,000
Test result	9.8%

Conclusion:
Since none of the test results equal or exceed 10%, the joint venture is *not* considered a significant subsidiary and summarized financial data is *not* required to be disclosed in the financial statements of the registrant.

(c) Periods Required

Insofar as is practicable, summarized financial information should be presented as of the same dates and for the same periods as the audited consolidated financial statements of the registrant.

However, this information is required only for those periods or portion of a period for which a joint venture is reported on the equity method of accounting. In other words, for any period or portion of a period that a joint ven-

EXHIBIT 11.5 A Registrant's Joint Venture Has an Investment
in Another Entity

	Registrant Consolidated	Joint Venture	Investee
Assumptions:			
Income, as defined	$4,000,000	$3,000,000	$4,500,000
Joint venture ownership of investee		40%	
Income Test:			
For the joint venture:			
Joint venture's income, as defined			$3,000,000
Registrant's ownership			50%
			1,500,000
Divided by registrant's income, as defined			4,000,000
Test result			37.5%
For the investee:			
Investee's income, as defined			$4,500,000
Joint venture's ownership			40%
			1,800,000
Registrant's ownership of joint venture			50%
			900,000
Divided by registrant's income, as defined			4,000,000
Test result			22.5%

Conclusions:
For joint venture:
Separate financial statements are required for the joint venture because the registrant's share of its income is 37.5%, which exceeds 20% of consolidated income.

For investee:
In addition, separate financial statements of the investee are required because the registrant's share of the investee's income is 22.5%, which also exceeds 20% of its consolidated income.

ture is perhaps consolidated, carried at cost, or not owned at all, no summarized financial information is required to be included.

(d) Need if Separate Financial Statements Included

The purpose of summarized financial information is to provide minimum standards of disclosure when the impact of joint ventures on the consolidated financial statements of a registrant is significant. If the registrant furnishes more information in its annual report than is required by these minimum disclosure standards, such as condensed financial information or separate audited financial statements, the summarized data can be excluded. The SEC's rules are not intended to conflict with the provisions of APB No. 18, specifically paragraphs 20(c) and (d), which provide that *either* separate financial statements of equity investees be presented *or* that summarized information be included.

(e) Omission for Immaterial Entities

The 10% measurement level of the significant subsidiary test was not intended by the SEC to establish a materiality criteria for omission, and the arbitrary exclusion of summarized information for selected entities up to a 10% level is not appropriate. However, the SEC staff recognizes that exclusion of summarized information for certain equity investees is appropriate in some circumstances where it is impracticable to accumulate such information and the summarized information to be excluded is de minimis.

11.7 SEPARATE FINANCIAL STATEMENT REQUIREMENTS

(a) General

As noted above, full financial statements are required for those joint ventures which individually meet any of the SX Rule 1-02(w) tests when 20% is substituted for the 10% threshold set forth therein (SX Rule 3.09). These financial statements must be in the same form that would be required if the joint venture itself was a registrant. This would include, in addition to the basic financial statements, a complete set of notes adhering to the requirements of SX and appropriate supporting schedules meeting the rules of Article 12.

If financial statements are needed for two or more joint ventures, they can be combined or consolidated if financial position, results of operations, and cash flows will be clearly exhibited. However, financial statements of unconsolidated subsidiaries and 50% or less-owned entities such as joint ventures cannot be combined with each other.

(b) Periods to Be Presented

SX Rule 3-09(b) provides that the separate financial statements of a joint venture be, if practicable, as of the same date and for the same periods as the financial statements of the registrant. However, these separate financial statements need be audited only for those years in which the appropriate 20% significant subsidiary test is met. Although certain years need not be audited, presumably audit tests would be required for the beginning of a year for which an audit is required, which follows a year for which no audit is required. If the joint venture was significant in an earlier year but is not significant in the latest year, the SEC staff will consider a waiver of the requirement to provide separate financial statements, if the registrant can demonstrate that the joint venture is likely to remain insignificant in future years.

Further, just as with summarized financial information, separate full financial statements are required only for those periods or portion of a period for which a joint venture is reported on the equity method of accounting as of the registrant's year-end. In other words, for any period or portion of a period that a joint venture is perhaps consolidated, carried at cost or not owned at all, no separate full financial statements are required.

(c) Differing Year-Ends

While it is preferable that a joint venture have the same year end as a registrant, many times that is impractical. Therefore, for purposes of filing a registrant's annual report on Form 10-K, SX Rule 3-09(b) provides some relief. Specifically, if the fiscal year of any joint venture ends within 90 days before the date of the filing, or if the fiscal year ends after the date of the filing, the required financial statements of the joint venture may be filed as an amendment to the report within 90 days, or within six months if the joint venture is a foreign business, after the end of such venture's fiscal year.

To illustrate, suppose that a registrant with a December 31 year-end has equity investments in three different joint ventures that are not foreign businesses, with fiscal year ends of February 28 (JV A), May 31 (JV B), and July 31 (JV C), the pertinent filing dates in satisfaction of the registrant's 19X7 Form 10-K requirements would be as follows:

- The registrant's December 31, 19X7 Form 10-K, including the July 31, 19X7 financial statements of JV C, would be due by March 31, 19X8
- The February 28, 19X8 financial statements of JV A would be due by May 29, 19X8
- The May 31, 19X8 financial statements of JV B would be due by August 29, 19X8

(d) Foreign Joint Ventures

The SEC, through FRR No. 44, has provided some accommodations to domestic registrants that are required to include financial statements of foreign joint ventures in their filings that meet the definition of a foreign business, that is:

- A business that is majority-owned by persons who are not citizens or residents of the United States and which is not organized under the laws of the United States or any state thereof and either:
  - More than 50% of its assets are located outside the United States.
  - The majority of its executive officers and directors are not U.S. citizens or residents.

The accommodations are that financial statements of such foreign joint ventures need only comply with Item 17 of Form 20-F, which allows the financial statements to be prepared on a comprehensive basis other than U.S. generally accepted accounting principles (GAAP) (e.g., international accounting standards). Quantitative reconciliations of net income and material balance sheet items to U.S. GAAP are required; however, the additional information specified by U.S. GAAP for disclosure in notes to financial statements is not necessary. Further, no reconciliations are required at all if the foreign business does not exceed the 30% level under the tests of significance which call for the inclusion of its financial statements.

If the foreign joint venture does not meet the definition of a foreign business, the registrant can file financial statements prepared in accordance with a basis of accounting other than U.S. GAAP, provided a reconciliation to U.S. GAAP, under Item 18 of Form 20-F is included regardless of the level of materiality.

If for some reason a domestic registrant furnishes separate financial statements of a foreign joint venture that are not reconciled to U.S. GAAP, the domestic registrant should furnish summarized financial data of the foreign joint venture pursuant to SX Rule 4-08(g), prepared in accordance with U.S. GAAP in its primary financial statements.

11.8   RELATED PARTIES

(a) What Constitutes Related Parties

The term "related parties," as used by the SEC in SX Rule 1-02(u), is the same as that defined in paragraph 24(f) of SFAS No. 57, *Related Party Disclosures* which is: affiliates of the enterprise and entities for which investments are accounted for by the equity method by the enterprise.

Obviously, a joint venture investment of a registrant would qualify as a related party as it is normally accounted for by the equity method.

(b) Related Party Disclosures

Requirements relating to public reporting of related party activities, such as transactions between a registrant and its joint venture investments, which are material, either individually or in the aggregate, and which affect a registrant's financial statements are provided by both SFAS No. 57 and SX Rule 4-08(k). These disclosure requirements include:

- The nature of the related party relationship(s).
- A description of the transactions, including those to which no amounts or only nominal amounts were ascribed, for each of the periods for

which income statements are presented and such other information deemed necessary to an understanding of their effects on a registrant's financial statements.

- The dollar amounts of transactions for each of the periods for which income statements and statements of cash flows are presented (to be shown on the face of these statements) and the effects of any change in the method of establishing the terms from that used in the preceding period.
- Amounts due from or to related parties as of the date of each balance sheet presented (to be shown on the face of the balance sheet) and, if not otherwise apparent, the terms and manner of settlement.
- The nature of control relationships that could result in operating results or financial position significantly different from those that would have been obtained if the enterprises were autonomous, regardless of whether there are transactions between the related parties.

11.9   SEC VIEWS ON JOINT VENTURE SPECIFIC ACCOUNTING ISSUES

(a) General

Although the SEC staff has never formalized its views relating to the accounting for many joint venture arrangements, the following sections attempt to provide insight into their views on some of the more significant joint venture accounting issues. These unofficial views have been obtained through consultations, discussions, and comment letters received from the staff relating to various registrants' public filings. As with any complex and significant issue, a careful evaluation of the individual facts and circumstances is critical in determining the proper accounting treatment. In addition, due to the fact that the following are unofficial views, advance clearance with the SEC staff of any questionable issues is advised.

(b) Gain Recognition on Formation

Many times, appreciated noncash assets are contributed to a newly formed joint venture in exchange for an equity interest when others have invested cash or other hard assets. In these cases, it has been argued that the investor contributing the appreciated noncash assets has effectively realized a part of that appreciation and that immediate gain recognition would be appropriate. Practice, as well as existing literature, is varied in this area.

The SEC staff has emphasized that any gain recognition in cases like this is heavily dependent on a careful analysis of the specific facts and circumstances involved. In determining whether any gain recognition is appropriate, it is helpful to view the formation of a joint venture in one of three ways:

- As the continuation or expansion of an existing business
- As a change in interest transaction, similar to that addressed by SAB No. 51 (Topic 5H)
- As the partial exiting or sale of a business (evidenced by the receipt of, or right to, cash in exchange for the assets contributed)

Determining which of the above most closely fits the formation of a particular joint venture is not always clear. Generally, the SEC staff would not accept gain recognition on formation of a joint venture under the first view since it represents the continuation of an earnings process, not the completion of one. Similarly, the staff is likely to resist gain recognition under the second view due to the difficulty in distinguishing such situations from the first. With respect to the last view or argument, the SEC staff will generally not object to gain recognition if all of the following conditions are met:

- *Measurability.* The fair value of the assets contributed to the venture must be clearly measurable. Generally, a significant amount of monetary consideration needs to be contributed on the part of one investor to clearly establish the fair value of nonmonetary assets.
- *Realizability.* The gain to be recognized must be realized. To be considered realized, the "seller" (i.e., the party contributing the noncash assets) must have received cash or other monetary assets which are readily convertible to cash without concern of collectibility. There cannot exist a requirement (legal, economic, or otherwise) for the seller to return the cash/monetary assets back to the venture, "buyer," or any related lender. Some examples of situations in which the gain would not be considered realized include:
  - A requirement to repay debt used to provide the cash consideration

- Debt or contract performance guarantees on behalf of the business contributed
- Partnership loss-sharing arrangements that require future cash contributions
- *Permanency and Irrevocability.* The risks and rewards of ownership for the portion sold must have been irrevocably transferred to the other investors with substantial certainty (i.e., permanency). There cannot exist any requirement (legal, economic, or otherwise) to reacquire the assets contributed to the joint venture.
- *Transaction Idiosyncrasies.* There cannot be any other unusual factors which would indicate that gain recognition is not appropriate. This necessitates a careful evaluation and consideration of the individual facts and circumstances surrounding establishment of the joint venture. An example of an arrangement which is problematic to gain recognition is an operating contract between the investor who contributed the noncash assets and the joint venture, such as a take-or-pay agreement.

(c) Restatement

There may be situations when a registrant's interest in a joint venture is reduced from one of control (and therefore resulted in consolidation of the venture) to a minority position that still enables it to exercise significant influence (and thereby apply the equity method of accounting). The question arises in these situations, whether this represents a change in reporting entity that should be reported by restating the registrant's prior-year financial statements (from consolidation to the equity method), or whether this represents a change in circumstances for which the equity method should be adopted prospectively (i.e., without restatement). While restatements in similar situations have occurred and been accepted in practice, the arguments used are less persuasive when taken in the context of contributions of assets to a joint venture and generally the SEC staff will object to any such reporting. Further, restatement of a registrant's financial statements would definitely not be appropriate when operating assets or divisions are contributed to a joint venture because those businesses had never been consolidated in the past as a separate entity by the registrant.

(d) Proportionate Consolidation

Proportionate or pro rata consolidation of joint ventures is a method whereby each investor combines its pro rata share of each of the assets, liabilities, revenues, and expenses of a joint venture with the similar items in its financial statements on a line-by-line basis. This method, which is advocated for jointly controlled entities by International Accounting Standard (IAS) No. 31, is not acceptable under U.S. GAAP, except under certain limited circumstances and in certain specialized industries where the practice historically has been accepted (such as oil and gas or mining). In those cases, proportionate consolidation is generally only appropriate where an investor owns an undivided interest in each asset and is proportionately liable for its share of each liability (i.e., no legal entity exists between the investor and the assets and liabilities of the joint venture).

11.10 ANTITRUST REGULATIONS

Antitrust issues typically associated with joint ventures include barriers to market entry, collusion, and loss of competition. Various regulations and agencies in the United States provide guidelines which attempt to deal with the antitrust implications of these types of issues. Some of the more significant follow:

- *The Sherman Act.* Directed toward existing monopoly power; prohibits all contracts, business combination, or conspiracies in restrain of trade in the United States or with foreign countries
- *The Clayton Act.* Prohibits mergers and acquisitions that would likely cause a substantial reduction in competition, or which tend to create a monopoly
- *The Federal Trade Commission Act.* Created the Federal Trade Commission (FTC) which issues various regulations relating to antitrust
- *The Robinson-Patman Act.* Enacted to prevent discriminatory pricing practices
- *The Hart-Scott-Rodino Antitrust Improvements Act.* Requires parties who plan to form a *corporate* joint venture meeting certain thresholds to notify both the FTC and the U.S. Department of Justice (DOJ) prior to its incorporation; generally, the thresholds are $10 million of annual sales or $100 million in total assets (this act is, however, not applicable to the formation of joint venture partnerships)

In addition, antitrust guidelines are also published from time to time by the DOJ as well as by virtually all 50 states within the United States and various foreign countries have adopted antitrust laws regulating the formation and operation of business organizations such as joint ventures affecting markets within their borders.

Due to the varied and complex nature of these acts and regulations, companies forming joint ventures would be advised to consult with appropriate legal counsel before entering into any joint ventures.

CHAPTER TWELVE

Joint Venture Accounting in Specialized Industries

Richard P. Graff
Coopers & Lybrand L.L.P.

12.1 Introduction
- (a) Scope of Chapter
- (b) Overview

12.2 General Accounting Principles in Specialized Industries
- (a) Accounting for Investments in Joint Ventures by the Venturers
  - (i) Introduction
  - (ii) Equity Method
  - (iii) Proportionate Consolidation
  - (iv) Cost Method
- (b) Differences between the Carrying Amount of an Investment and the Underlying Equity in the Joint Venture
- (c) Accounting by Joint Venture Entities
- (d) Venturer's Share of Losses in Excess of the Carrying Amount of Investment
- (e) Distributions Received in Excess of Investment
- (f) Intercompany Profits
  - (i) General
  - (ii) Venturer Sales to a Joint Venture
  - (iii) Joint Venture Sales to a Venturer
- (g) Cost-Sharing Arrangements

12.1 INTRODUCTION

(a) Scope of Chapter

Joint ventures are used extensively in the real estate, construction, oil and gas, and mining industries. This chapter will discuss broadly various joint venture accounting practices applicable to these specialized industries.

(b) Overview

Joint ventures enable companies to

- Share risks and rewards with their partners
- Enter and operate effectively in foreign markets aided by local expertise
- Obtain new technology or engage in research and development efforts
- Manage and finance major projects that are beyond the company's existing managerial and financial capabilities
- Finance the development of manufacturing facilities and products
- Engage in businesses in which one venturer provides special expertise or equipment and the other venturer provides capital

Accounting Principles Board (APB) Opinion No. 18, *The Equity Method of Accounting for Investments in Common Stock*, is the authoritative pronouncement on accounting for corporate joint ventures. APB No. 18 defines a corporate joint venture as

". . . a corporation owned and operated by a small group of businesses (the "joint venturers") as a separate and specific business or project for the mutual benefit of the members of the group. A government may also be a member of the group. The purpose of a corporate joint venture frequently is to share risks and rewards in developing a new market, product, or technology; to combine complementary technological knowledge; or to pool resources in developing production or other facilities. A corporate joint venture also usually provides an arrangement under which each joint venturer may participate, directly or indirectly, in the overall management of the joint venture. Joint ventures thus have an interest or relationship other than as passive investors. An entity which is a subsidiary of one of the "joint venturers" is not a corporate joint venture. The ownership of a corporate joint venture seldom changes, and its stock is usually not traded publicly. A minority public ownership, however, does not preclude a corporation from being a corporate joint venture."

The Accounting Standards Executive Committee (AcSEC) concluded in the July 17, 1979 Issues Paper, *Joint Venture Accounting*, that Section 3055 of the Canadian Institute of Chartered Accountants (CICA) Handbook should be adopted in substance as the definition of a joint venture. The CICA Handbook defines joint ventures as follows:

"A joint venture is an arrangement whereby two or more parties (the "venturers") jointly control a specific business undertaking and contribute resources toward its accomplishment. The life of the joint venture is limited to that of the undertaking which may be of short- or long-term duration depending on the circumstances. A distinctive feature of a joint venture is that the relationship between the venturers is governed by an agreement (usually in writing) which establishes joint control. Decisions in all areas essential to the accomplishment of a joint venture require the consent of the venturers, as provided by the agreement; none of the individual venturers is in a position to unilaterally control the venture. The feature of joint control distinguishes investments in joint ventures from investments in other enterprises where control of decisions is related to the proportion of voting interest held."

The above definition encompasses such arrangements as partnerships, undivided interests (unincorporated joint ventures), and project financing arrangements, as well as corporate joint ventures. However, it does not include arrangements between entities under common control. The definition also establishes joint control over the decision-making process as the most significant attribute of joint ventures regardless of the form, legal ownership, or voting interest held. Joint decisions in areas such as financing policy, dividend policy, significant asset sales, major acquisitions or divestitures, are imperative for there to be true joint control. Therefore, even if one of the parties manages the day-to-day activities of the venture, joint control can still exist.

International Accounting Standard (IAS) No. 31, *Financial Reporting of Interests in Joint Ventures*, also indicates that joint ventures can take many different forms and structures. IAS No. 31 defines joint ventures as contractual arrangements in which two or more parties undertake an economic activity which is subject to joint control. However, while IAS No. 31 is the most recent accounting standard to deal directly with joint ventures, it has no authoritative standing in the United States.

While APB No. 18 does not cover investments in unincorporated joint ventures (including partnerships), AIN-APB No. 18, No. 2 concludes that many of the provisions of APB No. 18 are also appropriate for investments in unincorporated joint ventures. Accounting for joint ventures is included in the Financial Accounting Standards Board's (FASB) project on consolidations and related matters. However, until a FASB pronouncement is issued, the authoritative pronouncements and other accounting literature listed below should be followed:

- APB No. 16, *Business Combinations*
- APB No. 18, *The Equity Method of Accounting for Investments in Common Stock*
- APB No. 29, *Accounting for Nonmonetary Assets*
- AIN-APB No. 18, Nos. 1 and 2
- Statement of Position (SOP) No. 78-9, *Accounting for Investments in Real Estate Ventures*
- AICPA Audit and Accounting Guide, *Construction Contractors*
- AcSEC Issues Paper, *Joint Venture Accounting* (7/17/79), and its addendum, *Accounting by Investors for Distributions Received in Excess of Their Investment in a Joint Venture* (10/8/79)
- Emerging Issues Task Force (EITF) Issue 89-7, *Exchange of Assets or Interest in a Subsidiary for a Noncontrolling Equity Interest in a New Entity*
- Staff Accounting Bulletin (SAB) Nos. 51 and 84 (Topic 5-H), *Accounting for Sales of Stock by a Subsidiary*
- Statement of Position (SOP) No. 92-1, *Accounting for Real Estate Syndication Income*
- FAS 94, Consolidation of All Majority-owned Subsidiaries
- EITF Issue 96-16, *Investor's Accounting for an Investee When the Investor Owns a Majority of the Voting Stock but Minority Shareholder or Shareholders Have Certain Approval or Veto Rights*

12.2 GENERAL ACCOUNTING PRINCIPLES IN SPECIALIZED INDUSTRIES

(a) Accounting for Investments in Joint Ventures by the Venturers

(i) Introduction. Investments in joint ventures are generally accounted for by the equity method or the proportionate consolidation method; in rare circumstances, the cost method may be appropriate. Another method that has been advocated is the combination method, in which one method is used in the balance sheet and another is used in the income statement. However, the use of the combination method is discouraged by the advisory conclusion in the *Joint Venture Accounting* Issues Paper which indicates that the same method should be used in the balance sheet and the income statement.

(ii) Equity Method. Accounting for investments in incorporated joint ventures is discussed in APB No. 18. A key distinguishing characteristic to be considered in accounting for joint ventures is that the significant influence criterion does not apply because of the underlying feature of joint control which is embedded in the joint venture concept. Accordingly, the equity method should generally be used for all interests in joint ventures, even if a venturer has more than a 50% interest or less than a 20% interest in the joint venture. In addition, AIN-APB No. 18, No. 2 states: "Many of the provisions of the Opinion would be appropriate in accounting for investments in . . . unincorporated entities. . . ."

(iii) Proportionate Consolidation. Accounting for an investment in a joint venture by the proportionate or pro rata consolidation method requires that the venturer's proportionate interest in the joint venture's assets, liabilities, revenues, and expenses be combined with each of the corresponding assets, liabilities, revenues, and expenses in the venturer's financial statements without separately distinguishing the amounts.

As indicated above, interests in joint ventures should generally be accounted for by the equity method. However, with respect to unincorporated joint ventures, AIN-APB No. 18, No. 2 states:

". . . because the investor–venturer owns an undivided interest in each asset and is proportionately liable for its share of each liability, the provisions of paragraph 19(c) [of APB Opinion No. 18] may not apply in some industries. For example, where it is the established industry practice (such as in some oil and gas venture accounting), the investor–venturer may account in its financial statements for its pro rata share of the assets, liabilities, revenues, and expenses of the venture."

The advisory conclusions to the AcSEC Issues Paper, *Joint Venture Accounting*, also state in paragraph 52(d) that "if an entity that otherwise meets the definition of a joint venture is not subject to joint control, by reason of its liabilities being several rather than joint [i.e., each venturer is responsible for its proportionate share of the joint venture's obligations] as in some undivided interests, investments in the entity should be required to be accounted for by the proportionate consolidation method."

In summary, the proportionate consolidation method should generally be used only if a venturer is individually responsible for its proportionate share of the joint venture's obligations or if it is the established industry practice. SOP 78-9 refers to the real estate, oil and gas, and mining industries as examples of industries wherein the proportionate consolidation method is appropriate.

(iv) Cost Method. Generally, the cost method is not used to account for an investment in a joint venture because there is a presumption that an investor has the ability to participate in the management of the joint venture. However, APB No. 18, as amended by FAS No. 94, precludes the use of the equity method when control of the investment is likely to be temporary or does not rest with the investors. The latter would include situations wherein an investee is in legal reorganization, in bankruptcy or operates under foreign exchange restrictions, controls, or other governmentally imposed restrictions so severe that they can question the investor's ability to control the investee.

An arrangement in which one party has control of an entity through a majority voting interest or otherwise may sometimes be referred to as a joint venture because it otherwise meets the definition. However, such an arrangement is not a joint venture, but rather a parent/subsidiary relationship in which one or a few entities have a significant minority interest in the subsidiary.

(b) Differences between the Carrying Amount of an Investment and the Underlying Equity in the Joint Venture

Frequently, there is a difference between the carrying amount (basis) of a venturer's investment in a joint venture and its underlying equity in the net assets of the joint venture. For example, this occurs when a venturer contributes (a) appreciated nonmonetary assets to the joint venture and records its investment at the book value of the contributed assets while the joint venture records these assets at their fair market value or (b) cash in an amount that exceeds its proportionate share in the recorded net assets of the joint venture (e.g., one venturer contributes cash, while the other venturer contributes an unidentifiable intangible asset such as "know-how" which is recorded at zero value at the joint venture level).

Paragraph 19(b) of APB No. 18 states: "A difference between the cost of an investment and the amount of underlying equity in net assets of an investee should be accounted for as if the investee were a consolidated subsidiary." Accordingly, the difference (after consideration of the need for an immediate write-down of the investment) should be attributed to the venturer's proportionate interest in specific assets of the joint venture and amortized over the estimated useful lives of the assets. No amortization would be recorded for difference attributable to nondepreciable assets (e.g., land). Paragraphs 87–92 of APB No. 16, *Business Combinations*, provide guidance in assigning the differences to specific assets. Any remaining amount in excess of amounts assigned to identifiable tangible and intangible assets (i.e., goodwill) should be amortized in a systematic manner related to the purpose and length of the venture. The period of amortization should not exceed 40 years.

(c) Accounting by Joint Venture Entities

Investors in joint ventures frequently contribute, singly or in combination, cash, tangible assets, intangible assets, or services. When cash is contributed, the entries recorded by both the venturer and the joint venture should be based on the amount of cash contributed. Cash contributions are generally the basis for determining the fair value of nonmonetary assets contributed by the other venturers. The accounting basis for recording contributed nonmonetary assets by the joint venture may differ from the basis used by the venturer for recording its investment. The accounting by the joint venture for contributed nonmonetary assets is complicated because of issues such as:

- Does the creation of a joint venture establish a reporting entity separate from its owners that requires a new basis of accounting for its assets and liabilities?
- Should assets or services contributed as capital to a venture by an investor–venturer be recorded at the investor–venturer's carrying amount, the amount agreed on by the parties, or the fair value?
- Are there any special problems associated with objectively determining the fair value of assets or services contributed by an investor–venturer?

The guidance available on these issues is summarized in the following paragraphs.

With respect to accounting by the joint venture, there is little authoritative guidance on accounting by a joint venture for contributed nonmonetary assets. The authors of the AcSEC Issues Paper, *Joint Venture Accounting*, paragraph 53, concluded, in a close vote, that:

(a) The creation of a joint venture establishes a reporting entity separate from its owners that requires a new basis of accounting for its assets and liabilities.

(b) Assets contributed to the joint venture should be recorded at the amount agreed on by the parties, which is assumed to be determined by reference to fair market value, but not in excess of the assets' fair market value.

Although the Issues Paper supported a new basis of accounting for nonmonetary assets contributed to a joint venture at the amount agreed on by the parties (not to exceed the fair value), the closeness of the vote indicates that the issue is very subjective. It is anticipated that the FASB will reconsider this Issues Paper as part of its project on consolidations and related matters.

In summary, accounting by joint venture entities continues to evolve and varies in practice. In 1979, when the Issues Paper was prepared, step-up accounting was fairly common. Since then, practice has been moving towards the carry-over of predecessor basis, especially in situations where there is little or no cash infusion into the joint venture. A primary consideration in determining the appropriateness of step-up accounting is whether there can be an objective determination of fair value.

The appropriate accounting for a joint venture depends on specific facts and circumstances such as the cash contributed by one or more of the venturers, the amount of such cash which remains in the joint venture, the nature of the assets contributed (i.e., tangible or intangible), whether the nonmonetary assets contributed to the joint venture were "just bought" property acquired from an independent third party and the availability of objectively determinable fair values. In situations where a step-up may be considered appropriate, the amounts agreed on by the venturers must be realistic and must be supported by appraisals or other acceptable methods of valuation. Intangibles should only be recognized as assets under circumstances where the value of the intangibles is objectively determinable with a high degree of reliability and where there is no doubt as to the ultimate recovery of such assets.

With respect to accounting followed by the joint venture partners, contributions of property, intangible assets, and services to a joint venture generally should be recorded in the investment account at the net book value of such assets unless there is an indicated impairment of value. This accounting is generally supported by paragraphs 30 and 32 of SOP No. 78-9, as amended by SOP No. 92-1, except in the case when real estate syndicators receive or retain partnership interests as compensation for performing syndication services. Although APB No. 29 indicates that it does not apply to transfers of nonmonetary assets between a corporate joint venture and its venturers, the author believes that it can be used as guidance for the above accounting. Paragraph 21 of APB No. 29 states:

> "If the exchange is not essentially the culmination of an earning process, accounting for an exchange of a nonmonetary asset between an enterprise and another entity should be based on the recorded amount (after reduction, if appropriate, for an indicated impairment of value) of the nonmonetary asset relinquished."

Paragraph 22 of APB No. 29 further states:

> "If a loss is indicated by the terms of a transaction described in paragraph 21, the entire indicated loss on the exchange should be recognized."

Some accountants believe that a venturer may record a gain, to the extent of the interest of the other venturers, for *appreciated assets* contributed to a joint venture. However, the author does not believe that a gain should normally be recognized (regardless of whether the other venturers contribute cash or other nonmonetary assets), because the contribution does not result in the culmination of the earnings process. However, if the venturer that contributes the nonmonetary assets receives cash as a part of the transaction, a gain may be recorded under the circumstances outlined in the following paragraph.

The Emerging Issues Task Force, in EITF Issue 89-7, reached a consensus on gain recognition in connection with a transaction involving the transfer by a company of its ownership of an individual asset (or assets) or its ownership in a subsidiary to a newly created entity in exchange for a noncontrolling equity ownership in that entity plus cash. The example transaction involves the transfer by Company A of a manufacturing plant with a book basis of $100 and an appraised value of $400 to a joint venture in exchange for a 50% interest in that entity. In the transaction, Company B purchases the remaining equity interest (50%) in the joint venture for cash of $200. The cash is subsequently distributed to Company A. Company A has no actual or implied commitment to support the operations of the joint venture, and there is no requirement for Company A to reacquire the assets contributed to the venture. Company A would recognize a gain of $150 as follows:

Fair value of interest in plant sold (50% of $400)	$200
Less book value of interest sold (50% of $100)	(50)
	$150

(Source: EITF Issue 89-7)

In the above example, the cash received equals the fair value of assets deemed sold. Although the consensus does not specifically address joint ventures, the author believes this guidance should be applied to those transactions otherwise meeting the conditions stated above. However, gain recognition in all cases is based on an evaluation of all facts and circumstances applicable to a particular transaction.

(d) Venturer's Share of Losses in Excess of the Carrying Amount of Investment

Judgment must be exercised in accounting for the losses of a joint venture in excess of a venturer's investment, including loans and advances. Specific guidance can be found in paragraph 19(i) of APB No. 18, which indicates that a venturer's equity in the losses of the joint venture in excess of its investment, including loans and advances, need not be recorded unless the venturer is liable for the obligations of the joint venture or is otherwise obligated to provide additional financial support.

When such circumstances do not exist, the venturer should generally stop recording its equity in the joint venture's losses when its investment, including loans and advances, is reduced to zero. If the joint venture subsequently reports net income, the investor should resume recording its share of the joint venture's net income only after its share of the net income equals its share of the net losses not previously recorded.

A footnote to paragraph 19(i) of APB No. 18, however, provides that a venturer should provide for additional losses in excess of its investment, including loans and advances, when the joint venture appears poised to return to profitability. For example, a material loss that is the result of an unusual and isolated event may reduce an investment below zero, although the joint venture's normal profitable operating pattern is not impaired.

Paragraph 15 of SOP No. 78-9 provides examples of circumstances in which a venturer should recognize losses in excess of its investment; however, the final determination must be based on the facts and circumstances of each individual case. The following are examples of such circumstances:

- The venturer has a legal obligation as a guarantor or general partner.
- The venturer has publicly indicated a commitment to provide additional financial support.
- The venturer's past performance indicates a commitment to provide additional financial support.
- The venturer's business reputation or credit standing indicates a commitment to provide support.

Sometimes one or more venturers are unable to bear their share of the joint venture's losses. In these situations, the remaining venturers should record their proportionate share of the losses otherwise allocable to the deficient venturers, if the provisions of FAS No. 5, *Accounting for Contingencies*, are met. If the joint venture subsequently becomes profitable, the remaining venturers should record their proportionate share of the venture's net income otherwise allocable to the deficient venturers until such income equals the excess losses they previously recorded. Once the excess losses are reversed, if the deficient venturers still have an interest in the joint venture, the remaining venturers should record their proportionate share of the net income of the venture in accordance with the joint venture agreement. The deficient venturers should continue to record their share of the losses unless they are relieved of the obligation to make payment by an agreement between the venturers or by law. In practice, if the remaining venturers fund the commitments of the deficient venturers, such deficient venturers would generally be required to reimburse the remaining venturers or surrender part or all of their interest in the joint venture. This accounting is supported by paragraphs 18 and 19 of SOP No. 78-9. Although this SOP only addresses accounting for investments in real estate ventures, the author believes that this concept generally applies to accounting for investments in all ventures.

(e) Distributions Received in Excess of Investment

The October 8, 1979 addendum to the AcSEC Issues Paper, *Joint Venture Accounting*, states in its advisory conclusion:

> "A[n] . . . investor in a real estate venture should account for cash distributions received in excess of its investment in a venture as income when (a) the distributions are not refundable by agreement or by law and (b) the investor is not liable for the obligations of the venture and is not otherwise committed to provide financial support to the venture."

Although AcSEC's conclusions relate specifically to real estate ventures, the author believes that they apply to all joint ventures. If any condition set forth above is not met, cash distributions received in excess of an investment in joint venture should be recorded as a liability.

(f) Intercompany Profits

(i) General.   Sales of goods or services from a venturer to the joint venture or vice versa often result in the recognition of intercompany profits by the seller of the goods or services. In applying the equity method, it is inappropriate to reflect 100% of such profits in the financial statements until the profits are realized by an ultimate sale to unrelated third parties.

(ii) Venturer Sales to a Joint Venture. Profits on a sale to the joint venture should be eliminated to the extent of the venturer's interest in those assets which were sold that remain on the books of the joint venture. For example, profits on sales of inventory should be eliminated to the extent of the venturer's interest, until the inventory is ultimately sold to an unrelated third party.

Similarly, a venturer's profits on sales of long-lived assets should be eliminated to the extent of the venturer's interest. Since there is generally no intent by the joint venture to sell such assets to other parties, the venturer may only recognize the deferred profits on sales as the assets are consumed (depreciated) in the operations of the joint venture. The deferred profits would be amortized into income over the estimated useful lives of the applicable assets as determined by the joint venture.

When costs for services performed for the joint venture are capitalized by the joint venture, paragraph 37 of SOP No. 78-9 states:

". . . profit may be recognized by the investor to the extent attributable to the outside interests in the venture if the following conditions are met:

(a) The substance of the transaction does not significantly differ from its form.

(b) There are no substantial uncertainties about the ability of the investor to complete performance (as may be the case if the investor lacks experience in the business of the venture) or the total cost of services to be rendered.

(c) There is a reasonable expectation that the other investors will bear their share of losses, if any."

The method of recognizing income from services rendered for the joint venture should be consistent with the method followed for services performed for unrelated parties. An investor should defer recognition of fees from services performed for the joint venture when the fees are being paid out of funds advanced by the investor, such as when the investor is funding the operating losses of the joint venture.

(iii) Joint Venture Sales to a Venturer. Because a venture cannot recognize profits on sales of assets and services to itself, its proportionate interest in such joint venture profits must be eliminated in the following way:

- The venturer's proportionate interest in profits from sales of inventory must be eliminated until the inventory is sold to an unrelated third party.
- On sales of long-lived assets, the venturer's basis in the assets must be reduced by its share of the profits. These profits should be recognized in income as the assets are depreciated over their estimated useful lives as determined by the venturer or when sold to an unrelated third party.
- If the venturer capitalizes the costs of services that are performed for it, the venturer's proportionate interest in the joint venture's profits from the transaction should be recognized as a reduction in the carrying amount of the capitalized costs. These profits should be recognized as the capitalized costs are consumed in the venturer's operations.

(g) Cost-Sharing Arrangements

If the intent of a joint venture is to serve as a source of supply to the venturers, and the venturers agree to purchase the joint venture's product in proportion to their respective interests, all intercompany profit should be eliminated. The intent of such an arrangement is to share costs, and until the product is ultimately sold to an unrelated third party, the earnings process has not been completed.

CHAPTER THIRTEEN

Joint Venture Accounting in the Real Estate, Oil and Gas, and Construction Industries

13.1 INTRODUCTION

(a) Scope of Chapter

In three particular industries, joint ventures have been extensively used as a way doing business, and the customs and procedures for accounting for joint ventures in these industries have received extensive coverage in accounting literature. These industries are:

- The real estate industry
- The oil and gas industry
- The construction industry

Although some of the practices and guidelines for use in accounting for joint ventures in these industries are contained in nonauthoritative accounting pronouncements such as various AICPA guides, they are generally accepted and followed in practice. This chapter discusses the guidelines and practices used in accounting for joint ventures in these industries, including detailed discussion of specific practices for joint venture accounting in the real estate, oil and gas, and construction industries. In some cases, the particular points noted are repetitive because those specific points are contained in the separate pronouncements that have been issued for more than one industry, and because much of the content of these pronouncements reiterates various requirements of APB Opinion No. 18.

13.2 ACCOUNTING FOR JOINT VENTURES IN THE REAL ESTATE INDUSTRY

(a) A General Business Perspective

Many real estate investments are made through joint ventures. Real estate joint ventures are usually formed for a limited life to combine the attributes of property ownership, financial resources, and industry knowledge needed to complete specific real estate projects. One of the joint venture participants, usually a developer or operator, controls the joint venture; although percentage ownerships and contractual provisions may result in the developer or operator not having control, as defined for accounting purposes. Whether or not control is present will determine if the developer or operator must consolidate the joint venture for accounting purposes.

Since real estate joint ventures can be structured to create tax benefits for investors, these ventures are often syndicated and funded through limited partnerships, which enables the funding investors to participate with limited liability. Real estate joint ventures are usually structured in the following forms:

- Corporate joint ventures
- General partnerships
- Limited partnerships
- Undivided interest ownerships

The first three forms previously listed should already be familiar to the reader. The fourth form refers to an arrangement in which two or more parties jointly own property, with the title held individually by each party to the extent of that party's interest. The approval of more than one of the investors in an undivided interest arrangement is usually required to commence specified actions with regard to the subject real estate. A key feature of this form of joint venture is that each investor is usually liable only for its own indebtedness incurred as part of the arrangement.

(b) Accounting for Real Estate Joint Ventures — Applicable Pronouncements

In 1978 the Accounting Standards Division of the AICPA issued Statement of Position No. 78-9, entitled *Accounting for Investments in Real Estate Ventures.* Although not an authoritative pronouncement, the Statement of Position has remained the primary professional guide regarding accounting for investments in real estate joint ventures. This pronouncement does not apply to regulated investment companies or other entities required to account for investments at quoted market value or fair value, however.

The Statement of Position indicates that the following accounting methods can apply to different forms of real estate joint ventures:

(a) The equity method applies to corporate joint ventures created to own or operate real estate.

(b) Investors in general or limited real estate partnerships should usually account for their investments in these joint ventures using the equity method, but in some cases the cost method or even consolidation may be appropriate.

(c) Real estate joint ventures structured as undivided interests should be accounted for using the equity method or pro rata consolidation, depending on the degree of joint control that is present.

In addition to the investments in undivided interest joint ventures for which the Statement of Position indicates that pro rata consolidation is acceptable, the Statement permits entities to continue a broader practice of pro rata consolidation if that practice was used prior to the issuance of the Statement in 1978.

In October, 1982, the FASB issued FASB Statement No. 66, entitled *Accounting for Sales of Real Estate*. This pronouncement established the current fundamental standards for recognizing profit or loss on sales of real estate, and governs the underlying principles of accounting to be used for the real estate transactions of real estate joint ventures. FASB Statement No. 66 carried forward a number of specialized real estate industry accounting principles that had been previously recommended by the AICPA in the following pronouncements:

Pronouncement	*Title*
AICPA Industry Accounting Guide	Accounting for Profit Recognition on Sales of Real Estate
AICPA Industry Accounting Guide	Accounting for Retail Land Sales
AICPA Statement of Position (No. 75-6)	Questions Concerning Recognition on Sales of Real Estate
AICPA Statement of Position (No. 78-4)	Application of the Deposit, Installment, and Cost Recovery Methods in Accounting for Sales of Real Estate

FASB Statement No. 66 carried forward most of the provisions of the foregoing nonauthoritative pronouncements into a single authoritative pronouncement. However, even prior to the issuance of FASB Statement No. 66, the recommendations included in these AICPA pronouncements were generally accepted and followed by the real estate industry and by the accounting profession.

A comprehensive review of the contents of FASB Statement No. 66 is beyond the scope of this book; the more relevant pronouncement to the specific subject of joint ventures, which will be discussed in detail herein, is the AICPA Statement of Position entitled *Accounting for Investments in Real Estate Ventures*. However, the following list indicates the general requirements for recognition of profit under the various methods used for accounting for profit recognition in the real estate industry. The following are the different methods of profit recognition:

- Full accrual method
- Percentage of completion method
- Installment method
- Cost recovery method

- Deposit method
- Reduced profit method

The general considerations in determining whether or not a real estate sale may be recognized on a full accrual basis, and if not, which alternative method should be used, are as follows:

1. Retail land sales
   a. The seller's receivables related to the transaction must be considered collectible.
   b. The seller must have no significant remaining obligations for construction or development.
2. Real estate sales
   a. A sale must have been consummated.
   b. The buyer must be committed to minimum investment requirements.
   c. The seller's receivable must not be subject to future subordination.
   d. The degree of the seller's continuing involvement with the real estate after the sale will impact the accounting method to be used.

The Statement contains many detailed requirements for applying and measuring the general criteria listed above and for applying the prescribed accounting methods.

Other FASB pronouncements that are relevant to certain real estate transactions are FASB Statement No. 26, entitled *Profit Recognition on Sales-Type Leases of Real Estate*, and paragraphs 23 through 25 of FASB Statement No. 28, entitled *Accounting for Sales with Leasebacks*.

The following sections focus on the important aspects of accounting for investments in real estate joint ventures as set forth in the AICPA Statement of Position entitled *Accounting for Investments in Real Estate Ventures*.

(c) Application of the Equity Method to Real Estate Joint Ventures

(i) General. The AICPA Statement of Position provides that the equity method should be generally used for real estate corporate joint ventures, and

because the equity method is essentially similar to the principles of accounting for partnerships, the fundamentals of the equity method generally apply to accounting for real estate joint venture partnerships. However, if an investor owns more than 50% of the voting shares of a real estate joint venture, and effectively controls the venture, the investee should be consolidated by that investor. It is interesting to note that in this case the venture will be reported as a subsidiary of that investor, and is technically not a corporate joint venture as defined in accounting rules. However, in practice, such arrangements are sometimes referred to as joint ventures nevertheless.

If a real estate joint venture does not prepare its financial statement in accordance with generally accepted accounting principles, an investor must make any adjustments required to make the financial statements conform with generally accepted accounting principles before recognizing its share of the joint venture's profit or loss.

The Statement of Position addresses a number of aspects of the equity method that should be applied in accounting for real estate joint ventures. These are discussed in the following sections.

(ii) Accounting for Joint Venture Losses.   An investor's share of losses reported by a real estate joint venture should be recognized by the investor, even if it is believed that the assets of the joint venture can be sold at a price that will enable the investor to recover an amount equal to or greater than the carrying value of the investment. Thus, unrealized increases in the value of real estate holdings of a joint venture do not overcome the requirement to account for an investment in a real estate joint venture in accordance with normal principles of profit and loss recognition under the equity method.

The Statement of Position discusses how an investor should account for losses in the following two situations:

1. If an investor's share of joint venture losses exceeds the carrying value of the investment in the joint venture

2. If it appears that another investor will be unable to bear its share of joint venture losses

If an investor's share of a real estate joint venture's losses exceeds the carrying value of the investment, that investor should continue to record its share of losses as reductions of any outstanding loans and advances made by that investor to the joint venture. Further losses should be recorded and presented as a liability in the investor's balance sheet if the investor is legally obligated to fund the additional losses as a guarantor or a general partner, or if the investor has indicated its intention to provide additional financial support to the venture. This may be indicated by statements or assurances given to other parties or to the joint venture, or by compelling adverse results (such as damage to an otherwise good business reputation or credit standing) that would occur if an investor were to withdraw financial support and allow joint venture obligations to go unpaid.

If the above circumstances are not present, and an investor does not recognize its share of losses in excess of the amounts of its investment, loans, and advances to the joint venture, then the investor should not recognize its share of any future income of the joint venture until the unrecognized share of income equals the unrecognized share of losses.

If it appears that another investor cannot absorb its share of the losses of a real estate joint venture, the other investors should recognize that investor's share of the losses on a pro rata basis. The AICPA Statement of Position recommends using the provisions of FASB Statement No. 5 entitled *Accounting for Contingencies*, in evaluating if it is probable that another investor will not be able to bear its share of the losses of the joint venture. In performing this evaluation, the Statement of Position permits the current market value of the other investor's share of the assets of the venture to be considered, as well as the extent to which the other investor's debt is nonrecourse. This may be difficult to measure if the nature and amount of the other investor's indebtedness are not known.

The need to recognize another investor's share of losses would not apply where the real estate joint venture is structured as joint ownership of property with undivided interests, and where claims against each creditor are limited to each separate investor's interest in the properties held by the venture and the individual indebtedness incurred related to the properties. If investors have recognized another investor's share of losses because of the other investor's apparent inability to bear those losses, future profits allocable to that investor should be recognized by the other investors until the amount of that investor's losses that were previously recognized by the other investors has been completely offset.

If one or more of the investors in a joint venture appears unable to meet its obligations, this may present evidence of other valuation considerations that could require accounting treatment, such as the possibility that the real estate joint venture might be forced to dispose of its properties under duress conditions. If this situation is so serious that it gives evidence of a decline in the realizable value of an investment, recognition of a loss may be required by the investors.

The Statement of Position also recommends that an investor that appears unable to bear its share of losses of a real estate joint venture should, nevertheless, recognize its proportionate share of the losses in its financial statements. This can result in the investors, as a group, recognizing in their separate financial statements losses equal to more than 100% of the losses of a real estate joint venture.

(iii) Permanent Decline in the Value of an Investment.   The Statement of Position specifically reiterates the equity method's principle that an indicated loss, other than a temporary decline in value of an investment in a real estate joint venture (including investments, loans, and advances) should be recognized currently as a loss. A decision by other investors to cease providing support or to reduce their financial commitment to a real estate joint venture can provide evidence of such situations.

(iv) Elimination of Intercompany Profits and Losses.   The Statement of Position indicates that the provisions of APB Opinion No. 18 regarding elimination of intercompany profits and losses under the equity method apply to purchases and sales of real estate between an investor and a real estate joint venture. Intercompany profits and losses can be eliminated to the extent of the investor's interest in a joint venture if the joint venture has acquired real estate from the investor. The entire profit or loss should be eliminated if the investor selling the real estate to the joint venture controls the joint venture.

If a sale of real estate from a real estate joint venture to an investor qualifies for current recognition, the investor should eliminate its share of the joint venture's profit on the sale. The investor's share of the profit should be recorded as a reduction of the carrying value of the real estate, and the unrecognized portion of the profit should be recognized when the investor sells the real estate to a third party or, alternatively, through a lower depreciation expense that would be recognized by the investor as the real estate is depreciated.

(v) Profit and Loss Allocation Ratios.   Real estate joint venture agreements frequently provide for specific allocations of profits, losses, expenses, and cash distributions from operations or liquidation. These agreements may also provide for changes in the ratios at specified times or upon specified events, such as at "pay-back," which refers to when a specified investor has recovered its investment.

These terms must be carefully evaluated to determine that profits and losses are allocated on a basis that is consistent with how the terms will affect cash distributions to the respective investors over the life of the venture.

(vi) Differences between an Investment Carrying Value and an Investor's Proportionate Share of Joint Venture Assets. The Statement of Position reiterates the fundamental provision included in APB Opinion No. 18 that differences between the carrying value of an investment in a real estate joint venture and an investor's share of underlying net assets should be accounted for as if the investee were a consolidated subsidiary. Accordingly, an investor should consider such differences in computing the share of joint venture income or loss to be reported.

Differences of this nature often arise from the contribution of real estate to a joint venture because the joint venture will carry the real estate at market value at date of contribution. In such cases, the difference should be amortized by the investor on a pro rata basis as the related real estate is depreciated or sold to third parties.

(vii) Sale of an Interest in a Real Estate Joint Venture. If an investor sells an investment in a real estate joint venture, the transaction should be viewed as a sale of the underlying real estate. Accordingly, the provisions of FASB Statement No. 66 apply to determining whether the profit on the sale should be recognized immediately.

If the sale is recognized, any deferred taxes that relate to the investment in the real estate joint venture and the underlying real estate should be included in the computation of gain or loss.

(viii) Accounting for Certain Transactions between an Investor and a Real Estate Venture. The Statement of Position contains guidance on accounting for a variety of transactions that frequently occur between investors and real estate joint ventures. These are discussed in the following sections.

Contributions of Real Estate to a Real Estate Joint Venture. Contributions of real estate to a real estate joint venture should be recorded in the investor's investment account at the investor's previous carrying value of the real estate, unless the transaction substantively constitutes the culmination of an earnings process. The earnings process should be viewed as completed only if the investor contributing the real estate, as part of the transaction, withdraws cash from the joint venture that was contributed to the joint venture by other investors who are, in substance, purchasing an interest in the real estate. A further condition to recognition of profit on such transactions is that the investor must not be obligated to reinvest the withdrawn cash in the real estate joint venture.

An investor may contribute real estate to a joint venture in exchange for a percentage interest in the joint venture as to which the proportionate amount of net assets of the joint venture is less than the previous carrying value of the real estate in the financial statements of the investor. Such an event may give evidence of a decline in value of the real estate, a decline which should be recognized by the investor.

Contributions of Services or Intangibles to a Real Estate Joint Venture. The contribution of services or intangibles should be accounted for in the same way as contributions of real estate to a real estate joint venture. That is, profit may be recognized only to the extent that cash contributed by other investors has been withdrawn by the investor contributing the services or intangibles, and only if the investor has no obligation to reinvest the cash in the joint venture. Otherwise, such contributions should be recorded at cost on the same basis that would be used if the services or intangibles were allocated to a wholly owned real estate project.

Income from Loans or Advances to a Real Estate Joint Venture. If investors are required to make loans or advances to a real estate joint venture in proportion to their respective ownership percentages in the venture, any interest paid by the venture in respect to these loans and advances should be reported by the investors as distributions rather than as interest income.

If loans and advances to a real estate joint venture are considered to be bona fide loans and advances, interest income may be recognized by the investors. However, interest income should not be recognized currently if there is doubt regarding collectibility of the interest or the principal amounts of the loans or advances. This may be indicated if the terms of the loans or advances are different from typical third party loans that would involve collateral or other protective measures. Interest income should also not be recognized currently if there is reasonable expectation that other investors will not bear their share of the joint venture's losses. This causes uncertainty regarding the joint venture's ability to pay the interest.

To the extent that interest expense has been capitalized by a real estate joint venture, an investor earning interest on a loan or advance should not currently recognize interest income. If interest income is recognized currently, the investor should eliminate the portion of the interest income that relates to its proportionate ownership of the joint venture.

Sales of Services to a Real Estate Joint Venture.   If an investor is compensated for services performed for a real estate joint venture, and the amount paid is capitalized by the joint venture, the investor may recognize profit, but must eliminate its proportionate share. Such profits should not be recognized if the substance of the transaction is not the performance of services in exchange for compensation, if there are substantial uncertainties as to collectibility, if there are substantial uncertainties as to the investor's capability to complete performance of the services, or if there is reasonable expectation that the other investors will not be able to bear their share of joint venture losses.

The timing of recognition and other accounting determinations for recognizing income from services provided by an investor to a real estate joint venture are the same as for services performed for third parties under generally accepted accounting principles.

Purchases of Services from a Real Estate Joint Venture.   If a real estate joint venture is compensated for services it performs for an investor and the investor capitalizes such amounts, the investor should eliminate its share of the profit on the transaction reported by the joint venture.

(ix) Financial Statement Disclosures.   The disclosure requirements contained in paragraph 20 of APB Opinion No. 18 apply to investments in real estate joint ventures. Further, the Statement of Position states that, except to the extent that a real estate joint venture's earnings have been distributed during the period or qualify as a current receivable, an investor's share of the joint venture's earnings should not be classified in the statement of changes in financial position under the section presented for working capital or cash provided by operations.

(d) Ownership of an Undivided Interest— Equity Method versus Pro Rata Consolidation

(i) General.   Some real estate joint ventures are structured with each investor owning an undivided interest in the underlying real estate, and with each investor being liable only for its pro rata share of joint venture liabilities (in other words, severally liable). Even though a real estate joint venture may be structured on the basis of undivided interests with the investors being severally liable, most ventures are subject to joint control by the investors. If joint control is present, the Statement of Position recommends that investors report their investments in a similar manner to reporting investments in noncontrolled partnerships. This is essentially similar to the equity method.

The Statement provides that if undivided interests are present but joint control is not (meaning that approval of more than one of the investors is not required for decisions regarding financing, development, sale, or operation of the real estate), and if each investor is entitled to only its pro rata share of income and is only responsible for its pro rata share of expenses and liabilities incurred regarding the property, an investor may report its investment and share of joint venture activities on a pro rata consolidation basis. It should be noted that because the equity method essentially produces the same profit or loss result as consolidation, the profit or loss reported under pro rata consolidation will generally be the same as would be reported under the equity method; the difference is in the financial statement classifications.

(ii) General Partnerships — Equity Method versus Consolidation. The Statement of Position recommends that an investment in a real estate general partnership by an investor that does not control the partnership should be accounted for using the principles of the equity method, with a one-line presentation in both the investor's balance sheet and income statement. This requires careful consideration of the tax implications of the partnership's revenues and expenses, as investors should provide income tax expense based on the pretax accounting income recognized in connection with the partnership, and not the actual tax liability or benefits that it realizes through the partnership tax return. Accordingly, special care should be given to the determination of time differences and deferred taxes.

If one of the general partners in a real estate joint venture has control over the general partnership, that partner should consolidate the partnership's assets and liabilities in its financial statements, and report the equity interests of the other partners as a minority interest.

The Statement indicates that if one investor holds more than 50% of the voting interests in the partnership, or greater than a 50% interest in the profits or losses of the partnership, this will normally give evidence of control. Additionally, other factors should be considered. These include contractual rights, leases, agreements with other partners, and court decrees that give evidence of control even though less than 50% of the voting rights or interest in profits and losses are held. Further, in some circumstances a general partner may own more than 50% of the voting interests, but may not have control because other partners must agree for major partnership transactions to take place.

If an interest in a real estate joint venture general partnership is consolidated, intercompany transactions should be fully eliminated under generally accepted accounting principles for consolidated financial statements.

(iii) Limited Partnerships — Equity Method, Cost Method, or Consolidation. The equity method is generally prescribed for accounting for a limited partners' interest in a real estate joint venture. However, the Statement of Position notes that for some limited partners' interests in real estate joint ventures, the cost method may be appropriate, and for others, consolidation may be appropriate. The cost method would be appropriate if an investor owns an insignificant percentage of a joint venture and effectively does not have the ability to influence its financial or operating policies. Consolidation is appropriate if a limited partner holds such a significant interest in a partnership that it has effective control.

If the cost method is used, distributions should be recognized as income by the limited partner, except that distributions that exceed the limited partner's share of earnings of the joint venture should be applied as a reduction of the carrying value of the investment until such investment is fully eliminated.

Determination should be made as to whether a general partner in a limited partnership effectively controls the joint venture, in which case the general partner should consolidate the partnership, with the limited partners reporting on the equity method or cost method, as appropriate.

Regardless of the method (cost, equity, or consolidation) used by a general partner or limited partner, the reporting investor should ensure that it has properly reported deferred taxes for timing differences related to the pretax income it has reported with respect to a real estate joint venture structured as a limited partnership.

It should also be noted that if a general or limited partner consolidates the joint venture, full elimination of intercompany transactions is required.

13.3 ACCOUNTING FOR JOINT VENTURES IN THE OIL AND GAS INDUSTRY

(a) A General Business Perspective

Joint ventures are formed in the oil and gas industry to carry out all phases of exploration and production of oil and gas. Reasons for this include the desires of the participants to share the high risks inherent in the oil and gas industry, and to raise the substantial funds required to do business in the industry. Some joint ventures in the oil and gas industry are funded by individuals, or by partnerships formed to provide the funds in the context of tax-advantaged investments. Larger joint ventures are often formed between large corporations in the industry to undertake major projects.

The various kinds of partnerships that are formed can be categorized by the purpose that the funds are intended to be used for and the degree of risk normally present at various stages of the oil and gas recovery process. "Completion fund" partnerships are formed to fund the completion of wells and the purchase of related equipment after it has been concluded that a previously drilled well is likely to produce acceptable levels of oil and gas. "Income fund" partnerships purchase existing producing properties. "Mezzanine financing" is provided for financing all activities of the oil and gas business process, from acquiring properties through completion. What distinguishes mezzanine financing arrangements is that the lenders normally take an equity position in the activities and accept a lower interest rate.

"Oil field services joint ventures" are formed between operators or owners holding properties with recoverable reserves, and various oilfield service vendors, including drillers, where the vendors receive an equity interest or a share of future revenues from the property, or a combination of the two.

"Exchange offers" are transactions in which interests in existing oil and gas properties are exchanged for interests in new, larger oil and gas ventures. These transactions may be subject to the jurisdiction of the Securities and Exchange Commission, which has issued rules for accounting for these transactions. In some cases, the interests in these entities trade on the open market, such as in the case of master limited partnerships.

(b) Accounting for Oil and Gas Joint Ventures

(i) General. An investor in an oil and gas joint venture must consider the accounting principles that are unique to the oil and gas industry that have been included in authoritative pronouncements issued by both the Financial Accounting Standards Board and the Securities and Exchange Commission.

An area of particular importance to oil and gas joint ventures relates to the accounting, procedural, and transactional practices that have evolved with regard to joint ventures and joint participations. A detailed review of all accounting principles applicable to accounting for oil and gas operations is beyond the scope of this book. The accounting principles and accounting procedures that are unique to oil and gas joint ventures are discussed in the following sections.

(ii) Accounting Procedures for Oil and Gas Joint Ventures. Most joint ventures in the oil and gas industry are governed by standard operating agreements that have been designed by the American Association of Petroleum Landmen. These operating agreements utilize specific accounting procedures and practices that were developed by an organization known as the Council of Petroleum Accounting Societies.

Under most oil and gas joint venture arrangements, one of the investors is appointed as the operator and given responsibility for running the day-to-day operations of the venture. The operator is normally required to provide the other investors with periodic (often monthly) reports on revenues and expenses, to collect funds required to be contributed by the investors, and to distribute revenues to the investors.

Joint Interest Billings. A joint interest billing (JIB) is a billing system maintained by the operator of an oil and gas property. In a joint interest billing system, the operator first records the expenses of the operation in total, and then allocates the charges to the joint venture participants as specified in the joint venture operating agreement. In addition to the normal central procedure that participants in an oil and gas joint venture utilize in verifying payments made for joint interest billings, it is customary for participants to audit the operator's financial records to determine the propriety of the charges and allocations. This procedure is commonly referred to as a "JIB audit," and accountants who are specialists in this area are referred to as "JIB auditors."

This is a critical function in the oil and gas industry, and is needed to supplement the normal controls a joint venture participant should have for reviewing joint interest billings prior to payment.

Unless there are obvious errors in a joint interest billing submitted to a joint venture participant by an operator, the participant is generally expected to make prompt payment of the amount billed, with any required adjustments made as an addition or reduction of a future billing.

For expenditures of a drilling or capital nature, a document known as an Authorization for Expenditure (AFE) is prepared by the operator, indicating the amount expected to be spent on a particular item. Frequently an AFE must be approved by the joint venture participants prior to the operator's commitment to incur obligations related to the expenditures.

Joint venture participants in the oil and gas industry normally receive a joint interest statement that details expenditures on a property-by-property and well-by-well basis that indicates the total expenditures and the portion payable by each participant.

Revenue Distribution.   The other major transactional requirement in oil and gas joint ventures relates to the computation of total revenues and the division of revenues among the joint venture participants. This process can require special metering procedures if certain wells on a property are covered by the joint venture and others are not. Furthermore, the distribution process is frequently complicated by revenue distribution percentages that change upon specified events, often connected with "pay-out," which is when one or more of the participants has fully recovered the amounts invested.

Another factor which must be considered in revenue distribution is that certain parties may be entitled to royalties based on a percentage of revenues derived from production from the joint venture's operations, or based on the profit after operating expenses. The latter arrangement is referred to as a "net profits interest."

(iii) Accounting Principles for Oil and Gas Joint Ventures.   Based on industry practice in the oil and gas industry, investors usually account for investments in oil and gas joint ventures using pro rata consolidation. Interpretation No. 2 of APB Opinion No. 18 specifically refers to this practice in the oil and gas industry, as follows:

Where it is the established industry practice (such as in some oil and gas venture accounting), the investor-venturer may account in its financial statements for its pro rata share of the assets, liabilities, revenues, and expenses of the venture.

However, depending on the circumstances, it may be appropriate to use the cost method or consolidation.

Pro rata consolidation is also the form of reporting usually used by general partners in general and limited partnerships in the oil and gas industry.

(iv) Accounting for Certain Transactions in Oil and Gas Joint Ventures. The following sections discuss generally accepted accounting principles and practices for certain transactions in joint ventures in the oil and gas industry.

Management Fees. The accounting treatment for management fees paid to a general partner or operator upon formation of a joint venture depends on whether the recipient utilizes the full cost method or the successful efforts method. If the full cost method is used, the fees may be recognized immediately as income only to the extent that related costs have been incurred and charged to expense. This is a specific requirement for public companies.

If the recipient uses the successful efforts method, management fees should be recognized as income when earned by the recipient.

Management Fees Received in the Form of an Interest in a Joint Venture. An interpretative response in SEC Staff Accounting Bulletin No. 47 discusses the proper accounting if the operator of an oil and gas joint venture receives part or all of its compensation in the form of an interest in an oil and gas joint venture for which the other participants provide funds. If the interest received relates to proved producing properties, the receipt of the interest may be recognized as management fee income if the value of the interest received is determinable. If substantial future development is required before the oil and gas can be recovered, public companies are required to follow the cost recovery method as described in SEC Regulation S-X, Rule 4-10(i)(6)(iii), which essentially results in the recognition of income as the properties are produced and cash accrues to the participant. It would appear that this accounting principle should apply as well to privately held companies.

Offering Costs. If a general partner receives a management fee that is a reimbursement of offering costs, the costs should be credited to expense. If a general partner is not reimbursed for offering expenses, the general partner may expense the costs immediately or amortize them over the life of the joint venture or over a shorter period. If a partnership pays the offering costs or reimburses a general partner for the costs, the partnership may amortize the costs over a reasonable period, expense the costs immediately, or simply record the partners' investments net of the offering costs.

Commissions.   Commissions paid to agents who market shares in an oil and gas venture may be paid by either a general partner or by the joint venture from the proceeds received from the investors. If paid by a general partner, it is acceptable either to expense the commissions immediately or to amortize them over the life of the venture or over a shorter period. If the venture absorbs the cost of the commissions, the cost of the commissions should be allocated to the participants, usually in accordance with terms included in the venture agreement, and the venture should record the amounts invested by the participants' net of the commissions.

Expense Reimbursements.   Direct reimbursements of expenses to an operator should be recorded as reductions of the related expenses by the operator. Amounts intended to provide a reimbursement of expenses, but that are structured as a management fee payable at a specified rate that does not necessarily equal the expenses, should be recorded as management fee revenues.

Windfall Profit Taxes.   Windfall profit taxes may be withheld from revenues at the partnership level, but this creates an unusual reporting situation. The partners, and not the partnership itself, represent the entities that are being taxed. The withholding of these taxes is generally recorded as a reduction of the capital accounts of the partners, as opposed to a partnership expense item.

(c) Financial Statement Disclosure Requirements

Private and public companies both must disclose the method of accounting for costs incurred in oil and gas producing activities (this generally will be the full cost method or the successful efforts method), and the method for disposing of the capitalized costs. FASB Statement No. 69, entitled *Disclosures about Oil and Gas Producing Activities*, established extensive disclosure requirements that generally apply only to public companies. The additional requirements that apply to public companies with significant oil and gas producing activities include specified information in the following areas:

1. Information on quantities and changes in proved reserves must be disclosed by geographic area.
2. Amounts of capitalized costs related to oil and gas producing activities and related allowances for depletion, depreciation, amortization, and valuation should be presented in total, and not by geographic area.
3. Amounts of total costs incurred, both capitalized and expensed, for oil and gas property acquisition, exploration, and development should be indicated separately for each geographic area for which proven reserves are disclosed. This disclosure excludes costs of production, which are included in the disclosure of results of operations described in item 4.
4. Results of operations of oil and gas producing activities including such information as revenues, production costs, exploration costs, depletion, depreciation, amortization, valuation adjustments, and income tax expense, should be reported.
5. A standardized measure of future net cash flows expected to result from existing proved reserves should be set forth, as to which the specific calculation requirements and definitions are set forth in SEC Accounting Series Release No. 253.

An entity's oil and gas producing activities are considered to be significant if one or more of the following tests are met:

1. Revenues from oil and gas producing activities are 10% or more of the reporting entity's consolidated revenues.
2. The pretax profit or loss from oil and gas producing activities is 10% or more of the greater of the combined pretax profit of all industry segments (as defined in FASB Statement No. 14, entitled *Financial Reporting for Segments of a Business Enterprise*) of the reporting entity that report pretax profits, or the combined pretax loss of all industry segments of the reporting entity that report pretax losses.
3. The identifiable assets of the reporting entity's oil and gas producing activities are 10% or more of the reporting entity's total consolidated assets.

These tests must be applied for each year for which a complete set of financial statements is presented.

FASB Statement No. 69 contains provisions that relate to how these disclosure requirements apply to investments in oil and gas joint ventures. Most of the provisions relate to investments in oil and gas joint ventures accounted for by the equity method, but the Statement also contains comments on applying the disclosure requirements to joint ventures that are consolidated (with presentation of minority interests), and proportionately consolidated investees. These are all discussed in the following sections.

(d) Consolidated Joint Ventures with Minority Interests

If a reporting entity fully consolidates the accounts of an oil and gas joint venture and a significant minority interest is present, the reporting entity must disclose the existence of the minority interest in consolidated oil and gas reserves and the portion of the reserves that relate to the minority interest.

(e) Pro Rata Consolidated Oil and Gas Joint Ventures

If a reporting entity has pro rata consolidated its interest in an oil and gas joint venture, the disclosures required by FASB Statement No. 69 include only the reporting entity's pro rata percentages of the items required to be disclosed. Such disclosures should be included along with the data presented for fully consolidated entities.

(f) Oil and Gas Joint Ventures Accounted for by the Equity Method

FASB Statement No. 69 has much to say about the application of the oil and gas disclosure requirements to investments in oil and gas joint ventures accounted for by the equity method. The items required to be disclosed are as follows:

1. An investor's proportionate share of oil and gas reserves of equity method investees

2. An investor's proportionate share of net capitalized costs of equity method investees

3. An investor's proportionate share of equity method investees' property acquisition, exploration, and development costs incurred in oil and gas producing activities

4. An investor's proportionate share of the results of operations of equity method investees engaged in oil and gas producing activities

5. An investor's share of equity method investees' standardized measure of discounted future net cash flows related to existing quantities of proved reserves for each year for which a full set of financial statements is required

The following is an example of footnote disclosure of the foregoing information with regard to a reporting entity's investments in oil and gas joint ventures accounted for by the equity method (with oil expressed in millions of barrels, gas expressed in billions of cubic feet, and dollars expressed in millions):

	Total		Country A		Country B	
	Oil	Gas	Oil	Gas	Oil	Gas
Company A's proportionate share of oil and gas reserves of oil and gas joint ventures accounted for by the equity method	100	150	75	100	25	50
	Total					
Company A's proportionate share of net capitalized costs of oil and gas joint ventures accounted for by the equity method	$ 75					

	Total	Country A	Country B
Company's A proportionate share of property acquisition costs, exploration costs, and development costs incurred by oil and gas joint ventures accounted for by the equity method	$100	$ 75	$25

	Total	Country A	Country B
Company A's proportionate share of operating profits of oil and gas ventures accounted for by the equity method	$ 10	$ 7	$ 3

	Total	Country A	Country B
Company A's proportionate share of the standardized measure of discounted future net cash flows of oil and gas ventures accounted for by the equity method	$60	$50	$10

13.4 ACCOUNTING FOR JOINT VENTURES IN THE CONSTRUCTION INDUSTRY

(a) A General Business Perspective

The construction industry is another industry well-known for a proliferation of joint ventures. In this industry, joint ventures are usually done on a project-by-project basis and enable contractors to share bonding capabilities and financial and other resources, including expensive construction equipment and engineering, design, and construction skills. Construction joint ventures are most commonly structured as corporate joint ventures and partnerships, although some undivided interest arrangements are found in the industry.

As in other industries, construction joint ventures are typically governed by a joint venture agreement that names one of the venturers as operator of the project, specifies the rights and obligations of the parties, and defines the basis for profit and loss distributions.

(b) Accounting for Joint Ventures in the Construction Industry

(i) General. The primary professional guidance on accounting for joint ventures in the construction industry appears in a nonauthoritative guide entitled *Construction Contractors* (the "Guide") that was prepared by the Construction Contractor Guide Committee of the AICPA in 1981. Although this is not an authoritative pronouncement, it is regarded as a source of established accounting principles for the industry.

The Guide covers in detail the accounting methods and principles used in the construction industry, such as accounting for performance of construction-type contracts on the percentage of completion and the completed-contract methods, and auditing procedures to be followed by auditors in audits of construction industry clients. The Guide also contains material on accounting for joint ventures in the construction industry, which essentially confirms the need to apply the principles of the equity method as set forth in APB Opinion No. 18 to construction joint ventures accounted for by the equity method. The Guide also discusses the application of other methods to construction joint ventures.

(ii) Accounting Methods. The Guide notes that there are at least five methods used in accounting for construction joint ventures:

- Consolidation with other investors' interests reported as a minority interest
- Proportionate consolidation
- The equity method
- Expanded equity method, whereby the reporting entity's share of the joint venture's current and long-term assets and liabilities and revenues

and expenses are presented separately in capsule form in the balance sheet and income statement of the reporting entity
• The cost method

The Guide notes that combinations of the foregoing methods such as an equity method presentation in the balance sheet and proportionate consolidation in the income statement have sometimes been used in the construction industry.

If an investor has control of a corporate joint venture or a partnership, the principles of accounting for subsidiaries should be followed, generally requiring consolidation.

For corporate joint ventures, control is generally established by ownership of more than 50% of the corporation's voting stock.

For general partnerships, control is usually indicated by ownership of more than 50% of the financial interests in profits and losses; however, control may alternatively be established by contract, agreement with the other partners, or by court decree. Conversely, control may be determined not to be present even though a partner owns more than a 50% interest in profits and losses if the other partners must approve major decisions of the joint venture.

Noncontrolling investors in general partnerships should generally account for their investments in partnership joint ventures by the equity method.

Limited partners would generally be expected to account for their investments in joint ventures on the same basis as general partners except that a limited partner may be more likely to have an insignificant interest in a joint venture, thus having little or no influence and making the cost method appropriate. Conversely, there are cases where a limited partner owns more than 50% of the partnership interests and has effective control, which would lead to consolidation as the proper reporting basis.

The Guide contains a discussion regarding joint ventures structured as undivided interests that expresses concepts similar to those contained in the discussions on the same subject in the AICPA Statement of Position on real estate joint ventures. The Guide states that for joint ventures in the construction industry that are structured on the basis of bona fide undivided interests, proportionate consolidation is acceptable. This practice has been widely used in the construction industry in recent years.

(iii) Determination of an Investor's Ownership Percentage.   The Guide notes that joint venture agreements often designate specific allocations of profits

and losses, revenues, costs and expenses, cash from operations, and cash from liquidation, and that the agreements sometimes provide for these allocations to change at future dates or upon occurrence of specified events.

(iv) Conforming Accounting Principles Used by a Joint Venture. If a construction joint venture uses accounting principles that are not in accordance with generally accepted accounting principles, appropriate adjustments to the amounts reported by the joint venture should be made before application of the equity method.

(v) Losses in Excess of Investment, Loans, and Advances. The principles for recognition of losses under the equity method by an investor in excess of that investor's investment, loans, and advances are the same in the construction industry as in the real estate industry previously discussed in this chapter.

(vi) Financial Statement Disclosures. The Guide highlights the following financial statement disclosures for inclusion in the financial statements of an investor in a construction joint venture:

- The name of each joint venture, the percentage of ownership, and any important provisions of the joint venture agreement
- If the joint venture's financial statements are not fully consolidated with those of the venturer, separate or combined financial statements of the ventures in summary form, including disclosure of accounting principles of ventures that differ significantly from those of the venturer
- Intercompany transactions during the period and the basis of intercompany billings and charges
- Liabilities and contingent liabilities arising from the joint venture arrangement

Index